D1825763

# Perspectives on Travel Writing

Edited by
Glenn Hooper and Tim Youngs

Studies in European Cultural Transition

Volume 19

General Editors: Martin Stannard and Greg Walker

ASHGATE

Published by
Ashgate Publishing Limited
Gower House
Croft Road
Aldershot
Hants GU11 3HR
England

Ashgate Publishing Company
Suite 420
101 Cherry Street
Burlington
Vermont, 05401–4405
USA

Ashgate website: http://www.ashgate.com

British Library Cataloguing in Publication Data
Perspectives on Travel Writing. – (Studies in European Cultural Transition)
   1. Travel writing. 2. Traveler's writings – History and criticism. I. Hooper,
   Glenn, 1959– .
   II. Youngs, Tim.
   809.9'3355

US Library of Congress Cataloging in Publication Data
Perspectives on Travel Writing / edited by Glenn Hooper and Tim Youngs.
   p. cm. – (Studies in European Cultural Transition)
   Includes bibliographical references and index.
   1. Travel writing. 2. Travel in literature. 3. Travelers' writings, European. I.
   Hooper, Glenn 1959– . II. Youngs, Tim. III. Series.
   G151.P485 2003
   208'.06691–dc21                                                        2003056044

ISBN 0 7546 0366 0

This book is printed on acid free paper.

Printed and bound in great Britain by MPG Books Ltd, Bodmin, Cornwall

# Contents

# Notes on Contributors

**Jan Borm** teaches English at the University of Versailles Saint-Quentin-en-Yvelines. He is co-editor (with Matthew Graves) of Bruce Chatwin's posthumous collection, *Anatomy of Restlessness* (London: Picador, 1997), and (with Jean-Yves Le Disez) of *Seuils et Traverses: Enjeux de l'écriture du voyage*, 2 vols (Brest and Versailles: Université de Bretagne Occidentale and Université de Versailles-Saint-Quentin-en-Yvelines, 2002). He has published numerous essays on British travel writing.

**Helga Quadflieg** has taught English Literature at the universities of Passau, Berlin, and Würzburg, and is presently acting Professor at the Pädagogische Hochschule Weingarten. She has published extensively on the short story, modern tourism, film, and multi-culturalism, and is currently completing two projects: a study of Tudor travel writing, and an introduction to the analysis of poetry.

**Betty Hagglund** is a Lecturer at the University of Birmingham. She has published essays on generic aspects of travel writing, imaginary voyages, travel writing and the eighteenth-century periodical press and on a variety of eighteenth- and nineteenth-century women travellers. She is currently editing the diaries of Mary and Martha Russell, two young British women who were captured by the French Navy during the Revolutionary Wars. She is Vice-President of the International Society for Travel Writing and co-edits the Society's newsletter, Snapshot Traveller.

**Glenn Hooper** is a Lecturer in the Department of English, Mary Immaculate College, University of Limerick. He is editor of *The Tourist's Gaze: Travellers to Ireland, 1800–2000* (Cork: Cork University Press, 2001), and *Harriet Martineau's Letters from Ireland* (Dublin: Irish Academic Press, 2001), and co-editor of *Irish and Postcolonial Writing* (Basingstoke: Palgrave, 2002), and *Ireland in the Nineteenth Century: Regional Identity* (Dublin: Four Courts, 2000).

**Jean-Yves Le Disez** lectures (in Literature in English and Translation Studies) at the University of Western Brittany, Brest, France. He is the author of *Étrange Bretagne* (Rennes: P.U.R, 2002). He is also a translator, notably of travel writing (Philip Glazebrook's *Journey to Kars*, Lawrence Millman's *Last Places*) and the founder and editor of *hopala!—débats de bretagne et d'ailleurs*, a Breton cultural magazine.

**Peter Hulme** is Professor in Literature at the University of Essex. His most recent books are *Remnants of Conquest: The Island Caribs and their Visitors, 1877–1998* (Oxford: Oxford University Press, 2000), the co-edited (with William Sherman) *'The Tempest' and Its Travels* (London: Reaktion Books, 2000), and the co-edited (with Tim Youngs) *Cambridge Companion to Travel Writing* (Cambridge:

Cambridge University Press, 2002). His current research relates to questions of history and fiction in the Caribbean.

**Erdmute Wenzel White** has taught at the University of Hamburg, and is currently an Associate Professor of French and Comparative Literature at Purdue University. She has published widely on poetry, music and modern dance, and her recent book is entitled *The Magic Bishop: Hugo Ball, Dada Poet* (Camden: Camden House, 1998).

**Loredana Polezzi** lectures in Italian Studies at the University of Warwick. Her research work concentrates on the genre and history of travel writing, and she has published on the subject in Italy and Britain. She is co-editor of *Fuzzy Boundaries? Reflections on Modern Languages and the Humanities* (London: CILT, 2001), and author of *Translating Travel* (Aldershot: Ashgate, 2001).

**Patrick Holland** teaches theory, nineteenth-century studies, and travel writing at the University of Guelph. With Graham Huggan, he is writing a study of travel writing in the age of globalization, and is also working on a book about the cult of Caravaggio.

**Graham Huggan** has a Chair in Postcolonialism at the University of Leeds. Previous publications include *Territorial Disputes* (Toronto: University of Toronto Press, 1994), *Peter Carey* (Oxford: Oxford University Press, 1996), *Tourists with Typewriters*, with Patrick Holland (Ann Arbor: University of Michigan Press, 1998), and *The Postcolonial Exotic* (London: Routledge, 2001). He is currently working with Patrick Holland on a 'sequel' to *Tourists with Typewriters*, and with Helen Tiffin on a book about postcolonialism, animals and the environment.

**Padmini Mongia** teaches literature in English at Franklin & Marshall College, USA. She has published on postcolonial and modern writing, and is editor of *Contemporary Postcolonial Theory: A Reader* (London: Arnold, 1996). She is currently working on a book entitled *Indo Chic: Marketing English India*.

**Tim Youngs** is Professor in English and Travel Studies at The Nottingham Trent University. He is founding editor of the journal *Studies in Travel Writing*, the author of *Travellers in Africa: British Travelogues, 1850–1900* (Manchester: Manchester University Press, 1994) and editor of *Writing and Race* (Harlow: Longman, 1997). He is co-editor with Peter Hulme of *The Cambridge Companion to Travel Writing* (Cambridge: Cambridge University Press, 2002).

# List of Illustrations

# General Editors' Preface

The European dimension of research in the humanities has come into sharp focus over recent years, producing scholarship which ranges across disciplines and national boundaries. This new series provides a major channel for this work and unites the fields of cultural studies and traditional scholarship. It will publish in the areas of European history and literature, art history, archaeology, language and translation studies, political, cultural and gay studies, music, psychology, sociology and philosophy. The emphasis is explicitly European and interdisciplinary, concentrating attention on the relativity of cultural perspectives, with a particular interest in issues of cultural transition.

Martin Stannard
Greg Walker
*University of Leicester*

# Chapter 1

# Introduction

## Glenn Hooper and Tim Youngs

### Europe, transition, and travel

One of the major aims of the series in which this volume appears is to add to the current of cross-disciplinary research on Europe, and to further an understanding of how Europe was constructed, as well as how it managed to construct its Others. We hope that *Perspectives on Travel Writing* will contribute to these discussions of differing European strands; of how ideas, people and customs operate within certain known, geo-political parameters, but also how they have come to influence – and be influenced by – other locales, jurisdictions, and cultures.[1] Indeed, given the emphasis within much of this research on mobility of one form or another, it seems appropriate that our contributors are scholars working within the broad area of travel writing, a form – as the following essays will demonstrate – that embraces many interests and themes, but which seems especially suited to the notion of *transition*, in all its guises. This sense of change is something we wish to underline.

A consequence of work in the past twenty or thirty years on how Europe has viewed and used other parts of the world has been to reinforce an impression of the continent as homogeneous. Yet there are differences within Europe – there are different Europes – and the ways in which those differences are enforced parallel the processes of Othering enacted elsewhere. To address these issues we have commissioned essays that between them (and in some cases on their own) cover diverse territories and periods. This is not to suggest that complete coverage has been attempted of the various geo-political identities historically linked with Europe, or which share even the vaguest connection with its development. Nevertheless, we do suggest that in their scope, and in the approaches they take, the essays presented here indicate some of the advantages to be gained from interrogating the generalizations made about Europe and its various Others. A more 'domestic' framework – represented by Scotland, Ireland and Brittany – is also opened up, while discussion of those regions distant from Europe, such as the Caribbean and Brazil, indicates how they have come under Europe's various influences. Our historical coverage ranges from

---

[1]    Other relevant volumes in the Studies in European Cultural Transition series are: Lynne Pearce, ed., *Devolving Identities: Feminist Readings in Home and Belonging* (Aldershot: Ashgate, 2000); Loredana Polezzi, *Translating Travel: Contemporary Italian travel writing in English translation* (Aldershot: Ashgate, 2001), and Katherine Turner, *British Travel Writers in Europe 1750–1800: Authorship, gender and national identity* (Aldershot: Ashgate, 2001).

the late fifteenth to the late twentieth century. Our methodologies reflect theoretical as well as more empirical interests and concerns.[2]

## The travelling genre(s)

Editors of essay collections usually have the advantage of knowing what it is that they assemble and introduce. Travel writing, however, remains a loosely defined body of literature. Whether this is despite or a consequence of the growing amount of critical energy expended on its study over the past couple of decades is debatable. One's ready assumption would probably be that travel writing is a factual, first-person account of a journey undertaken by the author. However, this is far from clear, and it is common to complicate such an argument by turning to the mediaeval example of *The Travels of Sir John Mandeville* (c. 1356): uncertainty about the author and what he claims to have visited remains strong.[3] Similar doubts have been raised about the truth of Marco Polo's account,[4] and even when we move into what we assume is more historically verifiable terrain – the eighteenth century – problems regarding veracity continue to exist. For example, Percy Adams has noted the high incidence of plagiarism among many travel writers of this period, and argues that much of what has been routinely accepted as 'truth' is in fact an amalgam of the historical, antiquarian and aesthetic jottings of many others.[5] An altogether different question is posed by a text such as Herman Melville's *Typee* (1846), which when first published was taken for what it purported to be: the self-told adventures of its sailor protagonist, but which was later, when Melville's writings became better known, reappraised as a novel. Nor is generic instability resolved simply by historical change or biographical information: to complicate the matter further, Melville's South Seas works have spawned their own travel texts.[6]

---

[2]    Several of the essays in this volume have their origins in a conference – 'Borders and Crossings', organized by Glenn Hooper and Tim Youngs – held in Magee College, Derry, in 1998. The success of that event – and of two follow-up conferences in Brest and Versailles, organized by Jean-Yves Le Disez and Jan Borm – led to this collection of specially commissioned essays. For the proceedings of the conference in Brest, see Jan Borm and Jean-Yves Le Disez, eds, *Seuils et Traverses: Enjeux de l'écriture du voyage*, 2 vols (Brest and Versailles: Université de Bretagne Occidentale and Université de Versailles-Saint-Quentin-en-Yvelines, 2002).

[3]    *The Travels of Sir John Mandeville*, trans. and intro. by C. W. R. D. Moseley (London: Penguin, 1983).

[4]    See David Henige, 'Ventriloquists and wandering truths', *Studies in Travel Writing*, 2 (1998), pp. 164–80.

[5]    Adams also discusses less formally derived tactics: 'And so the eighteenth century was a time in which people and ideas moved about … It was the age of gold for travelers, both real and imaginary. And, as a result, it was the age of opportunity for travel lies.' Percy Adams, *Travelers and Travel Liars, 1660–1800* (New York: Dover, 1980), pp. 8–9.

[6]    For example, Tim Severin, *In Search of Moby Dick: Quest for the White Whale* (London: Little, Brown and Company, 1999).

One of the most persistent observations regarding travel writing, then, is its absorption of differing narrative styles and genres, the manner in which it effortlessly shape-shifts and blends any number of imaginative encounters, and its potential for interaction with a broad range of historical periods, disciplines and perspectives. In much the same way that travel itself can be seen as a somewhat fluid experience, so too can travel writing be regarded as a relatively open-ended and versatile form, notwithstanding the closure that occurs in some of its more rigidly conventional examples.[7] Mark Cocker agrees that the 'enormous extension of style, content and intention in travel books has tended to confuse', but in a world where uncertainty is increasingly expected, if not courted, this has proved to be a bonus.[8] True, there is always the occasional sour note. At the beginning of *The Old Patagonian Express*, Paul Theroux, in an extension of the much quoted phrase that there is nowhere new for the traveller to visit, argues that travel writing itself has become an exhausted medium:

> The literature of travel has become measly, the standard opening, that farcical nose-against-the-porthole view from the plane's tilted fuselage. The joke-opening, that straining for effect, is now so familiar it is nearly impossible to parody. How does it go?[9]

Whether this is another exercise in bad faith on Theroux's part, a genuinely expressed difficulty, or a cover-up, is hard to say, for in a critical climate where the richness of repetition, irony and self-reflexivity are awarded high marks, none of what Theroux describes seems especially limiting. But not all writers are so jaded. W. G. Sebald's *The Rings of Saturn* (1998) employs memoir and historical and geographical digression within the narrative structure of a walk through the countryside of the author-narrator's East Anglia. Categorizing Sebald's work is impossible, and yet it is in its indefinability, as well as its textured prose, that much of its appeal lies.

Given these different styles of writing, as well as the fact that we are looking upon an unstable set of classifications generally, it hardly needs saying that the number of interpretive approaches required will be as varied as the primary sources themselves. As travel itself has changed – physically, as well as in terms of its perception[10] – so too has travel writing altered, reflecting the shifting aesthetic and cultural fashions of the day, as well as the power inequalities that lie between East

---

[7] Examples of open and experimental travel texts might include the writings of Bruce Chatwin; examples of more conservative ones those of Wilfred Thesiger.

[8] Mark Cocker, *Loneliness and Time: British Travel Writing in the Twentieth Century* (London: Secker, 1992), p. 8.

[9] Paul Theroux, *The Old Patagonian Express* [1979] (London: Penguin, 1985), p. 12.

[10] For a discussion of the effects of changes in the modes of travel on travel writing itself (in relation to gender) see Sidonie Smith, *Moving Lives: Twentieth-Century Women's Travel Writing* (Minneapolis: University of Minnesota Press, 2001).

and West, the history of empire, and the gendered spaces of home and abroad.[11] These factors, especially in the influence they directly have on the writer's thoughts and representations, make for an even greater sense of the random and fleeting than is usual with literary documents. And when we add to these the changes that have come about within the various disciplines and methodologies upon which we would routinely expect to draw – anthropology, historiography and English studies, for example – then we begin to have some sense of the complexities facing us in our task.[12]

## The essays

The question of loose borders is explored in the essays by Jan Borm and Tim Youngs that frame our volume. In the opening essay, Borm lists some of the many terms used to describe travel literature and asks what we mean by them; whether they even refer to the same object. Arguing against strict boundaries, he proposes that travel writing is not a genre, but comprises texts, both predominantly fictional and non-fictional, that have travel as their main theme. Travel writing might not be as strictly factual as some like to claim, he suggests, especially as it employs some of the most characteristic of fictional techniques. Indeed, even the presence of a non-fiction dominant is a complicated matter since ideas about non-fiction change over time. It is not only with the novel that travel writing crosses over, of course, but with autobiography also (and to complicate the matter further, developments over the past few years in the criticism of autobiography have tended to treat *that* genre as akin to fiction in its construction of character, its selection and relation of episodes, and its arrangement of plot – a point taken up by Loredana Polezzi in a later essay).[13] Besides the mixing of genres within travel writing that Borm describes,

---

[11] See, among many examples, Elizabeth Bohls, *Women Travel Writers and the Language of Aesthetics, 1716–1818* (Cambridge: Cambridge University Press, 1995); David Spurr, *The Rhetoric of Empire: Colonial Discourse in Journalism, Travel Writing, and Imperial Administration* (Durham: Duke University Press, 1993); Inderpal Grewal, *Home and Harem: Nation, Gender, Empire, and the Cultures of Travel* (London: Leicester University Press, 1996).

[12] See also Mary Baine Campbell, 'Travel writing and its theory', in Peter Hulme and Tim Youngs, eds, *The Cambridge Companion to Travel Writing* (Cambridge: Cambridge University Press, 2002), pp. 261–78.

[13] The nature of these relationships is commonly considered in general commentaries on travel writing, but there may be local circumstances to take into account also. It has, for instance, been argued that the line between travel writing and autobiography (as well as that between travel writing and fiction) is especially blurred in the case of Australia because of Australians' propensity to travel, and to write about it, and because overseas travel often forms a critical rite of passage. See also Ros Pesman, David Walker and Richard White's Introduction to their anthology, *The Oxford Book of Australian Travel Writing* (Melbourne: Oxford University Press, 1996), pp. ix–xxiv.

his essay crosses another boundary in that it draws on the work of European critics, notably Gérard Genette, Philippe Lejeune, Jean-Didier Urbain, and Jean-Marie Schaeffer, a reminder that despite the influence of continental European thinkers upon cultural theory in general, travel writing criticism still tends (in the US and Britain, at least) to be dominated by Anglophone critics. In considering what he describes as the hybrid nature of the travel book and travel writing Borm emphasizes the literary aspects. Youngs, too, while detailing some important cultural contexts and features of narratives that literary criticism ignores, concludes that specialist attention to literary characteristics is nonetheless essential to a fuller appreciation of travel writing. Where Borm reveals how travel writing crosses over with or accommodates other forms, Youngs demonstrates that a similar travelling occurs within its very study.

'Identity is largely constituted through the process of othering', writes Trinh T. Minh-ha. It is a process that can evolve within societies, but which is especially evident transculturally, at the point of contact, when our sense of Self is most under threat, frequently in need of reassurance, and likeliest to resort to binary modes of discourse as a form of defence.[14] In Helga Quadflieg's essay this process of Othering is seen as an almost necessary component of many early modern travel accounts, as the subject constructs himself – frequently as an English, Protestant, Colonizing Male – in contrast to the natives of Eastern Europe, Persia, North America, and the East Indies. Quadflieg's survey touches on several texts, including Hakluyt's *The Principal Navigations* and Purchas's *Hakluytus Posthumus*, and she notes that as with many modern travel accounts, for Tudor and early Stuart writers there is often a sense of unease about what they are producing, a form of discourse that manages to appear both intensely nuanced and naive. At once colonial discourse, autobiography and anthropological treatise, many texts, she argues, articulate a political perspective, while at the same time appearing conscious of the wider implications of their narratives. Moreover, because many of their evaluations fall within the period of the immediate pre- and post-reformation era, Quadflieg is able to show the extent to which religious difference was also deployed and seen as a convenient ethnic marker but also as an inevitable site of contention as the European powers fought to consolidate territorial gains, especially in the Americas and the East Indies. Facing the 'exotic', then, became a test for these early modern writers, but also a wonderful opportunity for self- (and national) (re)invention, a way of encountering, and then countering, difference.

Dealing with the exotic could, of course, prompt a variety of responses. James Duncan has examined the way in which sameness within difference can affect the self-perceptions of travellers, a troubling recognition within a site clearly unknown to them. Duncan discusses several Victorian travellers visiting the Kandyan Highlands

---

14 Trinh T. Minh-ha, 'Other than myself/my other self', in George Robertson *et al.*, eds, *Travellers' Tales: Narratives of Home and Displacement* (London: Routledge, 1994), p. 15.

of what was then Ceylon. Although fundamentally different, and recognized as such, Kandy startled many travellers because of its 'mountainous topography ... and the relatively cool climate', both of which acted on the imaginations of its visitors who saw it, sometimes needily, 'as a mirror of home'.[15] Something of this shared, or bifurcated, vision is evident in Betty Hagglund's essay, as she investigates the complex interleaving of self with place that is articulated by one particular traveller, Anne Grant. Born in Glasgow in 1755, Grant was an inspired and talented individual of modest means, but also a figure well-versed in the ethnographic change brought about as a result of travel. More interestingly, although a Lowland-born Scot, Grant was taken to live in the British colonies in Albany, New York, an experience that was to help shape her understanding not just of Native American culture, but also her own Highland society on her return to Scotland. On the outside of Native American life, yet part of a settler colony, on her return to a part of Scotland unfamiliar to her Grant found herself, as in America, at something of a remove. A hybrid figure who favoured a hybrid narrative voice, Grant appears as a complex character who gained an 'inside' perspective on Mohawk culture, who came to value the 'wilderness' of the frontier settlement of Albany, but who, in the Scottish Highlands, developed a romantic enthusiasm for the poems of Ossian, a convenient tool with which to deal with the challenges of her new surroundings.

The Scottish Highlands received increasing numbers of tourists from the middle of the eighteenth century, as did the south-west of Ireland, and North Wales. But closer to home, select parts of Derbyshire and Yorkshire also offered domestic competition to the Grand Tour.[16] Such a development might seem difficult to believe, but at just the point when enthusiasm for continental travel was at its peak (with the exception of the period of the Nine Years War), the more rugged and elemental parts of Britain and Ireland were witness to a noticeable increase in the number of travellers, and travel writers.

If Hagglund's essay investigates some of the motivation behind the fascination for the Home Tour – the advantages of scenic over grand tourism, a new-found confidence in the Celtic fringe – then one place in which this development would be played out more fitfully was in Ireland. Like Hagglund's, Glenn Hooper's essay

---

[15]   James Duncan, 'Dis-Orientation: On the shock of the familiar in a far-away place', in James Duncan and Derek Gregory, eds, *Writes of Passage: Reading Travel Writing* (London: Routledge, 1999), pp. 153, 152.

[16]   For some discussion of the development of the Home Tour, see Barbara Korte, *English Travel Writing: From Pilgrimages to Postcolonial Explorations* (Basingstoke: Macmillan, 2000), pp. 66–82. For an assessment of travel writing relative to Ireland, see Martin Ryle, *Journeys in Ireland: Literary Travellers, Rural Landscapes, Cultural Relations* (Aldershot: Ashgate, 1999). On the development of 'domestic' travel generally, see Malcolm Andrews, *The Search for the Picturesque: Landscape Aesthetics and Tourism in Britain, 1760–1800* (Aldershot: Scolar, 1989); John Gold and Margaret Gold, *Imagining Scotland: Tradition, Representation and Promotion in Scottish Tourism since 1750* (Aldershot: Scolar, 1995).

picks up on this theme of migrancy, although he takes as his starting point the Irish Famine of 1845–52, and shows how those disastrous years contributed to a re-evaluation of the country in the early 1850s. Hooper shows that an increasingly positive impression of post-Famine Ireland was endorsed by several British travellers and travel writers, well up until the late 1860s. More specifically, he argues that although the country was seen by many travellers to be in a deplorable state, several insisted that it was also time to see in its shattered economy an opportunity for investment, and in the place itself the most unlikely of opportunities: a resettlement option to rank with the Antipodes and the Americas.[17] Taking John Hervey Ashworth as an example of one of the most trenchant post-Famine settlers to Ireland, Hooper reveals how the travel narrative Ashworth composed became the perfect medium for the over-layering of a strident promotional rhetoric and he shows how adept Ashworth was at marketing Ireland to a wary British readership. *The Saxon in Ireland*, structured around a series of visits to Ireland made by Ashworth, deploys some of the most notorious of colonizing tropes while at the same time portraying the country as a somewhat disfigured extension of England, a feat that the travel narrative was able to discharge with arguably greater confidence than other forms. More attractive than places such as Australia, New Zealand and Port Philip, Ireland becomes, at least in the travel-settler mind of John Hervey Ashworth, a place from which an unpleasant and recent history might be excised, but also a region in which a new beginning may be allowed to emerge.

Jean-Yves Le Disez reminds us that there are margins within continental Europe as well as outside it. Brittany had at times been as peripheral to France as to Britain. Le Disez contends that the study of Victorian narratives of travel in Brittany illuminates the ideology behind the Victorians' relationship to their social/colonial Others, despite the fact that Brittany was neither British nor a British colony. Le Disez focuses on animal imagery as the site on which ideological values and confusions are especially evident. It is a truism that animals signify the border between nature and the wild on the one hand, and civilization and human on the other. Thus the presence of the beast can represent a threat to order, but its narrative expression contains it. Where Quädflieg discusses accounts from Hakluyt of the Algonquins as beastly, Le Disez shows that similar processes of Othering through discourses of animality operate within Europe. To travelling Britons, Brittany was a place both familiar and strange. It symbolized a rural England, looked upon with ambivalent feelings of nostalgic interest and of danger and discomfiture by those more used to modern, urban lifestyles. The echoes of revolution added an additional interest.

Ambivalent views about a wild Other are also discussed in Peter Hulme's essay, which takes as its starting point the description by Columbus in 1493 of the Caribbean in terms of its people's colour, the beginning of a classification that still

---

[17] See Glenn Hooper, 'The Waste Land: Writing and Resettlement in Post-Famine Ireland', *The Canadian Journal of Irish Studies*, 23:2 (1997), pp. 55–76.

reverberates. Focusing on Cuba and Dominica, Hulme selects texts from 1898 (the year of the US invasion of Cuba) and its aftermath, from the 1940s, and from the late twentieth century. Hulme's main theme is the perception of indigenous difference. He points to the growing US hegemony in the Caribbean and to the connections between the increase in guidebooks and travel writing and the rise of tourism post-1898, which was facilitated by technology derived from military developments. Hulme combines scrutiny of the material contexts of travel writing with analysis of the workings of textual descriptions that are produced by those contexts. He notes the lack of interest in the living Indians in Cuba, and the obsession with constructions of authenticity that privileged romantic ideas of the past at the expense of those in the present. The reality of transculturation was overlooked as visitors searched for – and rarely found – survivals of the authentic. The self-defeating quest for the authentic, when the reasoning that was adopted held that it had disappeared from the 1490s, lent itself to elegiac expression and ignored indigenous survivals (except as visible trace). Hulme's essay drives towards an attack on ideas of cultural purity and to a plea to allow definition according to self-perception.

Self-definition is also central to the essay by Erdmute Wenzel White. Early modern travel accounts of Brazil can be seen less as historical records of the New World than as source material with which to initiate a fresh beginning. Wenzel White provides an outline of sixteenth-century travel, missionary, ethnographic and political writing, showing how early impressions of Brazil helped shape a European view of the country that saw it as a site of pleasure, exoticism and barbaric rites. From these representations, however, many problems arise; although these early travellers to Brazil could accept, even promote, mutilation and their own violence, for example, they were horrified by tribal cannibalism. Yet it is precisely around these paradoxes and conflicts, amidst these stuttering European visions, that many Brazilian writers and intellectuals of the 1920s began to reconceptualize their own history and culture. Wenzel White demonstrates how these early accounts were reworked, then, and how an alternative set of 'national' representations were fashioned, a project that provocatively mixed the heady political strife of that era with experimental forms. Although coming a full century after independence from Portugal, modernist poets, ethnographers and novelists saw the re-birth of Brazil as a responsibility first and foremost, but as something that could best be achieved by a refutation of these earlier 'travel' accounts; versions of their history that they challenged by undertaking their own expeditions to the Amazon, from where they brought tales, dance, and songs. The intention, therefore, was to prove that from these non-coastal regions (some of the areas of the country from which the first colonists formed impressions) could come inspiration, a re-imagining and rediscovering of their own country for the twentieth century. Moreover, in Wenzel White's opinion, these writers not only appropriated the source texts of the 'discovery' of Brazil and reinterpreted them, but they realigned and rediscovered themselves at the same time. Criss-crossing the widely diverging regions of the country, the participants of *antropofagia*, in following in the footsteps of these early modern travellers, became travellers themselves, but also Brazilians in a way that set the country's future on a new and divergent path.

Travel writing's borrowings from, and sometimes outright dependency upon, other forms of discourse appears to be well established. Whether it is ethnographic writing, journalism or autobiography, travel writing displays a willingness to embrace these other forms, if for no other reason than that they supply it with an easy patina of texture and depth. Of course, there are potential dangers in unnecessarily blurring distinctions, and in Loredana Polezzi's essay an acknowledgement of the dangers of taking some of these similarities too far is evident. However, Polezzi also argues that accepting that comparisons between these forms exist can lead to useful, even unexpectedly beneficial results, and she discusses Estella Canziani as a case in point. Born in London to an Italian father and an American mother, Canziani was a complex, somewhat elusive individual who was on the council of the Folk-Lore Society, a member of the Royal Geographical Society, and an accomplished artist, traveller and writer. Of her writings it is her autobiography and her three earlier travel books – all of Italy – that Polezzi is most interested in, and which she investigates as profound examples of Canziani's efforts at identity construction. A bilingual and biculturally educated individual, Canziani offers us a sense of herself, but one that stands clear of easily defined notions of a unified or stable Self. Hovering between her work as retriever of local legends and superstitions, and her presence within the upper levels of Anglo-Italian London society, Canziani travels between different places and forms in a complex manoeuvre that appears like a type of performance, done as much for herself as for her reader. In her conclusions, Polezzi also points to a further layer of complexity, linked to the reception of Canziani's books over the years. While in Britain Canziani is almost forgotten or only remembered for her artwork, in Italy her travel books have recently been rediscovered, appropriated by the tourist industry, and even inscribed within contemporary regionalist discourses.

In their contribution, Patrick Holland and Graham Huggan revisit some ideas from their important study of contemporary travel writing, *Tourists with Typewriters*. Focusing on nostalgia in travel narratives of the second half of the twentieth century, they resist a reflex dismissal of this pervasive mood and demonstrate instead that it can be a force for critique as well as for conservatism. Close attention to this theme allows them to peer behind motifs that are often taken at face value. In particular, their gaze falls on the gentleman, a type whose appearance in latter-day travels is accompanied with a humour that is meant to be disarming. As Holland and Huggan observe, however, such self-deprecation is the smile of the supremely confident. Humour carries authority; it does not displace it. That which is ironized is often upheld rather than challenged.

To recognize this posture is also to discern the fictiveness of travel writing. The literary construction of a persona and the creation of a background mood of longing are closer to the strategies of fiction than to a straightforward documentary mode. Traveller, author and protagonist are all different, if related, entities. The evocation of a particular sensibility, so strong as to become a motif, resembles a strategy of the novel. What might at first look like an uncomplicated and sometimes humorous recitation of travels takes on the complexity of a text that is fabricated in both senses. Neither the place visited nor the person who went there is quite as it is presented to us. A mark of Holland and Huggan's investigation is their readiness to see in the apparent counter-examples of New Age and ecotravel a continuation of older traditions of pilgrimage and salvage. This suggests the view of travel writing, articulated by several critics, as a vehicle for the transmission and consolidation of 'colonial discourse'. As these critics recognize, however, travel writing remains a useful medium for the interrogation of ethnocentrism and for the displacement or estrangement of received ideas about 'other' cultures. Nostalgia holds the balance between these conflicting ideological purposes: first, by displacing the desire for domination and conquest onto 'benign' mythologies of loss or remembered pleasure; and second, by allowing for a critical reading of these self-serving mythologies and mechanisms of displacement.

The connections between (post)colonial and travel writing partly explored by Holland and Huggan are taken up by Padmini Mongia in an essay that reads Amitav Ghosh's *In an Antique Land* as a vibrant literary form: part 'subversive' history, travelogue, autobiography and novel. Mongia asks if *In an Antique Land*, a text that brings a whole range of literary devices and historical periods together, may be seen as a type of postcolonial travel writing, a blend of two worryingly unstable categories.[18] Beginning with an overview of the 'turn' that has come to dominate anthropological discourse since the 1980s, Mongia moves towards an appreciation of the ever-shifting arenas evoked by Ghosh, revealing the layered and multivocal narrative that is produced. Although Ghosh's text stems – in some part – from the archival sources themselves, Mongia argues that as Ghosh settles for a narrative that is finally marked by fragments and documents, scattered footnotes and ethnographic records, he produces a very partial and provisional outcome. Moreover, amidst the sense of uncertainty and unease generated by Ghosh over the 'veracity' of the story he writes, we find not only Bomma – the text's central character – but Ghosh himself. Eschewing narrative completion in favour of the intertwined histories of Indian and Egyptian subjects long traumatized by the colonizing ambitions of one imperial power after another, Ghosh reveals a layered and multivocal presence. A text that sits on the margins of literary categories, *In an Antique Land* broadens further the categories of 'postcolonial' and 'travel', while at the same time announcing itself as a possible candidate for the merging of both.

The volume closes with Tim Youngs's essay, which also has as its concern the broadening of the idea of travel. Youngs outlines recent developments in multi- and interdisciplinary approaches to the subject but asks what is left out when one looks

---

[18]    For further discussion of the intersections between travel and the history of imperialism, see Steve Clark, ed., *Travel Writing and Empire: Postcolonial Theory in Transit* (London: Zed, 1999).

at travel *writing*. Many aspects of the material contexts of travel, he argues, are omitted from discussions of its narratives. Criticism has tended to concentrate on discourse, images, and textual expressions of ideology rather than on the economics of travel. The adoption of metaphors of movement – notably nomadism – has removed these terms from the physical conditions they describe. Several types of travel are either not represented in most criticism of travel writing or are distorted through the adoption of figurative language. Yet although he calls for more notice to be taken of factors external to travel texts, and observes that to achieve this means to turn to the work of scholars in disciplines other than literary studies, Youngs suggests that close readings of narratives by specialists in literature can produce insights unlikely to result from the attentions of those in other academic fields. Paradoxically, the more that different disciplines combine to analyse the same body of work, the more useful is the employment of their own specialist tools.

Youngs's essay is not prescriptive. Attention to the different forms of travel reveals the need for a range of approaches, even within the field of literary studies alone, and as editors we hope that the present volume indicates some of the potential benefits. It would be wrong to impose a monolithic view on such a complex field of activity as travel (and therefore on its narration), or to force closure on ideas which, too, remain in transition. In the pages that follow, within the shared focus on travels (cultural as well as physical) from, to, and inside Europe, diverse regions, histories, and types of text are represented, as are various, though we hope complementary, ways of looking at them. Travel writing is fluid and versatile. It changes also according to who looks at it, and from where. We stress this provisionality and plurality in the title of our volume, *Perspectives on Travel Writing*, and turn to the title of the series, Studies in European Cultural Transition, to emphasize that changes occur in how we look, as well as in what we see: the transition not only of Europe but of Europeans, and of those who write about Europe. Besides the travelling and the writing, it is the criticism of these activities that is in process.

Chapter 2

# Defining Travel: On the Travel Book, Travel Writing and Terminology

## Jan Borm

From the amount of critical attention and the number of labels applied to travel writing in recent years, one may well wonder whether critics are discussing the same object. Among the wide range of terms in use are: 'travel book', 'travel narrative', 'journeywork', 'travel memoir', 'travel story', 'travelogue', 'metatravelogue', 'traveller's tale', 'travel journal', or simply 'travels' (*The Travels of Sir John Mandeville*), and, in a different vein, 'travel writing', 'travel literature', 'the literature of travel' and 'the travel genre'. While I do not refute the validity of any of these terms, their sheer abundance raises the question of what we actually mean by the *travel book* and *travel writing*. An answer in generic terms is far from being obvious, as Tim Youngs notes in his study, *Travellers in Africa*:

> Travel writing feeds from and back into other forms of literature. To try to identify boundaries between various forms would be impossible and I would be deeply suspicious of any attempt at the task.[1]

The point to determine, therefore, is whether *travel writing* is really a genre at all. I shall argue here that it is not a genre, but a collective term for a variety of texts both predominantly fictional and non-fictional whose main theme is travel. That said, the terms *travel book* or *travelogue* usefully describe a genre known in French as *récit de voyage*, and in German as *Das Reisebuch* or *Der Reisebericht*, a category of texts that are an integral part of travel writing. I will try to illustrate these points by looking at the hybrid nature of the travel book and travel writing, the role of the fictive and the referential, as well as at other works of representation. Finally, I would like to stress that the *literary* is at work in travel writing, and that it therefore seems appropriate to consider the terms *the literature of travel*, or simply *travel literature*, as synonyms of *travel writing*.

---

[1] Tim Youngs, *Travellers in Africa: British Travelogues, 1850–1900* (Manchester: Manchester University Press, 1994), p. 8.

**Travel writing as hybrid**

The problematic status both of travel writing and of the terms used to describe it becomes obvious as soon as one tries to define the object. Writing of the travel book, Mary Baine Campbell notes: 'This is a genre composed of other genres, as well as one that importantly contributed to the genesis of the modern novel and the renaissance of autobiography.'[2] In other words, the travel book does not seem to belong to any genre in particular, a fact that does not stop it from being a genre in its own right, as Campbell also points out.[3] Indeed, one may note, as Genette does, that 'the mixing of or contempt for genres is a genre amongst others'.[4] However, to consider *travel writing* as a genre seems to me highly problematic. To give but one example, Zweder von Martels suggests that:

> Travel writing seems unlimited in its forms of expression, but though we may therefore find it hard to define the exact boundaries of this genre, it is generally understood what it contains. It ranges from the indisputable examples such as guidebooks, itineraries and routes and perhaps also maps to less restricted accounts of journeys over land or by water, or just descriptions of experiences abroad. These appear in prose and poetry, and are often part of historical and (auto) biographical works.[5]

If some critics consider the travel book to be a genre in its own right, others look at it as being part of a larger genre. Paul Fussell claims that travel books 'are a sub-species of memoir in which autobiographical narrative arises from the speaker's encounter with distant or unfamiliar data and in which the narrative – unlike that in a novel or romance – claims literal validity by constant reference to actuality'.[6] While all travellers' accounts are autobiographical to a degree, there is no necessity for travellers to provide a retrospective overview of their life in the manner of the biographer.[7] Furthermore, to read travel accounts in this manner reduces the

---

2     Mary B. Campbell, *The Witness and the Other World: Exotic European Travel Writing 400–1600* (Ithaca: Cornell University Press, 1988), p. 6.

3     It appears that Campbell uses the terms *travel book* and *travel writing* as synonyms. On page 5 she considers 'the history of the travel book before the seventeenth century'; on page 9 she refers to the 'generic stabilization of travel writing that characterized the fourteenth century'. I assume that she is using both terms to speak about the same object.

4     Gérard Genette *et al.*, eds, *Théorie des genres* (Paris: Seuil, 1986), p. 158. (All translations from the French in this essay are my own.)

5     Zweder von Martels, ed., *Travel Fact and Fiction: Studies on Fiction, Literary Tradition, Scholarly Discovery and Observation in Travel Writing* (Leiden: Brill, 1994), p. xi.

6     Paul Fussell, *Abroad: British Literary Traveling Between the Wars* (New York: Oxford University Press, 1980), p. 203.

7     'Le texte doit être *principalement* un récit, mais on sait toute la place qu'occupe le *discours* dans la narration autobiographique; la perspective *principalement* rétrospective … le sujet doit être *principalement* la vie individuelle, la genèse de la personnalité.' Philippe

potential for imaginative readings of texts (or readings of imaginative texts) that do not at first glance fit the travel mode, such as Conrad's *Heart of Darkness* (1899/ 1902), Melville's *Moby Dick* (1851) and Darwin's *Voyage of the Beagle* (1839).[8]

One must next ask if *Heart of Darkness*, or *Moby Dick*, or any other number of such works, can be described as travel books or travelogues. Conrad's travels are at the origin of his novella (as Melville's shipboard experiences also shaped his writings), but one would be hard-pushed to affirm that a *referential pact* characterizes *Heart of Darkness* in a predominant way.[9] For some, such as Paul Theroux, it is the predominance of the referential pact between text and reader that defines travel writing:

> the difference between travel writing and fiction is the difference between recording what the eye sees and discovering what the imagination knows. Fiction is pure joy – how sad that I could not reinvent the trip as fiction.[10]

Theroux's remarks deserve some comment. Firstly, it seems reasonable to speak of the joys of travel writing in the same manner as the joys of fiction, whether in their creation or their reception. Historically, travel books have been read as much for pleasure as for instruction, a fact that remains today.[11] Secondly, Theroux's claim to record only what is seen by the eye in *The Great Railway Bazaar* is not to be taken literally. At the very least, one may point to the inevitable element of fiction in the recounting of conversations in the course of travel. Theroux, like other authors, makes use of fictional techniques in a manner characteristic of contemporary travelogues.[12] Critics have pointed to the use of 'free indirect

---

Lejeune, *Le pacte autobiographique* (Paris: Seuil, 1975), pp. 14–15. 'The text should be *mainly* a narrative, even if it is well-known that discursive writing is given considerable scope in narrative autobiography; the perspective should be *mainly* retrospective ... the subject-matter should be *mainly* concerned with the author's life, the birth and evolution of his or her personality.'

[8] Youngs has written that *Heart of Darkness* 'is best read as what it purports to be: a kind of travel narrative'. *Travellers in Africa*, p. 9.

[9] Joseph Conrad, *Heart of Darkness* with the *Congo Diary* (London: Penguin, 1995).

[10] Paul Theroux, *The Great Railway Bazaar: By Train Through Asia* [1975] (London: Penguin, 1979), p. 379.

[11] Charles L. Batten Jr, *Pleasurable Instruction: Form and Convention in Eighteenth-Century Travel Literature* (Los Angeles: University of California Press, 1978).

[12] Fictional techniques have obviously been used in travelogues before. For example, Mary Louise Pratt notes that a considerable number of eighteenth-century travellers and travel writers used or had imposed on them a professional writer to 'polish up' the original account: 'Travel literature did not remain immune to the professionalization of writing in the eighteenth century. Now that it had become a profitable business, traveler-writers and their publishers relied more and more on professional writers and editors to ensure a competitive product, often transforming manuscripts completely, usually in the direction of the novel.' Mary Louise Pratt, *Imperial Eyes: Travel Writing and Transculturation* (London: Routledge, 1992), p. 88. A famous example of such rewriting is Hawkesworth's version of Cook's travels (1773), imposed on the latter by the naval authorities.

style, scenic construction, present-tense narration, prolepsis, iterative symbolism, etc., [in] factual narratives'.[13] Finally, Theroux's clear-cut way of distinguishing between travel writing and fiction is problematic. Three examples may suffice: extended dialogue in travelogues is just one way to note the scenic construction (a fictional technique) that Lodge speaks of; apart from that, travel books may include fictional accounts or stories and myth; conversely, documents and discursive writing, as well as historical events, can also be used in novels (in the historical novel, for instance).

Another contemporary author, Jonathan Raban, has defined travel writing thus:

> As a literary form, travel writing is a notoriously raffish open house where different genres are likely to end up in the same bed. It accommodates the private diary, the essay, the short story, the prose poem, the rough note and polished table talk with indiscriminate hospitality. It freely mixes narrative and discursive writing.[14]

Raban's definition pleads in favour of a free mix of different kinds of writing within the category of travel writing. It is therefore more supple than Theroux's in stepping beyond the notion of clear-cut boundaries between fiction and non-fiction (difficult in any case to maintain with many texts), but Raban's definition also allows us to consider *Moby Dick*, with its numerous referential sections, and Chatwin's *In Patagonia* (1977), with its series of stories adapted from Charley Milward in the book's final sections, under the same heading of travel writing. However, Raban's definition again suggests that the terms *travel book* and *travel writing* are synonymous. Yet it seems to me that this is where a problem arises, for readings (and readers' expectations) of *Moby Dick* and *In Patagonia* are not identical. Captain Ahab is not a person that the reader supposes to have existed in life, whereas the narrator of *In Patagonia* obviously did. Or, to push the point by using another set of examples, it seems to me that one does not read *Gulliver's Travels* in the same way as one reads William Dampier's *A New Voyage Round the World*.[15] The former may indeed parody the latter, but the reader would not lend the same ontological status to Swift's fictive narrator, Gulliver, and to the British traveller William Dampier (1652?–1715), no matter how hard Gulliver tries to claim that he is Dampier's cousin.[16] Yet, both

---

[13]   David Lodge, *The Practice of Writing* (London: Penguin, 1997), p. 8.

[14]   Jonathan Raban, *For Love & Money: Writing – Reading – Travelling 1968–1987* (London: Picador, 1988), pp. 253–4.

[15]   Jonathan Swift, *Gulliver's Travels* [1726] (Oxford: Oxford University Press, 1994); William Dampier, *A New Voyage Round the World: The Journal of an English Buccaneer* [1697] (London: hummingbird press, 1998).

[16]   See Gulliver's letter to his cousin Sympson in *Gulliver's Travels*, p. xxxiii: 'I hope you will be ready to own publickly, whenever you shall be called to it, that by your great and frequent Urgency you prevailed on me to publish a very loose and uncorrect Account of my Travels; with Direction to hire some young Gentlemen of either University to put them in Order, and correct the Style, as my Cousin *Dampier* did by my Advice, in

Swift's novel and Dampier's travelogue can be studied within the framework of *travel literature*.

## Of forms and hybrid genres

While it seems misleading to distinguish between fiction and non-fiction in a dogmatic way, it does seem to be useful, at least in this context, to distinguish between the travel book and travel writing in order to clarify what may actually be meant by them. One way of doing so consists in looking for *dominant aspects* in a given work or genre, an idea suggested by Hans Robert Jauss: 'To introduce a dominant that organizes the system of a complex work, allows one to transform into a methodically productive category what one called "mixed genres."'[17] Thus, while certain genres consist of a mix of different genres and forms of writing, their identity can be defined in terms of dominant aspects. This idea may then allow us to attempt a definition of the travel book: *any narrative characterized by a non-fiction dominant that relates (almost always) in the first person a journey or journeys that the reader supposes to have taken place in reality while assuming or presupposing that author, narrator and principal character are but one or identical.* One may be hard-pushed to identify which element of a given text would be non-fiction or not. However, according to Jauss's theory, any work, no matter how original, 'supposes prior information or orientation of expectations against which originality will be measured'.[18] In other words, the reader has his or her horizon of expectations. Concerning the travelogue, the reader will presume that the author is *predominantly* concerned with the account of a journey he or she actually made. In the case of Captain Cook, one may follow his itinerary step by step, up to the point of being able to retrace his voyages oneself. In Dampier's case, this would be more difficult as his *New Voyage* sums up twelve years of travel around the world. Regarding some contemporary authors, the task may seem impossible as quite a number of the journeys in question are represented in a discontinuous way. Chatwin's *In Patagonia* is a case in point, and so is Jonathan Raban's *Coasting* (1986). Nonetheless, the reader continues to presume that Chatwin and Raban actually went on their journeys. In other words, the non-fiction dominant of the travelogue consists in readers presupposing that the text they are reading is predominantly non-fiction. Having said this, it has to be stressed that the degree to which readers presuppose the author of a travelogue to be writing non-fiction varies throughout

---

his book called, *A Voyage round the World*.' Dampier's account is the model for Gulliver's parody of the travelogue. Another matter of interest in this passage is the fact that Swift's text alludes to the same eighteenth-century practice of professional writers transforming manuscripts by travellers that Mary Louise Pratt speaks of (see note 12).

[17] Hans Robert Jauss, 'Littérature médiévale et théorie des genres' (1970), in Genette *et al.*, eds, *Théorie des genres*, p. 44.

[18] Jauss, 'Littérature médiévale et théorie des genres', p. 41.

the history of the genre. Indeed, as Paul Fussell has noted: 'In the seventeenth century the travel book was so commonly regarded as a repository of wonderful lies that in 1630 Captain John Smith felt obliged to modify the word *Travels* with the word *True* when he published *The True Travels, Adventures and Observations of Captain John Smith*.'[19] The situation does not seem to be the same today, the use of fictional techniques notwithstanding. Whatever the case may be, and to return to the definition of the travel book or travelogue suggested above, it seems to me that it allows us to read Columbus's *Journal* as the account of travels that really took place and which entailed enormous consequences, while being aware that his text invariably stresses – not to say exaggerates – certain aspects as part of an imperialist strategy. In a different vein, our definition allows us not to have to take Lucian's travel tale *True History* at face value. His narrator states from the start: 'Therefore, as I myself, thanks to my vanity, was eager to hand something down to posterity, that I might not be the only one excluded from the privileges of poetic licence, and as I had nothing true to tell, not having had any adventures of significance, I took to lying.'[20] His journey will then take him to the moon.

The meaning of some of the terms quoted in the introduction has been specified sufficiently to appear in a somewhat clearer light now. To take only one example, one may wonder whether the term *travelogue* is synonymous with the *travel book*, as suggested above. Given the current looser meaning of travelogue as a travel narrative, rather than just a 'film or illustrated lecture', as the entry in the OED runs, one might call Marco Polo's text a travel book or travelogue. But what if Frances Wood's theory that Polo made up the biggest part of his travel narrative were proven right?[21] Would one still call his narrative a travel book (or travelogue)? I believe that one might, while immediately specifying that it appears to be a *fictional* travelogue. And yet, one may have trouble affirming that William Golding's *Rites of Passage* (1980) is a travelogue without adding that it is a novel and thus predominantly fictional.

This is where I would like to go one step further. Both Golding's and Polo's narratives deal predominantly with the theme of travel, and it seems that the thematic aspect may serve to outline what one might understand by the term travel writing. French critics distinguish between the terms *récit de voyage* and *littérature de voyage*, just as German critics speak on the one hand of the *Reisebuch* or *Reisebericht* (travel report) and on the other of *Reiseliteratur*. In both French and German, one therefore distinguishes between the genre *travel book* (*récit de voyage*

---

[19]   Fussell, *Abroad*, p. 165.

[20]   Lucian of Samosata, 'A True Story, II', in Lucian, *Volume I*, trans. A. M. Harmon (Cambridge, Mass.: Harvard University Press, 'Loeb Classical Library', 1913; reprinted 2000), pp. 251–3.

[21]   Frances Wood, *Did Marco Polo Go to China?* (London: Secker & Warburg, 1995).

– *Reisebuch* or – *bericht*) or *travelogue* on the one hand, and, on the other, *travel literature* (*la littérature de voyage* – *Reiseliteratur*) as an overall thematic category (and not as a genre) that includes works of non-fiction and fiction. Given the French and German terms, I would like to suggest a similar distinction between the *travel book* or *travelogue* as a predominantly (and presupposedly) non-fictional genre, and *travel writing* or *travel literature* (*the literature of travel*, if one prefers) as an overall heading for texts whose main theme is travel. Thus, one may consider texts such as Ralegh's *Discovery* as part of the same group of texts dealing principally with travel as the *Odyssey, Beowulf, The Pilgrim's Progress, Robinson Crusoe*, or, in more recent times, some of Jack London's stories and books, Robert Byron's *The Road to Oxiana*, and works by contemporary travel writers such as Jonathan Raban and Redmond O'Hanlon. It remains to be seen to what extent texts that are characterized by the *dramatic mode* (drama) may be considered as travel writing or travel literature and which plays would come into consideration. A fair case might be made for arguing that *The Tempest* deals mainly with the theme of travel, and that a number of the tropes of travel writing can be recognized in Shakespeare's play.[22]

**Of various ways of representing travel**

Be that as it may, one might recognize in the list given above examples of what some French critics have termed a literature 'on the road' or a 'travelling literature'.[23] Others, such as Etienne Rabaté, have tried to deny the genre *récit de voyage* a literary status for its supposed lack of literary energy:

> The fact that the travel book is extraordinarily stereotypical is mainly a problem of writing (and not objective reality), which lies at the heart of the travel book's central mistake: as the world has to be represented as it is, there is no transformation, no literary energy involved. The best one can aim for is a touch of 'style.'[24]

---

[22] On *The Tempest* and travel see Peter Hulme and William Sherman, eds, *'The Tempest' and Its Travels* (London: Reaktion Books, 2000).

[23] Alain Borer *et al.*, eds, *Pour une littérature voyageuse* (Paris: Editions Complexe, 1992). Michel Le Bris writes in his contribution to Borer's volume ('Fragments du royaume', pp. 119–40): 'it may just so happen that the return to a truth too often forgotten in literature is enacted in the journey: to write means to always go away' (p. 121). He adds: 'After all, it may not be a coincidence that all the great "founding" texts, from the *Bible* to the *Odyssey* and I'd almost say from *Don Quixote* to *Moby Dick* are first of all travelogues' (pp. 135–6). Le Bris has also written on the concept of *écriture de voyage*, which he considers to be the equivalent of *travel writing*.

[24] Etienne Rabaté, 'Littérateurs de voyage', *Revue de littérature générale 2* (Paris: P.O.L., 1996), section 34.

Where Rabaté allows for a few stylistic effects as the little claim travelogues can lay to literature, some Anglo-American critics may argue that the style of certain travelogues goes too far in manipulating, as David Taylor does in Chatwin's case:

> The Chatwinian convention is to elide particularity, in contravention of the post-colonial insistence on overt recognition of cultural difference. A technique poignant in the representation of objects is disconcertingly reductive of persons, who are divested of contextualising discussion or life-narrative ... A style so committed to aesthetic purity cannot but highlight its extremity of manipulation.[25]

To what extent Taylor's remarks are accurate as far as Chatwin's representation of persons is concerned, may be only questioned here in passing. It is apparent enough, though, that Chatwin is not undertaking narrative ethnography,[26] as certain anthropologists might. For example, here is how Jean Malaurie describes representing the 'conscience of the other' – the North Greenland Inuit he stayed with in 1949–50 – in his spiritual autobiography *Hummocks*. The aim is 'to unravel the inner conscience, the essence and the hidden *grandeur* of these very strong personalities', and he adds:

> Any coherent understanding of a society relies on ... participant observation unravelling the most subtle resorts. ... Man and life. The silent moments, the gestures, the small and tiniest facts which only the quotidian of the quest allows to gather and which wipe out preconceived ideas by putting general views into perspective.[27]

To return to the travelogue, here is yet another definition, by Jean Roudaut. The model for his comments is André Gide's journey to the Congo:

> [T]he travel book is discontinuous. It juxtaposes also segments of texts which differ in tone ... The text is stratified: it consists of various layers of voices, vocabulary (the descriptions vary in kind: landscapes, habitats, clothing, works) and style ... The travel book combines the heterogeneous (using all in one the form of memoir, diary and the letter) and disparity. It aims at the mosaic.[28]

A lack of systematic representation of the Other's conscience may indeed be noted in certain travelogues, but if one accepts Roudaut's analysis even partly, one will note

---

[25]   David Taylor, 'Bruce Chatwin: Connoisseur of Exile, Exile as Connoisseur', in Steve Clark, ed., *Travel Writing and Empire: Postcolonial Theory in Transit* (London: Zed Books, 1999), p. 202.

[26]   On the links between the travel book and ethnography see my article 'In-Betweeners? On the Travel Book and Ethnographies', *Studies in Travel Writing*, 4 (2000), pp. 78–105.

[27]   Jean Malaurie, *Hummocks*, 2 vols (Paris: Terre Humaine/Plon, 1999), vol. 1, pp. 111, 113.

[28]   Jean Roudaut, 'La littérature et le voyage', *le magazine du Centre 94* (Paris: Centre Georges Pompidou, July/August 1996), pp. 7–8.

a certain variation in purpose between the travel book and narrative ethnography. What is striking in comparison to Rabaté's comment on travelogues and Taylor's remarks on Chatwin, is that Rabaté criticizes the genre for lacking literary energy, whereas Taylor detects too much of it in Chatwin, while Roudaut sees the mosaic as the genre's central structural device. It seems to me that some of the debate about what travelogues do, or fail to do, relies on misconceived ideas about mimetic processes in narratives. Indeed, time and again, Aristotle's concept of *mimesis* seems to be applied only to the field of fiction, even though his *Poetics* suggest that the transforming energy of *mimesis* or *representation* is at work in any narrative, be it mainly fictional or non-fictional. I use the term *representation* as a translation for *mimesis* in reference to a relatively recent French translation of Aristotle's *Poetics*,[29] in which the translators argue that *representation* is a more accurate translation for *mimesis* than the word *imitation*, traditionally used in French translations of the text.[30] Speaking of narratives, one will note that Aristotle considers the process of *mimesis* (or 'representation' – the term used in the English translation I quote from below) to be at work in any kind of narrative: 'Since the poet, like a painter or any other image-maker, is a mimetic artist, he must represent, in any instance, one of three objects: the kind of things which were or are the case; the kind of things that people say and think; the kind of things that ought to be the case.'[31] According to Aristotle, the concept of *mimesis* therefore does not only apply to fiction, but also to non-fiction ('the kind of things which were or are the case'). Indeed, Gérard Genette has suggested that 'one may include, without any harm in the notion of narrative, all forms of literary representation'.[32] Moreover, he has pointed out that texts of pure fiction or pure non-fiction are theoretical constructs

---

[29] Aristotle, *La Poétique*, Texte, traduction, notes par Roselyne Dupont-Roc et Jean Lallot (Paris: Seuil, 1980).

[30] This choice of translating *mimesis* by *représentation* rather than *imitation* has been criticized by Jean-Marie Schaeffer in his latest study, *Pourquoi la fiction?* (Paris: Seuil, 1999). He therefore quotes from an older French translation of the *Poetics* in which the word *imitation* is used. However, it may be pointed out that Schaeffer needs the word *imitation* in his theory of fiction in order to argue that fiction imitates, and that it is therefore a kind of 'playful feint' or trick ('feintise ludique'). In doing so, *mimesis* is a cognitive act, as he states: 'Il apparaît notamment que, contrairement à ce que soutenait Platon, la mimésis est bien une opération cognitive, au double sens où elle est la mise en œuvre d'une connaissance et où elle est source de connaissance' (p. 56). 'As opposed to Plato's arguments, however, it appears, notably, that *mimesis* is a cognitive act after all; it is both a way of making function some knowledge and it works as a source of knowledge.' For our purposes, the term *representation* seems more flexible. Whichever translation of *mimesis* may be more accurate, it seems apparent enough at this stage that travel books make more or less frequent use of mimetic devices, such as, notably, dialogue, and that some of them transform experience by using, for example, scenic construction.

[31] Aristotle, *Poetics*, trans. Stephen Halliwell (Cambridge, Mass.: Harvard University Press, 'Loeb Classical Library', 1995), pp. 125–7.

[32] Gérard Genette, *Figures II* (Paris: Seuil, 1969), p. 61.

that do not correspond to any given text.[33] In other words, there is no escaping *mimesis* in narratives. It is therefore at work *by definition* in any travel book and, more generally of course, in the field of travel writing. This is what V. S. Naipaul also seems to suggest when describing his most recent books:

> My books have to be called 'travel writing', but that can be misleading because in the old days travel writing was essentially done by men describing the routes they were taking ... What I do is quite different. I travel on a theme. I travel to make an inquiry. I am not a journalist. I am taking with me the gifts of sympathy, observation and curiosity that I developed as an imaginative writer. The books I write now, these inquiries, are really constructed narratives. There is the narrative of the journey and within that there are many little narratives that are part of the larger pattern.[34]

It is debatable whether travel writing in the old days was 'essentially' about describing routes. However, Naipaul also hints at the role of *mimesis* in his so-called works of non-fiction and his remarks illustrate the point. It may be added that few critics would deny that Naipaul's style may be characterized, amongst other things, as being literary.[35]

Whatever the case, there is no avoiding the literary dimension of travelogues.[36] Michel Morel has shown how the literary is invariably an expression of the dynamic role of individual *Style*:

> Style sheds light on the individual reenacting of a generic system. This is its individual dimension. At the same time, it also sheds light on the historical characteristics of the system at the moment a work appears. That is its collective dimension.[37]

At its most dynamic, Style is individual and opposed, to a certain degree, to generic norms.[38] Yet any set of such norms does not guarantee that the *literary* is at work in any one of the products of a particular genre. It can therefore be suggested that the travel book is no more, but also no less, a literary genre than any other. One can even say that the *romanesque* precedes any journey, and thus also the travelogue,

---

[33]   Gérard Genette, *Nouveau discours du récit* (Paris: Seuil, 1983), p. 11: 'Mais exista-t-il jamais une pure fiction? Et une pure non-fiction? La réponse est évidemment négative dans les deux cas.' 'But can a work of pure fiction ever exist? Or a work of pure non-fiction, for that matter? The answer is obviously no in both cases.' On the same page, Genette also states that a literary narrative need not necessarily be fiction.

[34]   V. S. Naipaul, in interview with Ahmed Rashid, 'Death of the Novel', *The Observer* (Review), 25 February 1996, p. 16.

[35]   Naipaul was awarded the Nobel Prize for Literature in 2001. The fact that the jury's choice leads to widespread debate every year is another question.

[36]   Whether this dimension is sophisticated or not, and to what extent a travel book does or does not transform both the Other and experience, is yet again another matter.

[37]   Michel Morel, *Praxis de la lecture*, unpublished Ph.D. dissertation, 2 vols (Paris: Université de la Sorbonne Nouvelle – Paris III, 1989), p. 350.

[38]   Morel speaks of the 'dynamic effect of linguistic invention' (*Praxis de la lecture*, p. 343).

as Jean-Didier Urbain does in *Secrets de voyage*: 'it would be … a mistake to underestimate the importance of the romanesque or more generally that of a narrative programme at the origin of a journey, of any kind of journey and to question not only its presence but efficiency'.[39] Speaking of Gavin Young following in Conrad's footsteps, Urbain notes: 'By proposing to rediscover, as though he were tailing it, the romanesque side of the real invented by another, Young invites one to travel less within a physical space than in the space of a narrative.'[40] It may be argued that this sort of travel and travel book characterizes particularly the contemporary period. But then again, one will note that literary references to other travel narratives, starting with the *Odyssey*, have characterized the travel book and travel writing for a long time. Thus, Urbain remarks that as a reader of Gavin Young 'one becomes a viator in fabula, a traveller travelling in a story',[41] just as the traveller travels in other travellers' stories. According to Urbain, at the origin of any journey there is 'a story, or another journey, or yet another story, in brief, there is a mediator of desire, a model to be translated that informs one's vision, governs one's action and feeds one's discourse'.[42] In other words, the transforming act of *mimesis* is present in a journey from its outset and remains so until the last full stop, or dash, of a travel book.[43]

An interesting case in point is the famous French series *Terre Humaine*, founded by Jean Malaurie in 1955, with his first title, *Les Derniers Rois de Thulé*.[44] The editorial policy of the series stresses the importance of narrative, and takes into consideration the role of mimetic devices in representing experience. Pierre Aurégan has analysed, among other aspects, the writing of a number of its titles in a recent study.[45] He lists the series' characteristics, that is, first-person narration, a 'refusal of academic jargon and professional anthropology's modes of arguing, the use of narrative and a personal implication of the author';[46] that is to say,

---

[39]   Jean-Didier Urbain, *Secrets de voyage: Menteurs, imposteurs et autres voyageurs invisibles* (Paris: Payot, 1998), p. 361. For an introduction to Urbain's work see Charles Forsdick, '*Viator in Fabula*: Jean-Didier Urbain and the Cultures of Travel in Contemporary France', *Studies in Travel Writing*, 4 (2000), pp. 141–64. An English translation of *Secrets de voyage* is forthcoming from Notre Dame University Press.

[40]   Urbain, *Secrets de voyage*, p. 362.

[41]   Urbain, *Secrets de voyage*, p. 362.

[42]   Urbain, *Secrets de voyage*, p. 372.

[43]   Jonathan Raban's *Coasting* (London: Collins & Harvill, 1986) ends with a dash, in reference to Sterne's *Sentimental Journey* (1768).

[44]   Jean Malaurie, *Les Derniers Rois de Thulé* (Paris: Plon/Terre Humaine, 5th edition, 1989; English translation *The Last Kings of Thule*, New York: E. P. Dutton, 1982). The second title in the series is Claude Lévi-Strauss's *Tristes Tropiques*, published that same year. Other famous works include translations of Wilfred Thesiger's travelogues *Arabian Sands* and *The Marsh Arabs*.

[45]   Pierre Aurégan, *Des récits et des hommes – Terre Humaine: un autre regard sur les sciences de l'homme* (Paris: Nathan/Plon, 2001).

[46]   Aurégan, *Des récits et des hommes*, p. 25.

'extensive use of the *I*, scenic representation of the *I* including mishaps and the use of narrative'.[47] The aim is to 'reconcile ethnography and the reader's emotion'.[48] Aurégan also comments on the fiction/non-fiction divide and dogmatic attempts to oppose discursive writing and fiction, as far as the representation of the Other is concerned, by stressing that *Terre Humaine* publishes various kinds of writing, including life-narratives, travelogues, narrative ethnography and fiction:

> The fact that a series like *Terre Humaine* publishes novels may come as a surprise and merits some consideration. And why not any novels? Why exclude from the outset romanesque fiction by denying it a dimension of documentary truth? In the name of a widespread preconceived view that there is a clear barrier between the ethnographic, sociological or historical narrative and a work of fiction. As though the former had been awarded a truth label outright. This is a heavy assumption that ignores the following three points to be observed:
> – that an ethnographic narrative bears the signs of a given period's limits and its observer;
> – that in spite of its intellectual honesty and its concern to proceed scientifically, the so-called documentary narrative is the result of classifying and ordering of facts, the hermeneutic value of which remains a matter of debate;
> – that there is no transparency between the subject writing and the object he or she is writing about. No doubt, reading Balzac will teach us as much – if not more – about post-revolutionary society as the historians of his time – forgotten today – did.[49]

Aurégan suggests that *Terre Humaine*'s policy consists in publishing texts that aim at breaking down 'the false dichotomy between the subjective and the objective'.[50] It is arguable, of course, to what extent an individual work manages to do so. The idea is interesting, nonetheless, in the context of our discussion of the travel book. An author's style does indeed transform and even manipulate experience by representing (and even by imitating) it. As we have seen above, the process is inevitable. This leads Aurégan to comment on one of the series' most famous titles, Jacques Lacarrière's travelogue *L'Été grec*,[51] in the following way:

> Jacques Lacarrière also clearly shows his point-of-view: he wants to show a different Greece, in parts, and partial; everyday, popular Greece as opposed to the scholarly Greece of ruins. Claiming an inner Greece to be truer than the impersonal Greece of historians and sociologists. Here, as with Thesiger, the observation and discovery of a culture are woven into a personal itinerary, caught within the net of an omnipresent *I*. The traveller therefore does not show *Greece*, but *his Greece*.[52]

---

47  Aurégan, *Des récits et des hommes*, p. 31.
48  Aurégan, *Des récits et des hommes*, p. 46.
49  Aurégan, *Des récits et des hommes*, p. 49.
50  Aurégan, *Des récits et des hommes*, p. 50.
51  Jacques Lacarrière, *L'Été grec* (Paris: Terre Humaine/Plon, 1975).
52  Aurégan, *Des récits et des hommes*, p. 52.

Incidentally, Chatwin also aims at showing *his Patagonia*, rather than *Patagonia*. Some readers will consider this a problematic act of taking possession and it is manifest that Chatwin's choice of (largely) leaving out the political context of his journey to Argentina in the 1970s presents certain difficulties.[53] Having said this, the aim in this essay has been to discuss various generic approaches to the travel book and to travel writing in Anglo-American and French criticism. What is striking is the extent to which the genre *travelogue* is criticized for very different and sometimes even opposing reasons.

If it seems to have been necessary to outline the space of the *travel book* or *travelogue* within *travel writing* or *the literature of travel*, it also needs to be stressed that the genre *travel book* mixes different forms of writing, while continuously crossing over into other genres. Concerning the overall sense given here to travel writing, it can help to establish numerous intertexts between various narratives whose principal narrative modes may not be of the same order, but which share the same archetype of the journey as a form of quest – to paraphrase Northrop Frye.[54] As seen above, a comparison between *Gulliver's Travels* and Dampier's *New Voyage*, or Conrad's diary and his *Heart of Darkness*, are methodically productive in taking into consideration an intertext whose components may vary in generic terms.

Not wanting to end on a sentimental tone, one may nonetheless refer again to Sterne and his Smelfungus, created in response to Smollett's personal mix of abuse against the French.[55] Having found a term for what undoubtedly existed before, that is, the sentimental journey, Sterne's text was to initiate countless so-called sentimental travel books, one of the best known of which is Mungo Park's *Travels into the Interior of Africa* (1799). As Mary Louise Pratt has pointed out:

> Though he certainly could have done so, Mungo Park did not write up a narrative of geographical discovery, observation, or collection, but one of personal experience and adventure. He wrote, and wrote himself, not as a man of science, but as a sentimental hero.[56]

This is perhaps where the heart of the matter lies. What form of travel writing one will practise depends on what kind of writer one is or wants to be. If I am uneasy about attempts to define travel writing as a genre, I do hope to have shown that

---

[53]   This is where he notably differs from Lacarrière; which does not mean, however, that *In Patagonia* does not develop any political themes. The disastrous effect of colonialism on the native population is one of its main concerns.

[54]   Northrop Frye, *Anatomy of Criticism* (Princeton: Princeton University Press, 1957): 'If archetypes are communicable symbols, and there is a center of archetypes, we should expect to find, at that center, a group of universal symbols ... Such symbols include that of food and drink, of the quest or journey' (p. 118).

[55]   Tobias Smollett, *Travels through France and Italy* [1766] (Oxford: Oxford University Press, 1981).

[56]   Pratt, *Imperial Eyes*, p. 75.

travel writing or travel literature can be a useful heading under which to consider and to compare the multiple crossings from one form of writing into another and, given the case, from one genre into another. In consequence, it seems appropriate to plead one last time in favour of the travel book's 'loose and shifting borders'[57] – shifting borders within that 'notoriously raffish open house' of travel writing which Jonathan Raban has described in such fitting terms.

---

[57] Jean-Marie Schaeffer, *Qu'est-ce qu'un genre littéraire?* (Paris: Seuil, 1989), p. 77.

Chapter 3

# 'As mannerly and civill as any of Europe': Early Modern Travel Writing and the Exploration of the English Self

Helga Quadflieg

When Richard Hakluyt set out in 1589 to praise the 'Principal Navigations, Voyages and Discoveries of the English Nation' in two voluminous folios, he could be said to have engaged in what modern linguistics might call a 'performative speech act'. English voyagers had just about begun their second attempt to establish an English colony overseas after the failure of the first colony three years before. Yet only a year after Hakluyt's publication this second 'Roanoke' colony had also to be abandoned, just like Martin Frobisher's and John Davis' attempts to find the North-West passage in the 1570s and 1580s, Humphrey Gilbert's attempts at colonization in Northern America (1578; 1583), and Walter Raleigh's desperate search for the legendary El Dorado (1584). As a maritime and colonial power, therefore, England could hardly compete with Spain, and in spite of various successful trading missions to Russia or Persia, the quantity and quality of successful 'navigations, voyages and discoveries' would have called for an octavo rather than two folios. Hakluyt's collection of whatever report about voyages to distant countries he could get hold of is a plea, therefore, for future successes more than a documentation of a glorious past; rather than describing the 'English nation' as the apparent protagonist of certain past deeds, it appears part of the discursive agenda of 'writing the nation' – a role it shares, amongst others, with Tudor historiographic, chorographic, judicial, architectural and literary discourses.[1]

The travelogues edited by Richard Hakluyt[2] and later by his literary 'executor'

---

[1] For the role of discourses, like the common law or chorography, see Richard Helgerson, *Forms of Nationhood* (Chicago: Chicago University Press, 1992); for the role of architecture and especially the 'country-house', see Bruce McLeod, *The Geography of Empire in English Literature* (Cambridge: Cambridge University Press, 1999), pp. 76–119. See also, Andrew Hadfield, *Literature, Travel and Colonial Writing* (Oxford: Clarendon Press, 1998) and Edwin Jones, *The English Nation: the Great Myth* (Thrupp/Stroud: Sutton, 1998).

[2] Richard Hakluyt, *The Principall Navigations, Voyages and Discoveries of the English Nation*, 2 vols (1589), later enlarged and published as *The Principal Navigations, Voyages, Traffiques and Discoveries of the English Nation*, 3 vols (1598–1600); reprinted in 12 vols (Glasgow: MacLehose, 1903–05). Unless otherwise stated all references are to

Samuel Purchas,[3] however, also give scope to the self-presentation of individual travellers. As the generic distinctions between the discourses of geography, ethnography, anthropology, sociology or historiography had not yet been academically institutionalized, and the individual self as both subject and object of autobiographical kinds of writing had not been generally established, Tudor travel writing participates in a number of discourses. In addition, these texts were produced in a historical phase in which people's perception of the universe and of the individual's place in this world changed in a radical way, and in which traditional systems of coherence had lost their binding force. The spatial, temporal and social co-ordinates that serve to position the individual with regard to particular systems of reference and coherence had to be redefined and adjusted to these new concepts. The writings of these Tudor and early Stuart travellers, therefore, can be analysed not only as examples of a particular kind of colonial discourse, but also as texts that are symptomatic of the changes in the perception of the world which took place in the sixteenth and seventeenth centuries and which constitute the 'modernity' of the early modern period. One aspect of this modernization is the increased differentiation between a public and a private sphere, and the necessity of establishing and defining one's individual place, function and identity in both spheres.[4]

This process was, of course, connected with changes in economic structures and principles, and the emergence of a 'state' as the agent and space of politics on the one hand, and a 'market' as the agent and space of economics on the other.[5] In constituting his or her identity in relation to various 'Othernesses', described in terms of increasingly unstable systems of reference and coherence, the Tudor individual had to engage in a complex system of redefinitions, both on a personal and on a social level. Moreover, the basic mechanics of exclusion and inclusion in the interaction of Self and Other, which are part of any process of identity formation, are multiplied for the traveller who encounters the Othernesses of foreign or even 'exotic' cultures. Tudor travellers were exposed to these kinds of foreign Otherness in a very pronounced and unprecedented way, and their reactions

---

the following edition: *The Principal Navigations, Voyages, Traffiques and Discoveries of the English Nation*, 8 vols (London: Dent, 1907).

    [3]    Samuel Purchas, *Hakluytus Posthumus or Purchas His Pilgrimes* (1625). All references are to the 20 vols edition (Glasgow: MacLehose, 1905).

    [4]    See Philippe Ariès, *Histoire de la vie privée*, vol. 3: *De la renaissance aux Lumières*, ed. R. Chartiers (Paris: Seuil, 1986); Norbert Elias, *The Civilizing Process*, 2 vols (Oxford: Blackwell, 1978–82). See also, Anna Bryson, *From Courtesy to Civility: Changing Modes of Conduct in Early Modern England* (Oxford: Clarendon, 1998).

    [5]    See, for example, L. Bauer and H. Matis, *Geburt der Neuzeit. Vom Feudalsystem zur Marktgesellschaft* (München: dtv, 1988); Hans Blumenberg, *Säkularisierung und Selbstbehauptung* (Frankfurt: Suhrkamp, 1974); Geoffrey Rudolph Elton, *England under the Tudors* (London: Routledge, 1991); David Palliser, *The Age of Elizabeth: England under the later Tudors, 1547–1603* (Harlow: Longman, 1992), and James Sharpe, *Early Modern England: A Social History 1550–1760* (London: Arnold, 1987).

towards confrontation with the 'Other' range from stressing 'difference' to the denial of Otherness. Early modern travelogues, therefore, can be described as one of the sites on which new concepts of subjectivity and identity on a personal, social and national level are negotiated. In exploring Others, these travellers explore themselves, and in describing Others they write themselves. In their discourse on the encounter with foreign Otherness, we witness the travellers' uncertainty of their own religious and cultural Selves, but we also face the discursive construction of an 'I' which struggles for new stability by positioning itself in a frame of reference defined by religion, civility and nationality.

# I

One of the most important sites for renegotiating early modern identity is religion and its social institutions. The turmoil following in the wake of the various reformations destabilized the British Christian community in a much more radical way than any of the diversifications of the pre-reformation era had done. Although Elizabeth had succeeded in calming the situation after Henry VIII's hesitating reforms, Edward VI's sweeping reformation and Mary's radical counter-reformation,[6] there was no new religious concept or institution which had developed a binding force strong enough to serve as a unifying and stabilizing co-ordinate for one's religious identity. Moreover, pre-Christian forms of belief, magic and ritual were still important for many groups of society, and whereas some of these pre-Christian rituals had had their niches within traditional Catholicism, the newly reformed churches were opposed to all kinds of 'heathen' magic.[7]

In their voyages abroad Elizabethan travellers came into contact with diverse forms of religious practice, and the confrontation with European or extra-European Others and their different forms of religiously motivated rites sometimes left them confronted with their own struggle for orientation. The perception and description

---

[6]   Crucial issues in all of these debates were the role of the saints and the various cults connected with them, of miracles, the purgatory, clerical celibacy, transubstantiation, forms and language of religious ceremony and of confession, etc. After having endorsed fairly strict reformatory positions in the 'Ten Articles' of 1536, Henry's 'Six Articles' of 1539 partly returned to 'Romish' forms (celibacy, transubstantiation, mass, auricular confession). They did, however, retain English as the language of both Bible and religious ceremonies. Edward VI's 'Second Book of Common Prayer' of 1552 and the 'Forty-Two Articles' of 1553 took a decidedly Protestant stance, abolishing all 'Romish' elements, introducing new forms of mass, and confirming the Monarch as the Supreme Head of Church. In winter 1554–55 Mary Tudor radically tried to enforce the re-establishment of a 'Romish' church under papal jurisdiction. Elizabeth's 'settlement' of 1559 successfully steered a middle course between religious conservatism and reformation.

[7]   See Alan Macfarlane, *Witchcraft in Tudor and Stuart England* (London: Routledge, 1970), and Keith Thomas, *Religion and the Decline of Magic* (London: Penguin, 1973).

of foreign forms of ritual were influenced partly by the motivation for establishing contact. A traveller who wanted to establish commercial relationships was likely to have a different perception than a potential colonizer: whereas the latter would focus on the fertility of the land and the tractability of the natives, the former might emphasize the mercantile potential of future trading partners. The screen of perception, however, was always defined by the traveller's own religious background, and the pattern for describing foreign religions was the pattern of differences between Catholicism and Protestantism. In other words, it is the insistence on the traveller's own Otherness which informs the reports of the Other's monotheistic religions, and the descriptions focus on differences rather than similarities, even when other Christian religions are described. The early reports about voyages into Russia, for example, dedicate long passages to ecclesiastical feasts and sacraments and the religious and political role of priests, as well as to the architecture and decoration of church buildings. Moreover, particular attention is paid to Orthodox monasteries whose very existence emphasizes the difference of the post-reformation traveller. Thomas Randolfe, the English ambassador to Russia, is particularly fascinated by the monks he encounters in Moscow (1568):

> [T]he apparell of the Monks is superstitious, in blacke hoods, as ours have bene. Their church is faire, but full of painted images, tapers and candles. … They lie apart, they eat together, and are much given to drunkennesse, unlearned, write they can, preach they doe never, ceremonious in their Church, and long in their prayers. (Hakluyt, vol. 2, p. 81)

Randolfe here is well aware that traditions in his own country, not very long ago, were similar to those in Russia, but his look back is free from nostalgia. With their proclivity to undisciplined consumption of drink and an education which is reduced to basic skills, the Russian monks appear as the equivalent of a less cultured or civilized form of religious practice which the traveller's own country has long overcome. This kind of rhetorical exclusion of foreign Otherness – by suggesting its proximity to less cultivated forms of existence – helps the traveller overcome the experience of finding himself the excluded one when he encounters monotheistic religions which in turn attribute absolute and universal validity to their own systems of belief:

> [T]hey hold opinion that we are but halfe Christians, and themselves onely to be the true and perfect church: these are the foolish and childish dotages of such ignorant Barbarians. (1553) (Clement Adams, Hakluyt, vol. 1, p. 291)

Encountering the stable and staunch convictions of Russian Orthodox Christians or Persian Muslims, Adams appears to experience a deep sense of uncertainty in the face of his own religious instability – a precariousness which was particularly marked in the year of writing, the year which also saw the transition from Edward to Mary Tudor. More specifically, Adams' comments dramatically indicate, by the accumulation of four derogatory terms in a half sentence of eleven words, the way in which various uncertainties can be channelled into the construction of a more stable Self: the threatening alterity of the Russians is packed off discursively to the world of undesirable Otherness. Thus the Russians now occupy the space of an Otherness which can easily be excluded from the traveller's world and which is marked by shortcomings of education, civilization and maturity, which, of course, leaves the English traveller's Self in a world replete with such cultural assets.

Other Tudor travellers, however, are less eloquent, and their reports document continued instability in the face of an Otherness that refuses to be integrated into the travellers' self-image. Anthony Jenkinson, for example, gives voice to the religious views of the Others he encounters in his journeys to Russia and Persia, even to the point of allowing himself to be catechized by them:

> [H]e reasoned with mee much of Religion, demaunding whether I were a Gower, that is to say, an unbeleever, or a Muselman … Unto whom, I answered, that I was neither unbeleever nor Mahometan, but a Christian. What is that, said he unto the king of Georgians sonne … and he answered that a Christian was he that beleeveth in Jesus Christ, affirming him to be the Sonne of God … Doest thou beleeve so, said the Sophie unto me? Yea that I doe, said I: Oh thou unbeleever, said he, we have no need to have friendship with the unbeleevers. (1561) (A. Jenkinson, Hakluyt, vol. 2, p. 22)

Jenkinson reports his observations on the religious beliefs of the Others he meets on his journey, but repeatedly we find him in the role of the observed rather than the observer. In providing space for the self-presentation of Muslim practice, he at least allows the possibility of an alternative set of beliefs to shine through, without necessarily adopting these beliefs as his own. This contact with foreign religions may thus imply a relativization of the traveller's own position, even more so when the traveller comes across phenomena which he cannot (yet) explain within the new concepts of his own religion, but which he cannot falsify either.[8] This applies especially to encounters with foreign forms of magic and ritual, an area with a considerable gap between 'official' Christian beliefs and the vestiges of older forms of belief. In 1556, for example, Richard Johnson witnessed a scene of sacrifice of the Samoids and watched the actions of the shaman, which he describes in all their technical detail. He emphasizes his endeavours to verify empirically what he claims to have seen:

> Then he tooke a sworde of a cubite and a spanne long (I did mete it my self) and put it into his bellie … Then he put the sword into the fire till it was warme, and so thrust it into the slitte of his shirte and thrust it through his bodie, as I thought, in at his navill and out at his fundament: the poynt beeing out at his shirt behinde. I layde my finger upon it. (Hakluyt, vol. 1, p. 355)

---

[8]   I use the masculine pronoun 'he' throughout because all the voyages and travels covered by Hakluyt and Purchas were undertaken by men.

Throughout the ceremony the observer hovers between his scepticism about the inexplicable 'magic' and his own observations:

> I asked them that sate by me what it was that fell into the water ... And they answered me, that it was his head, his shoulder and left arme ... Then I rose up and would have looked whether it were so or not, but they laid hold on me, and said, that if they should see him with their bodily eyes, they shoulde live no longer. ... and then at the last the Priest lifted up his head with his shoulder and arme, and all his bodie ... And I went to him, that served the Priest, and asked him what their God saide to him when he lay as dead. Hee answered, that his owne people doeth not know: neither is it for them to know: for they must doe as he commanded. (Hakluyt, vol. 1, pp. 355–6)

Although forty years later, in his editorial introduction to the text, Hakluyt clearly classifies these events as 'devilish rites', Johnson offers his narrative without comment. Throughout his description he oscillates between general doubtfulness of witchcraft, and a belief in what he sees and touches with his own eyes and hands. More importantly, Johnson seems to be fairly typical of the early Tudor travellers and their uncertainty with regard to these manifestations of the spiritual, an uncertainty that becomes even more marked when it is confronted with foreign forms of magic and ritual. Johnson appears to be so entangled in the field of tension between folkloristic belief in magic, traditional Christian belief in miracles, and more recent reformatory rationalism, that he accepts the denial of closer access to the scene of sacrifice without any obvious protest. What is particularly striking in the light of later reports, moreover, is that he also describes, without any comment or interpretation, the reservation of privileged knowledge for a small group of priests. He neither sees the events as the manifestation of 'good' supernatural powers nor assumes devilish mechanisms at work; he neither explicitly accuses the priests of betrayal nor interprets their secrecy as part of a Machiavellian device for maintaining power.

Johnson contrasts strongly, however, with later travellers such as Thomas Harriot, who in his *Briefe and true report of the New Found Land of Virginia* (1586) describes the religious creed of the Algonquins, especially the social and political function of their priests. When he comes across the function which the notion ('this opinion') of 'popogussa' – an Algonquian equivalent to Christian ideas of hell – has for the political and social order of the Indians, Harriot immediately refers this back to the role of the priests:

> What subtilitie soever be in the Wiroances and priestes, this opinion worketh so much in many of the common and simple sort of people, that it maketh them have great respect to their Governours, and also great care what they doe, to avoyd torment after death, and to enjoy blisse. (Harriot, Hakluyt, vol. 6, p. 189)

Stephen Greenblatt describes this passage as an insidious interpretation of religious rites which consciously or subconsciously undermines the basic conception of

Harriot's own religion by implicitly pointing out that such systems of belief can be functionalized politically.[9] Apart from that, however, the passage also refers to the central aspect of the presentation of the culture of the Others, which is the projection of the other religion onto the foil of the traveller's own religious and religio-political ideology. By insisting particularly on the importance of the priests for the practice of religion, Harriot's report points to the anti-clerical aspects of the reformation, and underlines the equation of Catholic with Indian rituals, which he had already implied in other passages:

> The Priests of the aforesaid Towne of Secoto ... are notable enchanters. ... They have comonlye coniurers or iuglers which use strange gestures, and often contrarie to nature in their enchantment.[10]

In Elizabethan times 'conjurer' had gradually become a synonym for Catholic priests who had refused to join the Anglican church, and the Puritan Henry Barrow generally used to refer to Elizabethan clerics as 'Egyptian chanters'.[11] When writing about Indian priests and medicine men in terms very similar to Barrow, then, Harriot rhetorically highlights the proximity of Catholicism and 'savage' religion. Similar discursive mechanisms can be seen at work in his description of the importance of tobacco (uppowoc) in a scene of sacrifice:

> This Uppowoc is of so precious estimation amongst them, that they thinke their gods are marvellously delighted therewith: whereupon sometime they make hallowed fires, and cast some of the pouder therin for a sacrifice: being a storme upon the waters, to pacifie their gods, they cast some up into the aire and into the water: so a weare for fish being newly set up, they cast some therin and into the aire. (Harriot, Hakluyt, vol. 6, p. 177)

In the same volume, Robert Transon reports on the Catholic Spaniards whom he encountered on a voyage to Nova Hispania in 1555, and Transon's description of their attempts to pacify a raging storm with various religious rituals is highly reminiscent of Harriot's descriptions of Native Americans' rituals of consecration and sacrifice:

> The friars cast reliques into the sea, to cause the sea to be still, and likewise said Gospels, with other crossings and ceremonies upon the sea to make the storme to cease: which (as they said) did much good to weaken the furie of the storme. ... By this men may see how the Papists are given to beleeve and worship such vaine things and toyes, as God, to whom all honour doeth appertaine, and in their needs and necessities do let to call upon the living God, who is the giver of all good things. (Hakluyt, vol. 6, p. 252)

---

[9]   See Stephen Greenblatt, 'Invisible Bullets', in Stephen Greenblatt, *Shakespearean Negotiations* (Oxford: Clarendon, 1988), pp. 21–65.

[10]   Harriot in his texts for *John White's paintings from Virginia*, cited in D. B. Quinn, ed., *The Roanoke Voyages, 1584–1590*, 2 vols (London: The Hakluyt Society, 1955), vol. 1, pp. 431–42.

[11]   See Thomas, *Religion and the Decline of Magic*, pp. 78–9.

Interestingly, this equation of Catholic and Indian religion becomes even more pointed in Richard Grenville's description of an Indian burial ritual:

> They of Weopomeiok should be invited to a certaine kind of moneths minde which they do use to solemnise in their Savage maner for any great personage dead. (1585) (Grenville, Hakluyt, vol. 6, p. 155)

A 'mon[e]th's mind' is the 'celebration of a catholic mass for the repose of the soul of the dead in the Roman Catholic Church'.[12] In this context, Harriot's insistence on the 'idleness' of the Indians, and his repeated complaints that they neglect the intensive agrarian use of soil, could also be seen as an implicit refusal of the more Catholic principle of contemplation, and a plea for Puritan activity and industriousness.

   If this kind of description may seem fairly plausible when applied to other Christian religions, the projection of such concepts onto Indian (and other non-Christian) religions should make clear that what is at stake here is neither the conflict between opposing trends within one and the same system of religion, nor the simple denigration of 'heathen' religions motivated by sheer ethnocentricity. What is at issue is the establishment of a new asymmetrical pair of binary oppositions – Christians and Idolators, instead of the mediaeval Christian vs Heathen paradigm.[13] More importantly, this new paradigm aims at equating Christians with 'reformed' Christianity and at excluding all kinds of non-reformed religions (be they Catholic, Islamic or Indian religions). In addition to the term 'heathen' (or 'gentile'), which continues to distinguish Christians from non-Christians and which is still employed for colonization, we now have the term 'idolator', which subsumes non-reformed Christians and non-Christians under one negative term. This form of exclusion of English Catholicism – in times of a strong counter-reformatory movement – transforms the meeting with the religion of the Others in a foreign country to a meeting with the religion in one's own country. In the disguise of a description of the American Other the travelogue becomes a place for direct religio-political struggle with the English 'own', an 'own' Self that gradually emerges to be indissolubly linked to Protestantism.

## II

There are, however, striking differences in the presentation of the Native Americans, depending on whether the text was in any way related to a project of colonization. The propagandists of colonization faced the dilemma of, on the one hand, justifying

---

[12]  Quinn, *The Roanoke Voyages*, vol. 1, p. 281.

[13]  See, for the concept of 'asymmetrisches Gegensatzpaar' (asymmetrical pairs of contrasts), Reinhard Koselleck, 'Zur historisch-politischen Semantik asymmetrischer Gegenbegriffe', in R. Koselleck, *Vergangene Zukunft* (Frankfurt: Suhrkamp, 1979), pp. 21–59.

their intended hegemony over the Native Americans by pointing out the savagery of the natives, and, on the other hand, not overemphasizing this for fear of scaring off potential investors. However, one way out of this dilemma was the re-activation of the old opposition of Christian vs Heathen/Infidel.[14] The patents for diverse potential colonizers always restricted colonizing activities to 'such remote, heathen and barbarous lands ... not actually possessed of any Christian prince, nor inhabited by Christian people'.[15] Although this opposition is an asymmetrical one by aiming at the exclusion of the Other, it involves a clearly marked temporal dimension: Heathens or Infidels are not necessarily excluded permanently from the community of Christians, but are rather potential 'not-yet-Christians'. This somewhat more 'optimistic' interpretation of the role of the natives therefore entails a slight change of perspective in the evaluation of the religious practices of these 'poore pagans' who so desperately seem to be waiting for Christianity:

> Is it not therefore (I say) to be lamented, that these poore Pagans, so long living in ignorance and idolatry, and in sort thirsting after Christianitie ... that our hearts are so hardened, that fewe or none can be found which will put to their helping hands, and apply themselves to the relieving of the miserable and wretched estate of these sillie soules? (G. Peckham, Hakluyt, vol. 6, p. 46)

In this type of discourse, colonizing projects are missionary projects, and although the natives are graced with at least the potential for the 'correct' religion, the colonists themselves have no doubt about what the correct religion might consist of: 'Some religion they have already, which although it be farre from the trueth, yet being as it is, there is hope it may be the easier and sooner reformed' (Harriot, Hakluyt, vol. 6, p. 187).

In a similar way the opposition of civility and beastliness is utilized for an affirmation of the traveller's own – and fairly new – values and criteria of civilization. In this context it might be useful to remember what has been described as the 'conquest of a private sphere' in early modern times: the increased importance attached to an individual's control of his/her affects and instincts, and the emergence of the notion of a 'private life' as explicitly opposed to an increasingly visible political and public life. This process is accompanied by more formalized and indirectly regulated forms of everyday life, where clothing, table manners, or other forms of social etiquette, can increasingly serve as an indicator of the social ranking of individuals. Indeed, hardly any of the travel reports from this period refrain from commenting on the clothing habits of the respective native populations, with special attention paid to the visibility and non-visibility of breasts and genitals.

---

[14] For a general discussion of the debates on colonization, see Anthony Pagden, 'The Struggle for Legitimacy', in Nicholas Canny, ed., *The Oxford History of the British Empire, vol.1: The Origins of Empire* (Oxford: Oxford University Press, 1998, pp. 34–54). See also, Hadfield, *Literature, Travel and Colonial Writing*, pp. 69–133.

[15] Cited in Hakluyt, vol. 6, p. 115.

Nevertheless, other criteria also mark a degree of civilization, or the lack of it: nutritional habits and table manners, houses and their interiors, agricultural habits, and so on. As with religious discourse (potential) colonists tend to be more optimistic in their discourse than other types of travellers and the scope of evaluations of the cultural achievements of the natives varies tremendously.[16] What the various reports have in common, however, is the set of concepts and values to which they keep referring in their description of the natives, and by which these travellers again define themselves more clearly than any of the natives of the countries they visit. What dominates descriptions here is the opposition of civility/courtesy and beastliness. In spite of their seeming disparity, for example, Dionise Settle's derogatory report on his encounters with the Inuit and Amadas and Barlowe's praise of the Algonquins share a common set of values:

> Their crafty dealing at these three several times being thus manifest to us, may plainly shew their dispositions in other things to be correspondent.
> …
>
> They weare their haire something long, and cut before either with stone or knife, very disorderly …
>
> They eate their meat all raw, both flesh, fish, and foule …
>
> If they for necessities sake stand in need of the premisses, such grasse as the Countrey yeeldeth they plucke up and eate, not deintily, or salletwise to allure their stomacks to appetite: but for necessities sake without either salt, oyles or washing, like brute beasts devouring the same. They neither use table, stoole, or table cloth. …
>
> They apparell themselves in the skins of such beasts as they kill, sewed together with the sinewes of them. (D. Settle, Hakluyt, vol. 5, pp. 148–9)

For Dionise Settle, who documented Frobisher's second expedition in search of the North-West passage in 1577, the Inuit are by implication little more than beasts: they do not eat cooked meals, they do not eat their greens nicely dressed as salads, and they make no use of what, for this traveller, are the most basic pieces of furniture. In addition, their dressing habits mirror their eating habits: they take whatever they find in nature and put it to immediate use without the refining or cultivating hand of nurture. In striking contrast to this, Philip Amadas and Arthur Barlowe seem to depict their natives as forerunners of the 'noble savage' of later centuries:

> [V]ery handsome and goodly people, and in their behaviour as mannerly and civill as any of Europe … when … the kings brother was present none durst trade but himself … And we noted there … that no people in the worlde would cary more respect to their King, Nobilitie, and Governours, then these do …

---

[16] For a short survey of some of these cultural assets, see Manfred Pfister, '"Man's Distinctive Mark": Paradoxical Distinctions between Man and his Bestial Other in Early Modern Texts', in Elmar Lehmann and Bernd Lenz, eds, *Telling Stories: Studies in Honour of Ulrich Broich on the Occasion of his 60th Birthday* (Amsterdam: Rodopi, 1992), pp. 17–33.

After we had thus dryed our selves, she brought us into the inner roome, where shee set on the board standing along the house, some wheate like furmentie, sodden Venison, and roasted, fish sodden, boyled, and roasted, Melons raw, and sodden, rootes of divers kindes, and divers fruites ... We were entertained with all love and kindnesse, and with as much bountie (after their maner) as they could possibly devise. We found the people most gentle, loving, and faithfull, voide of all guile and treason, and such as live after the maner of the golden age. (1584) (P. Amadas and A. Barlowe, Hakluyt, vol. 6, p. 128)

The hierarchical order and orderliness of the Algonquins, who, moreover, know of several ways of preparing cooked meals and serving them buffet style, contrasts sharply with the 'disorderliness' of the Inuit in Settle's text. While the Inuit are accused of essential dishonesty, the Algonquins appear as the very epitome of faithfulness and gentility. Despite the conflicting representations, however, what Settle's and Amadas and Barlowe's reports have in common is their system of reference within which they describe the respective natives: both attach primary importance to the forms and regulations of everyday life, and criticize or praise the natives for the lack or presence of these forms. What Amadas and Barlowe extol are not the virtues of living as closely as possible with nature, but rather the natives' expertise in nurture. Even in that, however, we can detect a suggestion of inadequacy: with the implication that although hosting English travellers as well as they possibly could, the Algonquins might have done better had their manner been a different one.

## III

When we move from the individual to the more social or 'national' level we observe similar mechanisms of identity construction at work. One of the most often applied criteria for evaluating natives is the question of whether or not the Elizabethan travellers detect the existence of a structured socio-political community – which is to say that many simply find something upon which they can project their own notions of political organization. Not surprisingly, this always implies hierarchical and monarchical structures, such as are described by Amadas and Barlowe, who praise the Algonquins for the strongly hierarchized image they presented to the English: the obedience paid to their native leader, the special respect paid to members of his family, the existence of trading privileges for family members, and the staged public display of power and rank. Another aspect that is important in this context is the existence of laws that regulate life within the social community. Here special attention is usually paid to laws referring to property and theft, which is certainly not accidental, considering the primarily mercantile clientele of these travelogues. The marked insistence on the well-orderedness of communities, and on the impressive staging of power, may point to the potential instability of the Tudor state; the desired private and public Self which emerges in these travelogues is the well-mannered, well-organized, 'cultivated', Protestant, trade-orientated European Self. It is, however, even more explicitly recognizable as a national, and, in this case, an English Self. Hakluyt's edition of texts had already been expressly devoted to the endeavours of what he, in his title and in his editorial, calls the 'English nation', irrespective of the fact that he also prints reports from Spanish or Portuguese sources. In his 'Preface to the Reader', for example, Hakluyt emphasizes that his project was undertaken for the 'benefit and honour of my country' and for 'the honour and benefit of this commonwealth' (vol. 1, p. 19).

The question of when we can satisfactorily discuss notions of 'nation' or 'nationalism' has been under debate for a considerable time, especially with regard to the early modern era.[17] Nevertheless, for our purposes, we can at least say that although Elizabethan and Jacobean England may not have been a 'nation state' in the nineteenth-century sense of the word, the concept of 'nation' had already enough binding force to provide a common system of reference for English travellers. As all kinds of identity are the result of processes of inclusion and exclusion, the concept of nation can also be described as the result of such processes in which what is conceived of as a coherent or common Self is discursively distinguished from various Othernesses. The 'Black Legend', as the common virulent anti-Spanish discourse of the 1580s and 1590s has come to be called, made Spain the villain of the piece, in which England claimed to play the part of the civilizer and missionary of the New World.[18] Unsurprisingly, therefore, in the texts published by Hakluyt it is mainly the Spanish nation which appears as a sort of counterfoil for an Englishness whose particular marks are Protestantism on the one hand, and on the other the insistence on more refined ways of dealing with the natives, coupled with the belief in trading expertise. The texts edited more than twenty years later in Purchas's collection often take a much more explicitly national tone, and it is not only Catholic Spain which appears as a rival in a competition of nations. When we examine, for instance, John Davis' report about his time as a master on a Dutch expedition to the East Indies, we see the Englishmen also favourably contrasted with the Dutch:

> [O]ur Baase came aboord with a Boat-load of Pepper; reporting words above credit, how the King had used him ... he further said, that the King did often demand of him, if he were not of England. ... He giving thankes, answered that he was not of England, but of Flanders, and at the Kings service. I have

---

[17] See Benedict Anderson, *Imagined Communities* (London: Verso, 1983); Ernest Gellner, *Nations and Nationalism* (Ithaca: Cornell University Press, 1983); Antony Easthope, *Englishness and National Culture* (London: Routledge, 1999); Adrian Hastings, *The Construction of Nationhood. Ethnicity, Religion and Nationalism* (Cambridge: Cambridge University Press, 1997); Eric Hobsbawm and Terence Ranger, eds, *The Invention of Tradition* (Cambridge: Cambridge University Press, 1983); Hans-Ulrich Wehler, *Nationalismus: Geschichte, Formen, Folgen* (München: Beck, 2001).

[18] See William Maltby, *The Black Legend in England: The Development of Anti-Spanish Sentiment, 1558–1660* (Durham: Duke University Press, 1971).

> heard of England, said the King, but not of Flanders: what Land is that? He
> further enquired of their King, State, and Government; whereof our Baase
> made large report, refusing the Authoritie of a King, relating the government
> of Aristocracie. He further made sute to the King, to give commandement
> that his subjects should not call him English: for it was bitterness unto him:
> which the King granted. (Davis, Purchas, vol. 2, pp. 313–14)

Davis's self-presentation as the only sober and reasonable character on board
a Dutch ship of disorderly fools is not primarily the staging of individual Self-
fashioning.[19] Davis is seen to act as a representative of Englishmen and of the
English nation in general. What is contrasted here are not the qualities of two (or
more) individual persons, but rather a pair of nations to whom particular qualities
are ascribed. The opposition of individual qualities like courage and cowardice, or
soberness and drunkenness, correlates with the political contrasts of order and chaos,
King and aristocrats, world-wide renown and insignificance. The individual derives
his qualities from his affiliation with his nation; being different from other nations
outside national borders also implies a degree of sameness within these borders.
Even qualities like 'apparell and fashion' are not (or not only) the personality
markers of an individual, or of his belonging to a particular class or rank within
society, but the expression of national identity.

Wherever it may take place geographically, the derogatory competitiveness of
nationalities, as soon as territorial or economic antagonisms become visible, is a
European affair. Moreover, the natives of the countries that become the site of this
rivalry of nations are reduced to little more than spectators in a staging of European
nationality. That said, they do appear as a necessary third party, for it is they who
spark off the spectacle of European travellers' national self-fashioning, no matter
how meaningless the insistence on national difference may be for the spectator. In
Java, for example, an English merchant named Edmund Scot, with a handful of
other Englishmen, stages a celebration on Coronation day to ensure the Javanese
are aware of the Englishness rather than the Dutchness of these men:

> the common people knew us not from the Flemmings, for both they and
> wee were called by the name of Englishmen, by reason of their usurping
> our name at their first comming thither to trade, wherein they did our nation
> much wrong … we began to think how wee might make our selves knowne
> from the Hollanders … we made a Flagge with the red Crosse through the
> middle, and because wee that were the Merchants would be knowne from
> our men, we edged our Scarfes with a deepe fringe of gold, and that was
> our difference. (1602/03) (Scot, Purchas, vol. 2, pp. 456–7)

Scot's public parade of nationality is motivated commercially as a stratagem
in the economic rivalry with the 'Flemmings' and he subjects his complete person
to the expression of his nationality. Again, clothes function as one of the most

---

[19]   See also the description of a 'carnival' on board the Dutch ship in Purchas, vol.
2, pp. 307–8.

important markers of national identity. He insists on being known for his rank, and he looks for lines of demarcation both within and outside national borders. More importantly, having travelled through a number of countries on his way from England to Java he ends up writing home about himself, and points out how different he is from others, as both a well-behaved Protestant, a respectable member of the merchant class, and an upstanding representative of Englishness. The English nation under construction, then, is a hierarchically structured one: Protestant, monarchic, renowned and respected for its courage, military expertise, orderliness, manners, reasonableness and sobriety. Scot's interest is quite openly not with the country in which he travels, for he does not explore, and there is nothing uncertain about his Self-perception. Indeed, for travellers like Scot the crossing of geographical borders implies the assertion or affirmation of a religious, 'civic' and national English self which has by now gained a Self-assurance it was not to lose for a very long time.

## Chapter 4

# 'Not absolutely a native, nor entirely a stranger':
# The Journeys of Anne Grant

## Betty Hagglund

'All literature of travel operates between notions of "here" and "there" and the audience for such writing may sometimes be in both places at the same time, just as the writer too may shift positions in significant ways', writes Dorothy McMillan in her study of early Scottish women travellers.[1] Anne Grant's response to the Highland landscape and to the Highland people was coloured not only by her own identity as a Lowland-born Scot of Highland parentage but, perhaps even more significantly, by her early experience of another culture and people as a young adolescent in the British colonies in Albany, New York.

Grant explored what it meant to be both a settler and a traveller. Her early writing about Scotland told of her travels but she settled in Laggan with her husband and took on the role of interpreter for the Highland people and culture she found there, learning Gaelic just as those she most admired in Albany had learned Native American languages. Her descriptions of Albany looked at the development of a young society of colonists but some of her most vivid writing about America was reserved for descriptions of her travel into the wilderness. In both places Grant had a peculiar position as both outsider and insider, simultaneously participant and observer.

Anne Macvicar [Grant] was born in Glasgow in 1755. In 1757 her father, a member of the 77th Foot regiment, went out to America. Later that year, Anne and her mother joined him and the next ten years were spent in and around Albany, a mixed community of Dutch, Scottish, English and native-born settlers. When she was five, Anne and her mother accompanied the regiment from Albany to Oswego, travelling by boat up the Mohawk River and sleeping sometimes in the woods, sometimes in the forts 'which formed a chain of posts in the then trackless wilderness'.[2] This early exposure to wilderness landscape would help to form Grant's later aesthetic sense. In 1768, the family returned to Scotland, and when

---

[1]    Dorothy McMillan, 'Some Early Travellers', in Douglas Gifford and Dorothy McMillan, eds, *A History of Scottish Women's Writing* (Edinburgh: Edinburgh University Press, 1997), p. 119.

[2]    Anne Grant, *Memoir and Correspondence of Mrs. Grant of Laggan*, ed. J. P. Grant, 3 vols (London: Longman, 1844), vol. 1, pp. 5–6. All subsequent references will be to MAC.

Anne was 17 her father accepted a post at Fort Augustus in Inverness-shire. The letters written on the journey from Glasgow to Fort Augustus form the first part of Grant's *Letters from the Mountains* and it is in these letters that we see the initial attraction to the Highland culture which was to become such a central part of Anne Grant's life.

Anne Macvicar married the Reverend James Grant, minister to the parish of Laggan in Inverness-shire, in 1779. She moved to Laggan, and her involvement with the Highland people, places and language truly began. Grant soon acquired sufficient knowledge of Gaelic to converse freely with her husband's parishioners and to begin to translate Gaelic poetry into English. She spent the next twenty-two years happily in Laggan, farming and raising the couple's nine children. When her husband died in 1801, Grant turned to writing as a means of financial support.

Given her early experiences, it is perhaps not surprising that travel soon became a main theme in Grant's writings. Her first foray into published travel writing came with the publication of her *Letters from the Mountains* in 1806,[3] a collection of letters sent to friends during her teenage journey from Glasgow to Fort Augustus and during the early years of her marriage. In 1808 Grant wrote and published *Memoirs of an American Lady; with Sketches of Manners and Scenery in America, as they existed previous to the Revolution*. Although purportedly a biography of Catalina Schuyler, the 'American Lady' of the title, the book's chief interest lay in its descriptions of the customs and mores of the infant colony and of the interplay between the Dutch, British, Native American and black slave populations who lived side by side. The two-volume work also included autobiographical narrative, generalized description of a kind we might now refer to as ethnography, reflections on the origin and nature of 'man', and descriptions of wilderness travel.

The Albany colony was comprised of a number of groups and cultures: Dutch, English, Scottish, black slave, various Indian tribes,[4] military personnel and civilians. Grant slips between these groups as she is writing, turning her focus first on one, then on another, and therefore moves constantly between the cultures she is describing. It is perhaps important to remember that Grant was a child at the

---

[3]    Anne Grant, *Letters from the Mountains: Being the real Correspondence of a Lady between the Years 1773 and 1803*, 3 vols (London: Longman, 1806). All subsequent references will be to LfM.

[4]    The question of what term to use when referring to indigenous American people is a problematic issue for both native and non-native peoples. As Robert F. Berkhofer, Jr has written, 'Since the original inhabitants of the Western Hemisphere neither called themselves by a single term nor understood themselves as a collectivity, the idea and the image of the Indian must be a White conception ... [which] neglect[s] or play[s] down the social and cultural diversity of Native Americans then – and now.' Robert F. Berkhofer, Jr, *The White Man's Indian: Images of the American Indian from Columbus to the Present* (New York: Vintage, 1978), p. 3. Grant, however, like many of her contemporaries, used the word 'Indian' in a general way and it is not often possible to identify to which group she is referring.

time of her stay in the American colonies,[5] arriving at the age of two and leaving when she was thirteen years of age. This obviously allowed her entrance to certain experiences – she writes in detail of berry picking and picnics among the children of the colony – but barred her from others. The book, however, is written from an adult's point of view and sees things largely through the eyes of the adult Grant then was.

Dorothy McMillan has written:

> [Grant's] position as a 'travel writer' is ... the reverse of the norm. Customarily travellers take a baggage of cultural assumptions to the new societies they are exploring. Anne Grant *returns* from Albany, armed with its culture, only to discover as she becomes acquainted with Britain, that much of what must have seemed natural to her is far from being so by old world standards. And so in order to write about Albany after forty years she has to learn to see, not just as is the case with all memoirs of childhood, with an adult eye endeavouring to recapture the sensations of childhood, but also with a culturally re-equipped sense of what her childhood and early adolescence must have been like to her then, and an acute awareness of how it will seem to her readers now.[6]

The book was not written until many years after the events and scenes described and seems to have been written from memory, Grant making no reference to owning diaries or other written records of her American sojourn.[7] She herself was aware of the difficulties of remembering accurately over such a long space of time, and included a disclaimer at the beginning:

> I do not mean to discredit my own veracity. I certainly have no intention to relate any thing that is not true. Yet in the dim distance of near forty years, unassisted by written memorials, shall I not mistake dates, misplace facts, and omit circumstances that form essential links in the chain of narration? Thirty years since, when I expressed a wish to do what I am now about to attempt, how differently should I have executed it.[8]

On the one hand, the disclaimer undermines any claims of authority or accuracy. On the other hand, Grant's use of the first person, her specific and detailed descriptions of customs and people, and her inclusion of personal childhood memories create in the reader a belief in the truthfulness of the portrayal. Unlike the accounts of later nineteenth-century travellers to America, there is no indication that Grant had

---

[5]  In this essay, I use the terms 'America' and 'American' to refer generally to the North American continent.

[6]  McMillan, 'Some Early Travellers', p. 131.

[7]  This is confirmed by the editor of the 1901 New York edition of the book, a descendant of Anne Grant's, who states: 'Mrs. Grant had neither the aid of letters, a diary, or data of any description in the preparation of the Memoir.' James Grant Wilson, Preface to 1901 edition of *Memoirs of an American Lady*, vol. 1, p. x.

[8]  Anne Grant, *Memoirs of an American Lady; with Sketches of Manners and Scenery in America, as they existed previous to the Revolution*, 2 vols (London: Longman, 1808), vol. 1, pp. 5–6. Subsequent references will be to MAL.

read any earlier or contemporaneous writings about the continent at the time she wrote her own book. Although Grant wrote about all of the groups and peoples who made up the colony, this essay will focus primarily on her depiction of the Indians and on her response to the wilderness landscape.

Shirley Foster, in her book *Across New Worlds*, divides nineteenth-century travellers to America into two groups, 'those who essentially rejected or tried to familiarise the wilderness, and those who were drawn to its otherness'.[9] She goes on to say:

> The first group, taking Europe as their standard, assessed it in terms relevant to their own culture or to their previous experiences of foreign landscape ... [or] sought to impose conventional literary or aesthetic images of beauty on the natural environment ... [or] look[ed] for signs of man's benevolent and practical intervention ... focusing on cultivated nature, in harmony with humanity. ... Others of the travellers were readier to embrace the challenge, psychological as well as physical, of the New World's uncompromising vastness. ... they welcomed the difference from an ordered landscape which represented the regular pattern of their home lives.[10]

Anne Grant's response to America fell into the second category. Looking back as an adult on the simpler society she had known as a child, it was the older, more refined society that she found inferior. At the age of five, she embraced the wilderness landscape with enthusiasm:

> In the month of October [my father] set out on this journey, or voyage rather, in which it was settled that my mother and I should accompany him. We were, I believe, the first females, above the very lowest ranks, who had ever penetrated so far into this remote wilderness. ... What joys were mine! to be idle for a fortnight, seeing new woods, rivers, and animals, every day; even then the love of nature was, in my young bosom, a passion productive of incessant delight. ... What a change from sitting pinned down to my samplar [*sic*] by my mother ... This journey, charming my romantic imagination by its very delays and difficulties, was such a source of interest and novelty to me, that above all things I dreaded its conclusion, which I well knew would be succeeded by long tasks and close confinement. (MAL, vol. 2, pp. 106–13)

Like Foster's second group of women travellers, the child Grant values the wilderness at least partly for its contrast with the restrictions of her daily life, a life constrained by female tasks and needlework, even within the frontier settlement of Albany.

The difficulties and physical challenges of making such a journey merely seem to have added to its charm for Grant and, writing with the distance of years, she translated its dangers into an experience of the sublime:

---

[9]   Shirley Foster, *Across New Worlds: Nineteenth-century Women Travellers and their Writings* (London: Harvester, 1990), p. 85.

[10]   Foster, *Across New Worlds*, pp. 85–9.

> In one place, where we were surrounded by hills, with swamps lying between them, there seemed to be a general congress of wolves, who answered each other from opposite hills, in sounds the most terrific. Probably the terror which all savage animals have at fire was exalted into fury, by seeing so many enemies, whom they durst not attack. The bull frogs, the harmless, the hideous inhabitants of the swamps, seemed determined not to be out-done, and roared a tremendous bass to this bravura accompaniment. This was almost too much for my love of the terrible sublime: some women, who were our fellow-travellers, shrieked with terror: and finally, the horrors of that night were ever after held in awful remembrance by all who haunt them. (MAL, vol. 2, pp. 116–18)

It is notable that the experience is *almost* too much and that the *other* women (but not, by implication, Anne) shrieked with terror. Eighteenth- and nineteenth-century women travel writers frequently use other women as a foil, defining their own achievements against other women's failures, timidity or inability to complete a journey. In this way they set themselves apart as special and highlight their own strengths and abilities. Although this rhetorical trope appears most frequently when women are writing about sublimity or about physically challenging or dangerous experiences, it can be found in descriptions of more domesticated travel. Dorothy Wordsworth, for example, in the journal of her second Scottish tour, repeatedly points out what she has achieved compared to her slower and more anxious sister-in-law.[11] Grant's subtext here is therefore a common one – others may be timorous but *I* am not overwhelmed. This implied self-possession in the presence of danger is often found alongside statements about being 'the first woman' or 'the only woman' to have achieved a particular adventurous goal, a claim also made by Grant for this particular journey.

Occasionally Grant anthropomorphizes the wilderness. This device seems to be on the one hand a way of expressing the vastness and power of the natural world, but at the same time an attempt to make it more comfortable or manageable. As the group travelled through the forest, for example, trees often fell across the stream, blocking the passage of the boat. Grant writes:

> In every tempestuous night, some giants of the grove fell prostrate, and very frequently across the stream, where they lay in all their pomp of foliage, like a leafy bridge, unwithered, and formed an obstacle almost invincible to all navigation. … Nothing remained for our heroes [the soldiers accompanying the party] but to attack these sylvan giants axe in hand, and make way through their divided bodies. (MAL, vol. 2, pp. 114–15)

'Sylvan giants', 'fell prostrate', 'divided bodies' – suddenly the journey narrative has become a child's fairy story with the trees as the villains and the simple foot soldiers transformed into heroes. At intervals throughout *Memoirs of an American Lady*, Grant uses this kind of storybook imagery. Consciously or unconsciously, she seems

---

[11]   Dorothy Wordsworth, *Journal of My Second Tour in Scotland, 1822*, ed. Jiro Nagasawa (Tokyo: Kenkyusha, 1989).

to recall the events of the past through the filter of her childhood imaginings. At the same time, redefining the obstacles of the natural world as mythical foes, against whom the human 'heroes' will always triumph, sets up an opposition between the natural and the human world in which potentially threatening situations are made safe and eventual victory over danger is assured.

The journey was punctuated with a visit to a Native American chieftain referred to by Grant as King Hendrick.[12] Grant's portrait of the native monarch is a sympathetic one and the child was presumably encouraged by her parents to treat the king with respect. Nevertheless, the king, although 'a princely figure' and 'a generous warrior', is defined by Grant as 'a primitive monarch' and not quite genuine royalty in the European sense:

> This primitive monarch … resided … in a house which the public workmen, who had lately built this fort, had been ordered to erect for him … His Majesty … not chusing to depart too much from the customs of his ancestors, had not permitted divisions of apartments, or modern furniture to profane his new dwelling. It had the appearance of a good barn, and was divided across by a mat hung in the middle. King Hendrick … was sitting on the floor beside a large heap of wheat, surrounded with baskets of dried berries of different kinds; beside him, his son, a very pretty boy … was caressing a foal, which was unceremoniously introduced into the royal residence. A laced hat, a fine saddle and pistols, gifts of his good brother the great king,[13] were hung round on the cross beams. He was splendidly arrayed in a coat of pale blue, trimmed with silver; all the rest of his dress was of the fashion of his own nation … All this suited my taste exceedingly, and was level to my comprehension. I was prepared to admire King Hendrick by hearing him described as a generous warrior, terrible to his enemies, and kind to his friends. … Add to all this, that the monarch smiled, clapped my head, and ordered me a little basket, very pretty … [I] am not sure but what I have liked kings all my life the better for this happy specimen, to which I was so early introduced. Had I seen royalty, properly such, invested with all the pomp of European magnificence, I should possibly have been confused and over-dazzled. But this was quite enough, and not too much for me; and I went away, lost in a reverie, and thought of nothing but kings, battles, and generals for days after. (MAL, vol. 2, pp. 110–14)

---

[12]  Earlier in the text, Grant herself links this visit with King Hendrick, also known as Theyanoquin, one of the four so-called Mohawk 'kings' who visited Queen Anne in 1710. (See Richmond P. Bond, *Queen Anne's American Kings* (Oxford: Clarendon, 1952) and Eric Hinderaker, 'The "Four Indian Kings" and the Imaginative Construction of the First British Empire', *William and Mary Quarterly*, 53:3 (1996), pp. 487–526.) Theyanoquin died in battle at Lake George on 8 September 1755, the year of Grant's birth, and therefore could not have been her host. I have been unable to identify the subject of her visit. It is possible that Grant, writing so many years after the event, conflated memories of seeing Theyanoquin's portrait, which featured him in a lace-trimmed coat, with her memories of the visit.

[13]  A term used several times by Grant to refer to the British monarch when discussing Indians.

Three primary ways have been identified in which colonialist writers define and document the alien: by screening the incomprehensible out of the picture altogether, by naming and foregrounding the strangeness, and therefore acknowledging it, or by subverting terms of cultural familiarization so as to debase or ridicule, thereby reinforcing rather than obliterating difference.[14] Grant's description of her encounter with King Hendrick is ambivalent. On the one hand, as already suggested, she is respectful and acknowledges him as an important figure. At the same time, much of the detail she reports creates a sense of incongruity about the scene. Hendrick lives in a European house, but one built by European orders, not one he has initiated himself. The king chooses not to furnish his house in the European style, and to Grant's eyes, therefore, it appears like a good barn, divided by a mat hung in the middle, and with European gifts hanging from the rafters. The king sits upon the floor, and his son has a horse within the house, therefore reinforcing the barn image. This is a storybook fantasy, a pretend king for a child, 'level' to the five-year-old's understanding.

Grant frequently depicted Native Americans in glowing, idealized terms. Describing them as 'the high spirited rulers of the boundless wild, who, alike heedless of the power and splendour of distant monarchs, were accustomed to say with Fingal, "sufficient for me is the desert, with all deer and woods"' (MAL, vol. 1, p. 30),[15] she wrote of their 'strength and sublimity' (p. 33), their 'sonorous, musical, and expressive' language (p. 17), and their 'generous and elevated sentiments, heroic fortitude, and unstained probity' (p. 17).

Shirley Foster has argued that idealization of the primitive often works as a distancing strategy, preventing the traveller from actually 'seeing' the Native American as a real human being.[16] Grant, however, despite her habit of ennobling the Native Americans, does seem to go beyond that tendency to a more complex depiction. Unlike those whose encounters with Native Americans occurred purely on touristic journeys, Grant frequently experienced long periods of interaction between the Native Americans and the white settlers and was particularly influenced by encounters between women of the two groups:

> Some detached Indian families resided for a while in summer in the vicinity of houses occupied by the more wealthy and benevolent inhabitants. They generally built a slight wigwam under shelter of the orchard fence on the

---

[14]  See Elleke Boehmer, *Colonial and Postcolonial Literature* (Oxford: Oxford University Press, 1995), especially chapter 2. I would also like to express my appreciation to Shirley Foster, whose 1998 conference paper, 'The depiction of Native Americans in the early nineteenth century', helped to develop my thoughts on this matter (25 April 1998; 'Literature and Travel, 1750 to the Present', University of the West of England, Bristol).

[15]  Grant's choice of a quotation from *The Poems of Ossian* to describe the self-sufficiency of the Indians is an interesting conflation of Highland and Indian imagery, a conflation which recurs throughout Grant's writings and which is discussed in more detail below.

[16]  Foster, *Across New Worlds*, pp. 102, 104.

shadiest side; and never were neighbours more harmless, peaceable, and obliging; I might truly add, industrious; for in one way or other they were constantly occupied. The women and their children employed themselves in many ingenious handicrafts ... The summer residence of these ingenious artisans promoted a great intimacy between the females of the vicinity and the Indian women, whose sagacity and comprehension of mind were beyond belief. ... It was necessary then that all conversations should be held, and all business transacted with these females, by the mistress of the family. In the infancy of the settlement the Indian language was familiar to the more intelligent inhabitants, who found it very useful, and were, no doubt, pleased with its nervous and emphatic idiom, and its lofty and sonorous cadence. Conversing with those interesting and deeply reflecting natives, was to thinking minds no mean source of entertainment. Communication soon grew easier; for the Indians had a singular facility in acquiring other languages; the children I well remember, from experimental knowledge, for I delighted to hover about the wigwam, and converse with those of the Indians, and we very frequently mingled languages. (MAL, vol. 1, pp. 121–6)

As a child, Grant had possibly not yet absorbed European stereotypes of female beauty or accomplishment against which to measure the appearance and behaviour of the Indian women. In addition, values of utility in a wilderness settlement made the Indian women's craftwork more valuable and appreciated in that context than it might have been otherwise. This gendered mixing of Indian and settler families enabled Grant to come to know them as individuals, just as she would later come to know and value the Highlanders of her husband's parish in Laggan. Grant's early experience of an 'alien' culture, therefore, took place within a wider circle of female commingling and mutual acceptance, and her emphasis on the industriousness of the Indian women seems consciously designed to counter the accusation common in contemporary travel writing of 'picturesque idleness'. She herself believed that she had a more accurate picture of the Indians than did casual travellers:

> One must have seen these people, (the Indians I mean,) to have any idea what a noble animal man is, while unsophisticated. Voyagers, who have not their language, and merely see them transiently, to wonder and be wondered at, are equally strangers to the real character of man in a social, though unpolished state. (MAL, vol. 1, pp. 87–8)

Furthermore, adult travellers often used distancing strategies to deal with new cultures or landscapes, attempting to minimize the perceived threat to their own stability of the known. Life for any young child is filled with novelty and difference, and Grant's 'known' – her parents and a sense of being included and cared for – travelled with her, minimizing any sense of risk in new encounters or experiences.

In a letter to a friend in 1821, Grant depicted her relationship with the women of Laggan in terms that were strikingly similar to those she used when describing her Albany experience:

> Long days have I knit my stocking or carried an infant from sheaf to sheaf, sitting and walking by turns on the harvest-field, attentively observing conversation which for the first years of my residence in the Highlands I

was not supposed to understand. Seldom a day passed that I did not find two or three petitioners in the kitchen respectfully entreating for advice, medicine, or some petty favour. Often I sat down with them, and led them to converse, captivated with the strength and beauty of their expressions in their native tongue. (MAC, vol. 2, p. 264)

Unlike Mary Louise Pratt's 'contact zone', which she describes as 'the space of colonial encounters, the space in which peoples geographically and historically separated come into contact with each other and establish ongoing relations, usually involving conditions of coercion, radical inequality, and intractable conflict',[17] Grant's descriptions of 'gendered contact zones' (my term) depict encounters between women and children from separate communities, based on mutual respect and acceptance.

In 1768, Grant returned to Scotland. As a Lowland-born young woman, and one who had spent most of her childhood in the colonies, she found the Highlands to be as much unknown as Albany had been. Despite her early exposure to – and appreciation of – wilderness landscape, her first impression of the Highlands was one of disappointment:

Determined to like the Highlands, a most unexpected occurrence carried me, in my seventeenth year, to reside there … it is not easy to say how much I was repelled and disappointed. In vain I tried to raise my mind to the tone of sublimity. The rocky divisions that rose with so much majesty in description, seemed like enormous prison walls, confining caitiffs in the narrow glen. These, too, seemed like the dreary abode of solitude and silence. These feelings, however, I did not even whisper to the rushes.[18]

Eventually, however, she grew to appreciate her new wilderness. Grant's romantic enthusiasm for the poems of Ossian was one of the tools that enabled her to deal with the challenges of her new surroundings, as she populated the landscapes she saw with imaginary figures:

I began to grow a little savage myself … and when I grew acquainted with the language and the poetry of the country, I found a thousand interesting localities combined with those scenes where the lovely and the brave of other days had still a local habitation and a name: cherished traditions, and the poetry of nature and the heart shed light over scenes the most gloomy, and peopled solitude with images the most attractive and awakening. When, after a long residence in this land of enthusiasm, I left the abode of ghosts and warrior hunters and heroines, to come down to common life in a flat country, you cannot imagine how bleak and unsheltered, how tame and uninteresting it appeared. (MAC, vol. 1, p. 197)

---

[17] Mary Louise Pratt, *Imperial Eyes: Travel Writing and Transculturation* (London: Routledge, 1992), p. 6.

[18] Anne Grant, *Essays on the Superstitions of the Highlanders of Scotland: to which are added Translations from the Gaelic; and Letters Connected with those formerly published*, 2 vols (London: Longman, 1811), vol. 2, pp. 335–6. Further references will be to *Essays*.

In this passage, Grant defines her path into an appreciation of the scenery as 'language and poetry'. The 1760 publication of James Macpherson's *Fragments of Ancient Poetry, Collected in the Highlands of Scotland, and Translated from the Gaelic or Erse Language*[19] had provided non-Highland readers of the poems with new ways of seeing and representing the Scottish landscape. Leah Leneman has suggested that the effect was threefold. Firstly, the poems of Ossian 'provided a new way of looking at wild and desolate scenery'.[20] Hugh Blair, author of *Critical Dissertation on the Poems of Ossian* in 1763, wrote on the subject of sublimity, using quotations from the Ossianic poems as illustrations, and it has been suggested that Blair's work on sublimity was a direct influence on Gilpin's later writings on Scottish landscape. Secondly, travellers began to associate the scenery directly with Ossian, peopling the landscape with blind bards and heroes created by their own imaginations, just as Grant depicts herself doing. Thirdly, the poems, feeding into Enlightenment ideas about the 'nobility' of 'primitive' societies, caused a re-evaluation of present-day Highlanders, making them acceptable and even admired:

> The surroundings in which they lived were said to have had a profound effect on the Ossianic heroes, and those surroundings had not changed significantly over the centuries, so it followed that eighteenth-century Highlanders possessed many of the same qualities as their noble ancestors.[21]

Paul Baines has reminded us that 'Ossian was always at least partially a geographical phenomenon'.[22] Claiming to be 'fragments ... collected in the Highlands of Scotland', the poems were from the outset intimately linked with the Highland landscape. Many eighteenth- and early nineteenth-century tourists treated the poems as historically and geographically verifiable fact. While they travelled through the Highlands, they searched for the sites described in the poems. At the same time, they peopled the landscape in their imaginations with Ossianic figures and endeavoured to respond to the landscape with true Ossianic fervour.

Having 'taught' herself to appreciate the Highland landscapes, albeit through an Ossianic lens, Grant took it upon herself to interpret the Highlanders and their lives to the outside world. Although Lowland born, she presented herself as 'a true Highlander', uniquely qualified to comment, 'not absolutely a native, nor entirely a stranger, but [one who] has added the observant curiosity of the latter to the facilities of enquiry enjoyed by the former' (*Essays*, vol. 1, p. 10). In Albany, the people Grant had most admired had occupied an ambiguous position, part of the local community but at the same time outside it. This had been perhaps particularly

---

[19] James Macpherson, *Fragments of Ancient Poetry, collected in the Highlands of Scotland, and translated from the Galic or Erse Language* (Edinburgh: Hamilton, 1760).

[20] Leah Leneman, 'The Effects of Ossian in Lowland Scotland', in Jennifer J. Carter and Joan H. Pittock, eds, *Aberdeen and the Enlightenment* (Aberdeen: Aberdeen University Press, 1987), p. 358.

[21] Leneman, 'The Effects of Ossian', p. 360.

[22] Paul Baines, 'Ossianic Geographies: Fingalian Figures on the Scottish Tour, 1760–1830', *Scotlands*, 4 (1997), p. 44.

true of the female Indian-Dutch relationships which the child Grant had so closely observed. Taking up her position as 'minister's wife' in her husband's parish, Grant positioned herself in a similar way. Regarding the Highlanders as a noble but primitive race, just as she and others around her had regarded the Indians, Grant learned the local language but always stayed at one remove, never fully identifying herself with her farming neighbours.

Despite living for many years among them, Grant's picture of the Highland peasantry and landscape remained a deeply idealized one. In 1811 she published *Essays on the Superstitions of the Highlanders*, her most formal attempt to represent Highland culture to the outside world. Although it purported to be a book about 'superstitions', leading many of its contemporary readers to expect a book on folklore and traditional beliefs, it coincided far more closely with another strand of study and thought in late eighteenth- and early nineteenth-century Scotland. Fiona Stafford has traced the way in which, during the eighteenth century,

> the Apocalyptic model ... ceased to be the dominant influence on ideas of ending and ... it is possible to discern a growing interest in disappearing families, tribes, and communities. The trend reflects a new awareness of cultural relativism, which involved not only ideas of time and history, but also of race. For the first time, works began to emerge in which the central characters derive their significance from being members of a vanishing group, and are referred to specifically as 'the last of the race'.[23]

This coincided with a growing interest in primitive peoples and cultures and in conjecture about the origins of the writer's own society. The concept that all societies passed through a number of stages based on different modes of subsistence (hunting and gathering, domestication of animals, agricultural, commercial) was taking hold, replacing an earlier ethnography which mapped differences between cultures onto a taxonomy of 'peoples'.[24] Both the Highlands and islands of Scotland and the American Indians were frequently given as examples of society in its most primitive form.

In *Memoirs of an American Lady*, Grant had proposed a theory of societal development wherein a culture passes from primitive contentment to 'a higher state of society' via a difficult, intermediate state created by contact with more 'civilized' groups. She believed this process to be a universal one, and described its effects in the American colonies, in the Middle East 'where the cradle of our infant nature was appointed' (MAL, vol. 1, p. 219), and in the Highlands of Scotland. Linking the Highlanders with the American Indians as examples of primitive and savage peoples was not of course unique to Grant.[25] In 1755 William Robertson,

---

[23] Fiona Stafford, *The Last of the Race* (Oxford: Clarendon Press, 1994), p. 83.

[24] For a detailed discussion of the 'four stages theory', see Ronald L. Meek, *Social Science and the Ignoble Savage* (Cambridge: Cambridge University Press, 1976).

[25] See Meek, *Social Science and the Ignoble Savage*, particularly chapters 2 and 4, and Robert Crawford, *Devolving English Literature* (Oxford: Clarendon, 1992).

the historian and clergyman, preached a sermon in which he stated that in the Highlands and islands of Scotland 'society still appears in its rudest and most imperfect form';[26] later the same year he approvingly quoted William Douglass's comment that 'America may with much Propriety be called the youngest Brother and meanest of Mankind'.[27] Boswell found the Highlanders in Auchnasheal 'as black and wild ... as any American savages'.[28] Nevertheless, Grant was one of the few writers who had direct personal experience of both cultures upon which to base her observations. Just as she had depicted the Indians as a noble but primitive race, she likewise represented the Highlanders as examples of a primitive people worthy of study in order that more 'civilized' cultures might be better appreciated, and so that her contemporaries might understand their origins. She was keen to emphasize that the Highlanders, although 'primitive', were not complete savages:

> Were we to land on some savage island, where the foot of man has never trod, nor his hand removed incumbrance or opened access, we should be harassed with fears and perplexed with intricacies. ... The solitary, cruel, selfish, and capricious savage, far from forming an object of amusing speculation, fills us with sensations of mingled horror and disgust, such as we feel at the Yahoo pictures of Swift; and make us, like his reader, shudder at owning our fellow nature with a being so degraded. But among a people, whose progress towards civilization, is so far advanced, that the feelings of the heart, and the powers of the imagination have been called forth, preceding the light of science, as the morning star and the dusky dawn do the effulgence of the sun. Among such people, the mind finds something to dwell on that is soothing and satisfactory. (*Essays*, vol. 1, pp. 3–5)

At the same time, she saw both the Highlanders and the American Indians as examples of cultures which were rapidly disappearing: 'The fair form, where inspiration has for so many ages, awaked the bard, animated the hero, and soothed the lover, is fast gliding into the mist of obscurity, and will soon be no more than a remembered dream' (*Essays*, vol. 1, p. 9).

To Grant, both the Indians and the Highlanders of the nineteenth century were identical to those of the ancient past. 'What has been said of the immutability of Oriental customs, is, in a great degree, applicable to those of the highlanders', she wrote. 'Wherever they remain in undisturbed possession of their own language, and the prejudices connected with it, they think and act pretty much as they would have done a thousand years ago' (*Essays*, vol. 1, p. 117). Grant's Highlanders appear as a highly romanticized community. They are a 'warlike, musical, and poetical people' with a 'chivalrous dignity, and refinement of sentiment' (*Essays*,

---

[26]  William Robertson, *The situation of the world at the time of Christ's appearance and its connection with the success of His religion considered: a sermon*, 5th edition (Edinburgh: John Balfour, 1775).

[27]  William Robertson, *Edinburgh Review*, 1755, p. 42.

[28]  James Boswell, *The Journal of a Tour to the Hebrides with Samuel Johnson* (Edinburgh: Canongate, 1996), p. 260.

vol. 1, p. 12). Courageous, spirited and unafraid of hardship, loving their wives and children, and unselfishly committed to the common good, their 'imagination was exercised and called forth. … This is exactly the period in which heroic poetry is born: and these are the scenes fitted to awake the sensations that nurse its infancy' (*Essays*, vol. 1, p. 14). Poetry was described as natural to the Highlanders, and their primitive lifestyle was credited with having created the climate in which poetry could flourish. *Essays on the Superstitions of the Highlanders* also included translations of contemporary Gaelic poetry. Grant used her readings of eighteenth- and nineteenth-century Gaelic verse to support her argument that the Highlanders were truly a 'poetical' people, with untaught bards still composing poetry.

Grant's idealized Indian and Highland worlds were also frozen worlds, worlds where older values still prevailed and where progress was a negative quality. Both groups were depicted as caring little for material comfort because of the compensation of their communal life. Grant perceived both 'primitive' groups as being dangerously at risk of extinction, or of corruption by exposure to more 'civilized' societies. She saw those risks as coming equally from the avarice and lust for gain of the American fur traders, and from those in Scotland who wished to give the Highlanders 'a lowland education', and she believed both the Indians and the Highlanders to be in equal need of protection from those who could offer them a kind of parental care and guidance:

> We contemplate nations in this state, with a feeling like that which every unspoilt mind derives from the innocent prattle of such children as are not confined in artificial trammels, but allowed to express their own thoughts in their own words. We feel all the comparative consciousness, that we can think deeper, and express ourselves better; yet, making the due allowances, we wonder how they think so soundly, and speak so well. To this wonder is added the never failing charm of simplicity, and the delight we take in detecting the first motions as they arise in the untutored breast; and assisting the retrograde view, we love to indulge of our own feelings and opinions, during that guileless period. (*Essays*, vol. 1, pp. 3–5)

Grant's early experience of the communities and ways of life that she encountered in Albany gave her a set of perspectives with which to view – and depict – the community she later found in the Highlands; her Highlands experiences enabled her to make sense of her American memories. Her exposure to the Indians developed her belief in the possibility of strength and 'nobility' in a simpler culture. At the same time, her life in Laggan affected her retrospective view of Albany, and her writings about America are filtered through her later experiences and perceptions. An 'implicated spectator' (McMillan, 'Some Early Travellers', p. 134), writing simultaneously from within and without the communities she describes, Grant's experiences allowed her to analyse the cultures she found on both sides of the Atlantic with particular sharpness and acuity.

Chapter 5

# The Saxon in Ireland: John Hervey Ashworth on the Emigrant Trail

## Glenn Hooper

### Travails in Ireland

Throughout the first half of the nineteenth century Ireland received more tourists
and travellers than at any other time in its history. The Act of Union of 1800,
which brought the country into Union with England, Scotland and Wales, created
unprecedented enthusiasm for Ireland, especially among British travellers, who were
encouraged to see the new-found political relationship as a sign that the country
could now be safely visited and sampled, much as the Scottish Highlands, North
Wales and parts of the Lake District had been from the late 1760s onwards.[1] Like
other parts of the Celtic fringe, Ireland was associated with the sublime and the
romantic, and its frequently depopulated landscapes and antiquarian treasures helped
to entrance many a visitor. But the country's turbulent history, and its inhabitants'
adherence to the Roman Catholic faith, as well as a distinct linguistic tradition,
became additional stimuli, ensuring for many travellers a sense of the exotic, despite
its close proximity to the 'mainland'. Ireland was like Britain, yet utterly different.
It had for generations been governed by English laws, yet it consistently proved
itself resistant to those laws, and remained stubbornly unassimilated, especially in
the more remote regions. Hardly surprising, then, that all an 'adventurous' traveller
had to do was board the next steam-packet from Holyhead to Dublin, for the delights
of such an encounter to be made almost instantly available.

Publications such as John Carr's *The Stranger in Ireland* (1806), Sir Richard
Hoare's *Journal of a Tour* (1807), James Hall's *Tour through Ireland* (1813), William
Reed's *Rambles in Ireland* (1815), and Anne Plumptre's *Narrative of a Residence in
Ireland* (1817), revealed how many travellers connected the political transformation
brought about by the Act of Union with an incentive to visit the place, and to ponder
the fate of this little understood, yet constitutionally absorbed 'Sister Isle'. That
said, while many managed to convey to a largely British audience the attractions
of Ireland, in some instances a degree of narrative unease with the still politically

---

[1]    See, for example, John Bush, *Hibernia Curiosa* (London: Flexney, 1769),
Richard Twiss, *A Tour in Ireland in 1775* (London: privately printed, 1776), Arthur Young,
*A Tour in Ireland, 1776–79* (London: Cadell, 1780), and Charles Topham Bowden, *A Tour
through Ireland in 1790* (Dublin: Corbet, 1791), although even this growing eighteenth-
century interest was overshadowed by the far greater numbers who visited in the immediate
post-Union era.

unsettled nature of the island filtered through their pages. The disappointment expressed by Ireland's Catholics at the lack of progress over Emancipation (not granted until 1829), the often appalling condition of the peasantry, and the sense of a generally widespread and increasing political dissatisfaction, were just some of the issues with which many of these writers engaged.[2] In other words, whatever else they may have written, travel writers who visited in the early nineteenth century developed an interest in a whole range of Irish social and cultural matters, and showed how the travel narrative could be one of the most useful methods of representing Ireland to a largely incredulous English public.

The year 1845 will be long associated in Irish memory with the arrival of *Phytophora infestans*, the potato blight that first appeared in the west of Ireland, and which would recur annually until 1850, with the after-effects of famine continuing until 1852.[3] With a majority of the population heavily dependent upon the potato for sustenance, the result throughout these years was some one million deaths from starvation and disease, with roughly the same number emigrating to Britain, North America, and further afield. Politicians and political economists, as well as a host of on-the-ground activists drawn from agricultural science, philanthropy, missionary and outdoor relief work, became heavily involved in Ireland's tragedy. But the country was also swamped with writers, journalists, and travel writers, some of them voyeuristically in search of rich copy, others dedicated to disseminating knowledge of Irish misery for more benevolent purposes. Writings such as Mrs West's *A Summer Visit to Ireland* (1847), William Bennett's *Narrative of a Recent Journey* (1847), John East's *Glimpses of Ireland* (1847), James Hack Tuke's *A Visit to Connaught in the Autumn of 1847* (1847), and Sidney Godolphin Osborne's *Gleanings in the West of Ireland* (1850), all reveal how the travel narrative became one of the most effective means of conveying information about a range of economic, agricultural and social issues. Indeed, the use of interview, and the fieldwork format adopted by several, emphasize how well adapted the travel narrative was to this type of work. Since the experience of famine was what many wished to convey to their

---

[2]  One traveller, Mary Grant, who travelled throughout Britain and Ireland in the years immediately following the Act of Union, remarked forcefully on the agitated state of the country: 'We have been here [Loughrea] some weeks, but do not find it near so pleasant, in point of scenery, as our last quarters […] G. has been refused leave of absence, in consequence of the state of this country, it seems to cause general alarm, and a second rebellion, it is feared, will be the result of the Catholic Petition being refused. Nothing but the military keep the people in any kind of awe.' Mary Anne Grant, *Sketches of Life and Manners, with delineation of scenery in England, Scotland and Ireland* (London: Cox, 1810), p. 248.

[3]  The history of the Irish Famine has been very well documented, especially over the last decade or so. For some of the most informed writing on the subject, see the following: Mary Daly, *The Famine in Ireland* (Dublin: Dublin Historical Association, 1986), Cormac Ó Gráda, *The Great Irish Famine* (Dublin: Gill and Macmillan, 1989), and Christine Kinealy, *This Great Calamity: the Irish Famine, 1845–52* (Dublin: Gill and Macmillan, 1994).

readers, the journalistic style frequently employed – in its immediacy, 'realism' and documentary mode – appeared like an especially useful narrative method with which to capture, and represent, human tragedy.

But if travel writers of the Famine years wrote with something of the journalist's eye (and the relationship between journalism and travel writing has always been close),[4] then the early 1850s, when the effects of famine were on the wane, saw an even more interesting development: the coalescence of travel writing with an especially strident form of promotional rhetoric. Indeed, as soon as the first instalments of the 1851 census figures were printed in London, travellers made plans to visit Ireland, many of them with the intention of reporting on the opportunities the country now afforded to thrifty and industrious settlers. In John Forbes's *Memorandums made in Ireland* (1853), the narrator remarks on 'the English colonists' settled around Clifden, and of the 'fertile-seeming, English looking homesteads' they inhabit.[5] Meanwhile Harriet Martineau, sent on a tour of Ireland in 1852 by the *Daily News* – the paper founded by Charles Dickens – wrote of the 'western wilds' as 'the region for English settlers', and of the new houses, the gardens and the 'really verdant fields' they have created.[6] Martineau's *Letters from Ireland*, originally published in article form, was such a success with the British public that a complete reprint was almost immediately called upon. It is true that not everything discussed by Martineau or Forbes was so positive, with both acknowledging the economic and political difficulties that still faced the country.[7] Nevertheless, in many immediate post-Famine accounts an emphasis on the advantages of settling in Ireland became a key feature of their writings. For example, even though Francis Bond Head, in *A Fortnight in Ireland* (1852), opened his text with a distribution map detailing the number and location of Irish constabulary stations (a gesture that must have raised, as much as quelled, settler anxieties), he still emphasized the confidence of British migrants to Ireland, especially to parts of Co. Mayo, throughout this period:

---

[4] Although more concerned with the modern connections between journalism and travel writing, a lively and provocative discussion is nevertheless offered by Patrick Holland and Graham Huggan in *Tourists with Typewriters: Critical Reflections on Contemporary Travel Writing* (Ann Arbor: University of Michigan Press, 1998), esp. pp. 1–27. See, also, David Spurr, *The Rhetoric of Empire: Colonial Discourse in Journalism, Travel Writing, and Imperial Administration* (Durham: Duke University Press, 1993).

[5] John Forbes, *Memorandums made in Ireland in the Autumn of 1852*, 2 vols (London: Smith, 1853), vol. 1, pp. 259–60.

[6] Harriet Martineau, *Letters from Ireland*, ed. Glenn Hooper (Dublin: Irish Academic Press, 2001), pp. 90–91.

[7] Although Martineau was very clear about how improved Ireland could be, and what potential existed, she was also never less than outspoken about its limitations: 'The western coast of Ireland is very beautiful … But a few days are enough. A few days of observation of how the people live, merely by our going to see them, are sad enough to incline one to turn away, and never come again.' *Letters*, p. 115.

> In front of Mr. Butler's lawn and gardens was a small rocky eminence,
> on which from a slight flag-staff I saw revelling in pure air the British
> Union Jack, beneath which several children were gambolling. The young
> plantations were thriving very luxuriantly.[8]

Lawn, gardens, gambolling children, the Union Jack, pure air; this is less a description of a moment or place, than a fantasy of empire, a reinscribed landscape that conveys the benefits of the paternal hand. And like many imperial fantasies its impact is largely achieved by simply reconfiguring, or overlaying, one (native) reality with another (settler) one. In this case swapping lazy beds for lawns, bogs for gardens, ophthalmic for healthy children, Irish militantism for the Union flag, and the prevailing stench of pestilence for 'pure air'.

However, of the several travel writers who visited Ireland in the 1850s and 1860s, and who emphatically endorsed this notion of post-Famine resettlement, the Rev. John Hervey Ashworth was possibly one of the most trenchant. Ashworth's *The Saxon in Ireland: or, the Rambles of an Englishman in Search of a Settlement in the West of Ireland*, published in 1851 and republished the following year, exudes all the ebullience of settler discourse: outgoing, positive, and full of the detail of a potentially profitable landscape. Educated at Oxford, in his mid-fifties by the time of his migration to Co. Clare, Ashworth composed a travel narrative marked by an especially strident marketing rhetoric. Moreover, by recommending Ireland to potential investors by comparing it to less favourable destinations further afield, but also by focusing on the material benefits to be gained from settling in the country, he constructed his own version of the Home Tour.[9] Ireland is not exactly 'home' to Ashworth, nor indeed is it to many of his readers, but the intention throughout his narrative is to convert their shared unease over the 'state' of Ireland into something positive; to suggest that if one individual can overcome his/her fears and reservations about the place, then how much more successful would the efforts of hundreds, or thousands, be to the benefit of Ireland, but also to the benefit of British national security.[10]

---

[8]    Francis Bond Head, *A Fortnight in Ireland* (London: John Murray, 1852), p. 177. Interestingly, Head is one of the more enlightened visitors to South America discussed by Mary Louise Pratt, who writes of his 'unmitigated enthusiasm for free-wheeling pampa life', and of how the 'deathly exploitation of the Andean miners inspired his profound horror'. Mary Louise Pratt, *Imperial Eyes: Travel Writing and Transculturation* (London: Routledge, 1992), p. 153. As the quotation above suggests, however, Head cut a much more conservative figure during his tour of Ireland.

[9]    For recent commentary on the Home Tour, see Barbara Korte, *English Travel Writing: From Pilgrimages to Postcolonial Explorations* (Basingstoke: Macmillan, 2000), especially pp. 66–82. See, also, Malcolm Andrews, *The Search for the Picturesque: Landscape Aesthetics and Tourism in Britain, 1760–1800* (Aldershot: Scolar Press, 1990), John Glendening, *The High Road: Romantic Tourism, Scotland, and Literature, 1720–1820* (London: Macmillan, 1997), and John Harrington, *The English Traveller in Ireland* (Dublin: Wolfhound, 1991).

[10]    The concept of 'home' is, of course, a notoriously complex category, not just because our sense of what it implies is rarely shared by others, or because it can be frustrated or overridden by attachments to region or community, but because in the case of a place

In this essay I want to examine the presumed opportunities afforded Britain in the aftermath of Irish famine by looking specifically at the example of John Hervey Ashworth, a figure who saw travel as a way of overcoming his anxieties about Ireland but, more importantly, as a way of inducing others to do likewise. Composed at a time of significant change in Irish history, Ashworth's text is an act of testimony as well as a persuasive instruction manual for those who would like to imagine the country to be free of pestilence, but free, also, of much of the troubled politics that had hampered and frustrated its progress for so long.

## Making the pitch

So, how exactly does Ashworth convey to wary British investors, more accustomed to stories of famine and contagion, the notion that Ireland is an ideal place to which to emigrate? How does he overcome years of prejudice, and which tactics does he feel best articulate the idea of Irish renewal, the sense that the country can afford fresh opportunities to potential emigrants? From the very outset Ashworth bases his appeal to intending emigrants on the fundamentals of geography, reminding readers that Ireland is considerably less remote than many of Britain's other 'colonies', and arguing that the proximity of Ireland to Britain is one of the least appreciated of its advantages. The overall design of his work, he states simply in his preface, 'is to direct the attention of persons looking out either for investments or for new settlements, to the vast capabilities of the Sister Island'. But his ability to persuade potential emigrants that Ireland is worth considering, that it is now politically as well as economically stable, involves reminding them in the first instance of where the country actually is. Indeed, almost as though the idea of uncomplicated travel between Ireland and Britain is one of his major concerns, Ashworth structures the first part of his text around a series of journeys that takes the narrator from England to Ireland, then back to England, and finally back to Ireland again as a resolute emigrant embarking on a voyage of discovery. The narrative opens with Ashworth sitting under an oak tree, near his home, contemplating his future in England with some anxiety.[11] His options

---

such as Ireland – like, but not quite – the category presents more than the usual number of challenges, especially to British narrators. For a fuller, more sustained discussion, see Rosemary Marangoly George, *The Politics of Home: Postcolonial Relocations and Twentieth-century Fiction* (Cambridge: Cambridge University Press, 1996). See, also, Joseph Childers, 'At Home in the Empire', in Murray Baumgarten and H. M. Daleski, eds, *Homes and Homelessness in the Victorian Imagination* (New York: AMS, 1998), pp. 215–17.

[11]   The oak tree acted as a quintessentially 'English' motif, and within the context of Ashworth's text reinforced the appropriate national and gender priorities. William Shenstone, for example, referred to the oak as 'the perfect image of the manly character: in former times I should have said, and in present times I think I am authorised to say, the British one'. Cited in Tom Williamson, *Polite Landscapes: Gardens and Society in Eighteenth-Century England* (Baltimore: Johns Hopkins University Press, 1995), p. 128.

are limited. He feels he can do nothing but emigrate, possibly to the Antipodes, but is prompted into a reconsideration by the wise counsel of a friend: 'Will nothing but New Zealand, or Australia, or icy Canada, or the burning Cape suit you? ... what do you think of Ireland?'[12] The question appears initially ludicrous, then less so, as arguments in favour of Ireland as a resettlement option – convenience to major markets, comparable climate, largely English-speaking – become increasingly convincing. Within a mere three pages Ashworth has absorbed all the descriptive, historical and statistical information on Ireland he can lay his hands on, has packed his bags, and is ensconced at the Imperial Hotel, Dublin.

Ashworth's efforts to 'sell' Ireland to the more sceptical British settler are both exhausting and compelling. As suggested above, one of the principal methods of enticing potential investors is to emphasize how well Ireland fares when compared with other colonies. Indeed, before long, he insists, 'the English will discover how much better it is to settle in Donegal or Mayo, than to seek their fortunes beneath burning suns, or in the land of the wild Indian'. It is more attractive, he tells us, than 'Australia or the Canadas', while even New Zealand, the Cape, and Port Philip cannot hope to compete with all that Ireland has to offer (p. 104). However, these strategies, designed to dispel what might otherwise have been unfavourable comparisons with Ireland, are frequently supported by extensive agricultural data, such as the suitability of certain soil types for reclamation or drainage.[13] In other words, Ashworth is aware of the need to discuss Ireland within the larger, colonial setting, but is at the same time alert to the practicalities of everyday life. Settlers, he rightly gauges, will need to be persuaded to think of Ireland in broad terms, as an alternative to other locations, but they will also require specific details of what exactly it is that makes it a realistic substitute.

Which is why Ashworth develops a semi-confessional approach during the initial stages of his narrative, declaring himself effectively bankrupt, before inviting a close friend to advise him in his hour of need. This presentation of the narrator as a desperate and sceptical individual combines precisely the sort of elements necessary to overcome the doubts of those readers thinking of Ireland as a resettlement option, yet nevertheless still fearful of its reputation and history. Ashworth clearly realizes that Ireland is not the first place one might think of emigrating to, suggesting to

---

[12]  John Hervey Ashworth, *The Saxon in Ireland: or, the Rambles of an Englishman in Search of a Settlement in the West of Ireland* (London: Murray, 1851), pp. 4–6.

[13]  This agricultural interest, aside from its importance to Ashworth as a potential emigrant, was part of an ongoing debate, with many politicians and political economists trying their hand at resolving Ireland's seemingly intractable difficulties. Although they each have their own agendas and interests, the following texts give a flavour of how widespread concern for Ireland's agri-economical problems had become: James Caird, *The Plantation Scheme; or, the West of Ireland as a Field for Investment* (Edinburgh: Blackwood, 1850), George Preston White, *Three Suggestions for the Investment of Capital* (London: Trelawney, 1851), and William Webster, *Ireland considered as a Field for Investment or Residence* (Dublin: Hodges, 1852).

his friend that 'the midnight attacks of armed ruffians – the abduction of females – the lifting of cattle – [and the] forcible abstraction of crops' would be enough to dishearten the hardiest settler (p. 6). And yet no matter how many obstacles he puts in his – and our – way, Ashworth nevertheless insists that the country's potential attributes are kept very firmly centre-stage. Indeed, even when the narrator turns the discomforts of distant colonies into comparative assets, with Ireland seen in less favourable terms, all is not lost. 'We could bear the solitude of the backwoods of the Western Continent, or the chill air of Canada, or the sultry winds of South Africa', remarks an uninitiated and sceptical Ashworth, 'but the poverty, the squalidness, the degradation of the lower orders in Ireland, as described by travellers, we could not endure to witness' (p. 7). But there are *other* reasons, argues Ashworth's friend, for travelling, and ultimately living, in Ireland:

> It is idle to blame individuals; the social system of the country is rotten to the core; it has grown up under misgovernment; it must and will be altered; and the day is not far distant, nay, it has already arrived, when the axe will be laid to the root of that tree, and a finer and fairer be planted in its stead. When we consider the progress of the human mind, can we doubt that Ireland will yet be righted? Do not therefore decide too hastily. I will send you a few books and sundry documents to which I have alluded; look them over carefully, and without any of your John Bull prejudices, and then we can discuss the subject with a better chance of arriving at a right decision. (p. 8)

Not only is Ireland a source of untapped wealth, then, just hours away by steam-packet from Britain, and arguably cleansed of much of its recent disorder, but there is also a responsibility on potential emigrants, argues Ashworth's friend, to consider it a serious alternative. And this moral imperative, developed within only a matter of pages, becomes a central element in Ashworth's resettlement programme. Clearly, enticing Britons to travel to Ireland because of rich pickings, especially in the West, is one thing, but to suggest to them that the country requires their participation in the development of its resources, in the building of its infrastructure, and in the establishment of a more stable political system, provides additional leverage of the sort necessary to inspire a particular type of Victorian reader.[14]

Not surprisingly, then, Ashworth develops a very hands-on, no-nonsense approach, stating that the 'following pages were principally written amid the scenes which they attempt to describe', and that they convey 'the passing impressions of the moment' (Preface). Composed, we are led to believe, in the manner of a report, with situations and personalities fixed briefly within Ashworth's gaze, the text asks us to regard everything we are being told as verifiable and truthful, not only because from truth comes trust, but because it is trust that Ashworth primarily needs to establish between himself and his reader. Ireland must be promoted as a desirable and bounteous place in which to live, but there is an awareness that for

---

[14] I allude here to the 'mission civilisatrice' that governed the efforts of many settler-colonists, that aspect of imperial ideology that encouraged them to associate their emigration in the light of how useful, or helpful, their 'contribution' and residence might be.

Figure 1. *Protestant Missionary Settlement, Isle of Achill.* Courtesy of the National Library of Ireland.

a certain class of reader it might be useful to base that 'plea' on sound, empirical evidence. And if that 'evidence' also happens to be explicitly identified with the notion of tangible and likely profit, in terms of what can be got out of the country, how quickly, and on what terms, all the better.

## From the urban to the rural

Ashworth's arrival in Ireland is marked by a compression of sights and sounds, with the city of Dublin presented as a myriad of frenzied, sometimes unappealing activity: 'The public buildings, the streets, the shops, the hotels, all striking and handsome [I] was well pleased with everything I saw, save the crowded and filthy purlieus of this otherwise fine city' (p. 12). Dublin, for all its architectural and cultural interest, however, is despatched in less than a page, clearly of little use to the task in hand, and Ashworth sets off on a number of excursions towards the west of the country, taking the train from Dublin to Mullingar, and then the mail to Galway, a 'kind of Seville', he remarks, full of Moorish associations (p. 17). But even Galway is only a stopping point, a place where information and advice can be gathered, and it is not until he has properly departed, 'taking the road that skirts the western shores of Lough Corrib', that his 'tour of observation' begins (pp. 18–19).[15]

These tours, in which the narrator casts himself in something of the explorer mode, rarely fail to convince him of Ireland's limitless potential, and he rhapsodizes about the country's attributes and how accessible they seem:

> I have been again much gratified with my excursions today in the neighbourhood of Westport. What may be done by patient industry is here manifested on every side; and I am convinced that persons wishing to leave England may here find an asylum to suit their inclinations and their means (p. 52).

Even when Ashworth steps off dry land, departing for what he terms an 'aquatic excursion', there is more than a feeling of well-being about his experiences, a fit between his sense of place and his sense of Self, and a corresponding belief that his economic difficulties will be shortly at an end (p. 89). In fact, everywhere Ashworth travels prompts comments from him on the extractive or agricultural potential of the place, on how it requires only modest investment and a little imagination to make it truly profitable. Indeed, at the beginning of his narrative he confirmed that

---

[15] Dublin always featured as part of any traveller's itinerary, not just because most people arrived at Kingstown (now Dun Laoghaire), a few miles away, and because it was the instinct among many to compare Dublin with London, but also because Dublin was used as a cultural marker to set against the Irish countryside, which was regarded as potentially dangerous, if topographically rich. Although Ashworth's hasty departure for the western seaboard, and his focus on a very particular region in the west, is a little unusual, it does give his text an immediacy of purpose not all travellers are able to convey.

this was his main objective, that he was there largely to comment on the country's agricultural capability, and that his high-energy efforts would be directed towards an evaluation of Irish fields and bogs, and on their likely transformation.

Nevertheless, sensing that such efforts might be better supported by testimony other than his own, Ashworth produces a series of facts and figures regarding the potential profitability of the place, but chooses to have them narrated by other settlers, or 'witnesses', who come forward – not unlike subsidiary characters in a novel – to recite their personal experiences, and give evidence of how attractive Ireland really is. This type of witness narration, perhaps not surprisingly, had a real appeal for those ideologues looking to promote Ireland in the aftermath of famine. One such figure, Thomas Miller, who published *The Agricultural and Social State of Ireland in 1858*, compiled a text that was almost entirely comprised of extracts from correspondence he had had with various settlers throughout Ireland in the mid-1850s. Like Ashworth, Miller was keenly aware of the need to persuade potential investors in England of the necessity of considering Ireland as a settlement option, but he also knew that by 'collecting the sentiments of [his] fellow-countrymen' he might be able to present precisely the sort of documentary evidence to clinch such a deal, to show readers that these were not fantasies, but empirically supported – and proven – 'facts'.[16] And for Ashworth, whose efforts in this regard are nevertheless more restrained than Miller's, the effects of such manoeuvring are just as effective ('I have never, however', he continued, 'repented my choice of a home, and never intend to leave it [Ireland]') (p. 128). Moreover, just as Ashworth is persuaded in the first instance by a friend to overcome his own prejudice about Ireland, Ashworth now in turn pressurizes his reader, by gathering around him figures who corroborate his impressions of the country, and who then go on to verify the attractions of Ireland in their own right.

Yet no matter how enthusiastic Ashworth becomes about Ireland, or about the native Irish (especially their labouring skills), or how much he warms to the economic potential of the place, one point is emphasized time and again: the fact that not only have communications improved in Ireland, but that physical contact between Britain and Ireland has also advanced. Ireland, Ashworth is keen to stress, is no longer deficient in transport networks, but rather progressing daily:

> Now that internal communications are daily opening out, and the proximity to England is so marvellously increased by railways in every direction, it becomes a self-evident fact that Ireland *cannot* remain as it is. (pp. 114–15)

At a certain level this might seem like a straightforward enough statement about the effects of an 'improving' Irish modernity, and yet the emphasis on communications

---

16  Thomas Miller, *The Agricultural and Social State of Ireland in 1858, being the experience of Englishmen and Scotchmen who have settled in Ireland ... With an Appendix, consisting of Letters from Scotch and English Proprietors and Farmers resident in Ireland* (Dublin: Thom, 1858), p. 10.

that occurs throughout the text demonstrates an awareness of the necessity of such a transformation for Ireland, especially for potential emigrants. The Irish canal system had seen significant developments since the mid-eighteenth century, with the Grand Canal links between Dublin and the Barrow and Shannon rivers being completed by 1791 and 1805 respectively. But the really big change – and hope – lay with the railways, which expanded throughout the 1830s, but which saw dramatic advances throughout the 1840s and 1850s. Of course, railways and a generally improved infrastructure meant one very obvious thing: easier access to the British markets for those settlers dependent upon the export of livestock or crops. But improved infrastructure also suggested increased security, and provided precisely the sort of guarantee a nervous investor might need before considering Ireland as a resettlement option. Getting potential travellers, settlers and investors to re-imagine the country in the aftermath of Famine, by stressing the sense of physical proximity between Britain and Ireland, was one way of initiating interest. But by emphasizing how developed infrastructural links are, or could be, Ashworth takes this issue one stage further. The physical space of Ireland is being made better known to many British readers as a result of Ashworth's narrative and explorative efforts, but the transformative power associated with these new colonists becomes an increasingly dominant element of his text. Having relocated what many took to be an imperceptibly situated entity, Ireland, and especially its landscape, must now be brought to life.

## Views of Ireland

While Ashworth declares an interest in publicizing Ireland's physical capabilities above all else, his motives for doing so could not be simpler: to keep the potential settler's mind focused on several core issues, but also to maintain a distinction between the type of journey he is conducting, and the more scenic or picturesque tour.[17] As an early reviewer of the text suggested, the 'value of this book (which may be strongly recommended to the perusal of intending emigrants) consists mainly in the excellent view it gives of the actual resources of the soil in the districts traversed by the author'.[18] Ashworth may be travelling around some of the most scenic parts of the west of Ireland, but his intentions remain focused on promoting that landscape at all times, and in this he may be regarded as diverging from other travellers, whose purpose is largely to entertain and amuse.

While he journeys across parts of the west of Ireland, then, striking out on each occasion from Cong, his 'headquarters', Ashworth adopts an increasingly

---

[17] For an overview of the historical development of tourism in, and travel writing about, Ireland, see Martin Ryle, *Journeys in Ireland: Literary Travellers, Rural Landscapes, Cultural Relations* (Aldershot: Ashgate, 1999).

[18] *Fraser's Magazine*, August 1851, p. 224.

proprietorial air, stopping to comment on the altering profiles of hills, on the paucity of woodland, the layout of Irish village life, and the fact that much of what he sees is in need of economic rejuvenation. And perhaps unsurprisingly the twin-track approach chosen by Ashworth – conveying impressions of Ireland to his readers, while deciding on a location in which to settle with his family – is aided by an extensive use of maps, to which Ashworth constantly refers throughout, and which appear to occupy an increasingly legitimizing role. As a way of coming to terms with the specificities of the Irish landscape, of course, maps are the ideal tool, able to image the landscape in terms of scale and perspective, while showing enough of the sort of natural detail that would be of use to someone with Ashworth's interests: determining whether land is being used for cultivation, rough-grazing or waste, showing the location of towns, waterway systems and bogland. Seen in this way, maps are an indispensable aid for the more serious-minded traveller, a means of appreciating the fullness of the terrain over which s/he travels, while providing a more 'scientific' edge to his/her narrative. But maps have other purposes too. As J. B. Harley suggests, 'maps are never value-free images; except in the narrowest Euclidean sense they are not in themselves either true or false'.[19] They are not unambiguous displays of technicality and admeasurement, in other words, but rather texts upon which are inscribed whole histories of possession and territoriality.

However, although a type of cartographic discourse is employed by Ashworth at a number of junctures in his text ('The whole of Achill lay below me like a map'), one especially memorable moment sees it displaced onto an imaginary realm, allowing for the possible reinvention not just of the Irish landscape, but of the very identity of John Hervey Ashworth himself (p. 155). As with so much of Ashworth's writing on Ireland, the aim here is simply to convince the reader of the prospect for limitless self-advancement, of the transformations that can be fulfilled, and how beneficial to Ireland, but also to Britain, a settler's efforts might be. Ashworth climbs to the top of Ballycroy mountain, near Newport, Co. Mayo, in the company of a local Irish guide, only to express the following sentiments. 'I could have stood and gazed for hours', he enthuses, 'It was Nature's own map, and I soon, from my geographical knowledge of the district, made my eye familiar with my position' (p. 140). Having finally dispensed with an actual map, Ashworth chooses to rely on his own expertise for clarification, establishing himself as the authority he would dearly love to be, capable of comprehending the scene that lies before him without any textual aids or prompts. Indeed, so keen is he to make the transition from traveller to settler that he engages his guide in a sort of duet, in which they each take it in turn to name the various mountains and villages that lie beneath their gaze:

---

[19]   J. B. Harley, 'Maps, Knowledge and Power', in Stephen Daniels and Denis Cosgrove, eds, *The Iconography of Landscape: Essays on the Symbolic Representation, Design and Use of Past Environments* (Cambridge: Cambridge University Press, 1988), p. 278.

'We are now,' said my companion, 'in Shrahduggane; and that lake to the left, as well as the dark one below us, are the sources of the Owenduff river, which empties itself yonder into Turlogh Bay.' 'Yes,' said I, 'close by Croy Lodge, where is the celebrated salmon fishery. That black and gloomy range to the left, in the far distance is, I suppose, Currawn Achill; and beyond are Slievemore and Croaghan, with Saddle Head to the north'. 'Right, Sir,' interrupted Macguire; 'and look off to the sea as far as your eye can reach – that rock is called Deevelaun ...' 'And,' continued I, 'yonder far bay, on which the sun is just now shining, is Blacksod Harbour, and beyond is the Mullet, and this lovely creek, that penetrates so beautifully inland, is Tulloghan Bay ... What a glorious map is this!' (pp. 140–41)

And not for nothing does this epiphany take place on the top of a mountain. Mountain views, of course, provide a feeling of mastery, and are central to many colonial narratives. Indeed, in Mary Louise Pratt's *Imperial Eyes* the term 'prospect', among just one of many physical aspects prized by a type of nineteenth-century European traveller, is given an unusual spin, recalling 'the European subject who scans landscapes and dreams of their transformation'.[20] In Pratt's opinion, the 'promontory description', an especially nuanced method of landscape appreciation favoured by a number of famous Nile explorers including Speke, Burton and Grant, articulates a 'particularly explicit interaction between aesthetics and ideology'.[21] In other words, those travellers or explorers who take to gazing enviously from great heights upon what they frequently describe as 'virgin' territory, are reconfiguring that territory as much as appreciating its scenic attractions, thinking of it as a potentially lucrative investment as well as a place of beauty. And it is at this interface between aesthetics and ideology, between a view of Ireland that is appreciative, and another that exploits that view in the interests of capital, that we find Ashworth: gazing, viewing, seeing, sometimes just presiding over a largely uninhabited landscape:

Take the large map of Ireland I have sent you, and draw a circle around this mountain, as far as you think the human eye can range, and you may have some idea of the glorious prospect I now enjoyed. The objects were infinite, and the view embraced one of the most interesting and picturesque tracts, I had almost said, on the world's surface. (p. 46)

Although Ashworth's appreciation of Irish potential, then, largely involves re-imagining the place for British readers, his effort to extol the wonders of the west of the country are especially noteworthy. Noted for its romantic aspects, though conversely also for its association with some of the worst effects of the Famine, the west of Ireland is presented by Ashworth as a settler's delight, capable of generating untold wealth, prosperity and happiness. And this rapturous appraisal, directed at the very heart of the intending emigrant experience, is highly effective, largely because of the 'seeing', recording authority that accompanies it. For example,

---

[20] Pratt, *Imperial Eyes*, p. 104.
[21] Pratt, *Imperial Eyes*, pp. 202, 205.

when he stands alone, almost delirious with the potential that lies just outside the village of Clifden, he is prompted to comment on how the 'richness' of the views, and the 'sublime scene', have left him entranced (p. 39). But on the northern shore of Lough Corrib, after he has ascended to the highest point from which to appraise its worth, Ashworth comments on its 'magnificent view', and more interestingly, how 'gazing ... upon a vast extent of country' prompts the mind to 'speculate upon the rapid changes which must soon come over this fertile, but hitherto almost unknown region' (p. 71). Indeed, as a specific location the Lough Corrib region appears especially bountiful, inviting 'the eye of the improver [to see] ... much to attract his attention', a space of rich, if unexplored, potential amidst some of the worst of the Irish wastelands: 'A more delightful location for a settler than that I can scarcely conceive; everything is made to his hand, and the future prospects of this district are certainly most encouraging' (p. 72). As a place apart, then, the west of Ireland has become many things to John Hervey Ashworth: a physical entity, a potential investment, a metaphysical salve, and an Edenic realm on the brink of modernity.

## From home to home

When Ashworth, approximately half-way through his text, arrives back in England, determined to settle in Ireland, he announces to his family that the 'delightful and convenient Mullingar railroad has lost Australia or the Canadas a right worthy and desirable emigrant. To reach Galway from London in four-and-twenty hours certainly sets a new face on things' (p. 104). At certain moments throughout his tour Ashworth made use of the exoticizing qualities of the Irish, and of how the country differed spectacularly from Britain, in cultural as well as geographical ways. It sometimes suited him, in other words, to tempt the potential traveller or emigrant with salacious tales of Irish life, and especially with claims of how at odds with so much British cultural practice he found the place to be. Ultimately, however, Ashworth must turn away from this potentially worrying form of presentation, and project a vision of Ireland that satisfies basic travel-emigrant criteria. He must draw Ireland, and the Irish, closer to Britain. Fortunately, a number of technological advances make the presentation of such an argument that bit easier to convey, and he begins with an appeal to logic: 'the power of steam has almost annihilated distance', reasons Ashworth, 'and now brings the Irish proprietor within a few hours' journey of the English metropolis' (p. 106). A strong argument, the reader might think. However, no matter how much Ashworth tells himself that Irish railways are a necessary development, that England can be easily reached, and communications are generally improving, these arguments seem, finally, to sound less convincing than he would wish, and he decides on an altogether different strategy. Ashworth, in other words, decides to play safe, which amounts not so much to telling readers how easily Ireland can be transformed, or how easy it is to travel from there to Britain, but to reminding them how much like England Ireland *really is*. 'You cannot', he asks rhetorically of the emigrant experience, 'call this banishment, when the same breezes blow over both islands – the same laws are observed, and the same legislature governs, and exchange of communication is the work of only a few hours?' (p. 108). Indeed, in the final pages of the book, after some time spent persuading readers of the attractions of Irish difference, he makes the following announcement:

> [T]his is not like a new country. It is historical all over – full of the associations of olden times, yielding the same fruits, raising the same crops, inhabited by the same animals, birds, and fishes, as merry England – similar in climate, and occupied by a people intermixed with our own race, and speaking our own language. In about sixteen hours we may at any time step on English ground, and in eight hours more, pace the streets of London. The recent improvements in travelling seem almost to annihilate time and space, and ere long, people will think as little of journeying to the shores of the Atlantic, and locating themselves among the green mountains or fertile plains of Mayo, as they used to think of a tour in Devonshire, or even a trip to Margate. (pp. 260–61)

Ireland is not just *like* England, so the reasoning runs, but really an *extension* of England, a place in which one's neighbours, as well as the laws they observe, the food they eat, and the language they speak, are as your own. Indeed it is at this point that we feel that Ashworth really has taken us on quite an Irish excursion, with the country lit up from one, slightly jarring, perspective after another: seen as relatively unknown, then increasingly explored and understood; comprehended as a region of almost endless economic possibilities, but also as a somewhat vandalized – though salvageable – version of England.

John Hervey Ashworth sincerely believed in Irish economic potential, and felt the best way for it to be realized was by encouraging thrifty English and Scottish settlers to Ireland in the aftermath of Famine. True, the country was in a sorry state, but he believed it was possible to transform it, and to take advantage of its proximity to British shores, an advantage that Ireland had over many of its competitors. Realizing that generating interest in Ireland was going to be a struggle, not least because of the discontent that continued to prevail in the country, he made the most of its scenic attributes, but especially of his own not inconsiderable marketing abilities. Ashworth may have been back in Britain by the late 1860s, his dream of an Irish home cut short by disappointment or homesickness, but his enthusiasm for the country, at a time when most people thought of it in terms of extreme hardship and deprivation, constitutes one of the most engaging pieces of travel-emigrant literature to emerge from nineteenth-century Ireland:

> The Owenduff and one of its most considerable tributaries watered this plain with their meanderings, the former descending from the mountains overhanging the distant valley of Shrahmore, and the latter visibly rushing down the precipitous sides of Nephin Beg, from the Lake of Scardaun. I could at the moment have fancied myself amid those lovely scenes of

Asia Minor described by travellers. The eye of fancy speedily crowded this solitary plain with flocks and herds, perched on each rising knoll some quiet pastoral home, covered the rocky sides of the mountains with dark forests, or converted their sunny slopes into green pastures, or joyous fields of corn. (pp. 230–31)

Chapter 6

# Animals as Figures of Otherness in Travel Narratives of Brittany, 1840–1895

## Jean-Yves Le Disez

It was the oppressed, exploited, alienated, or repressed part of humanity that kept on reappearing in the imagination of Western Man as the Wild man, as the monster, and the devil – to haunt or entice him thereafter. Sometimes this oppressed or repressed humanity appeared as a threat and a nightmare, or other times as a goal and a dream ... but always as a criticism of whatever security and peace of mind one group of men in society had purchased at the cost of the suffering of another.[1]

### Introduction

Brittany proved a popular destination for British Victorian travellers.[2] Of their many accounts of the region published between 1840 and 1895 few are as sensitive to the Other as 'A tour through Brittany' by the Reverend Thomas Price. One object, however, fails to seduce Price, and that is the *sabot*, or wooden shoe, which the author describes as 'the disgrace of civilization': 'I know not which is the most offensive object in a civilized country, that of actual barefoot squalor, or this remnant of the rudest and most uncouth efforts of barbarian ingenuity.'[3] The association between the Breton people and primitivism is not confined to their appearance, however. Indeed, several British travellers made use of animal imagery in their responses to the region and its inhabitants, an element in this writing that has been largely overlooked. This neglect is due perhaps to the following facts: their works were published at a time hardly regarded as prestigious in the history of travel (too late to belong to the tradition of the Grand Tour, too early to interest the student of mass tourism); they related to a peripheral and not very exotic part of Europe; and, finally, even within France, narratives of the regions failed to excite particular curiosity amongst critics.[4] It is

---

[1]   Hayden White, 'The Forms of Wildness', in *Tropics of Discourse. Essays in Cultural Criticism* (Baltimore: Johns Hopkins University Press, 1978), p. 180.

[2]   Jean-Yves Le Disez, 'L'Autre des Victoriens. Récits de voyageurs britanniques en Bretagne (1830–1900)', Ph.D. thesis, Université de Bretagne Occidentale (Brest), 1997. For a revised version see *Étrange Bretagne* (Rennes: P.U.R, 2002).

[3]   'A tour through Brittany made in the year 1829', in *The Literary Remains of the Rev. Thomas Price, Carnhuanawr*, 2 vols (Llandovery: William Rees, 1854), vol. 1, p. 105.

[4]   Cultural relations between marginal parts of Europe (or between the centre and the peripheries) have often received little attention partly because metropolitan histories tend to erase them. Thus, only four of at least 27 Victorian travel narratives of Brittany are

my contention, however, that it is in these apparently nondescript narratives that the ideology of the time can be best observed, in part because more sophisticated literary works are rather better at hiding their political values.

To put this in some kind of perspective, let me say that although there are a number of important narratives of travel in Brittany by French authors, including prestigious ones – notably Maupassant, Mérimée and Flaubert, author of the superb *Par les Champs et par les Grèves* (1855) – more was published within the genre in English than in French. The reasons for this have more to do with the relative lack of interest for, and low status of, travel writing as a genre at the time in France than with an indifference towards the region (the vogue for Brittany expressed itself mainly in painting). The attitude of French authors to Brittany and its inhabitants did not differ *fundamentally* from that of their counterparts but British travellers have more to say about the landscape – and a finer brush to paint it – and a different agenda, linked to the specific religious and political configurations of their own society, and their complex relationship with a part of France which is French, yet in many ways reminiscent of Britain.

Although the Reverend Price, as a friend and (Welsh) 'cousin' of the Bretons, tries to console himself by insisting that the *sabot* is by no means the privilege of the province, it will nevertheless haunt him forever:

> [T]here are two descriptions so domiciled in my ears, that I imagine I can never entirely forget them, or their accompanying localities. The one is the noise made by the march of the cows through the village of Chamouni ... the other is the noise caused in the streets of Morlaix by the tramp of the sabots in the market-place, and which, in fine weather, commences early enough to surprise the weary traveller before he has finished his morning nap, and increases more and more as the peasantry arrive from the country, until at length even sleep and fatigue give way to the more powerful effect of curiosity. (p. 106)

Of course, as Linda Colley has shown, the wooden shoe was for the British the symbol of the backwardness of the Continent.[5] It is no coincidence that the sound of the *sabots* is associated with Morlaix, the Breton town Price ranks above all others because it is where Lédan, the major Breton printer, has his shop. The

---

(briefly) mentioned in the major study of Victorian travel in France, Sylvaine Marandon's *L'image de la France dans l'Angleterre victorienne* (Paris: Armand Colin, 1967). Very few travel books concerning the peripheries can be found under entries such as 'Brittany' or 'Auvergne' in the catalogues of Europe's national libraries.

[5] 'Imagining the French as their vile opposites, as Hyde to their Jekyll, became a way for the Britons – particularly the poorer and less privileged – to contrive for themselves a converse and flattering identity. The French wallowed in superstition: therefore, the British, by contrast, must enjoy true religion. The French were oppressed by a bloated army and by absolute monarchy: consequently, the British were manifestly free. The French tramped through life in wooden shoes, whereas the British – as Adam Smith pointed out – were shod in supple leather and, therefore, clearly more prosperous.' Linda Colley, *Britons, Forging the Nation* (London: Pimlico, 1992), p. 368.

intruding *sabot* reminds the town dweller that the Enlightenment is fragile, and that the wildness of the peasantry is still a threat to 'civilization' and 'improvement'. A close reading of the text reveals strange associations. Not only are the *sabots* associated with hooves (perhaps under the influence of the French language, which uses the same word for hooves and wooden shoes) but the wooden shoe is deemed more offensive than the naked foot of the savage. Clearly, something crucial is at stake here, which has to do with the frontier between wildness and civilization, and with the line between the human and the animal.

My belief is that because of its intermediate position between the foreign (France) and the domestic (British) – as Matthew Arnold reminded his readers, Brittany was the only Celtic country that 'was not ours' – Brittany served for the Victorians who visited it (and sometimes lived there) like rural Britain itself, but even more so, as a 'psychic balance wheel', to borrow Martin J. Wiener's apt phrase.[6] Being both close and distant, very different and sometimes oddly familiar (and not just in terms of landscape), it alternatively offered travellers an opportunity to work out their own contradictions or, on the contrary, added to the confusion that comes, as Freud has shown, from the emergence of the 'Unheimlich' (the uncanny).[7] As a consequence, they represented Brittany as either very wild or very sweet, until Mrs Norton, in her immensely successful poem *The Lady of La Garaye* (1861), came up with an oxymoron that summed up her contemporaries' response to the region when she marvelled at 'those Breton songs so *wildly sweet*'.[8]

The uncanny *sabot* is Price's fetish object, repulsive yet oddly attractive, because it symbolizes for him, consciously or unconsciously, the contradictory nature of his encounter with his Breton 'cousins'. But for most authors the revelation will come in the guise of an animal. Almost systematically, the emergence of an animal in the narrative – a dog, a horse, wolves, sheep, cows, or even sardines – signals a (wild) subtext that constantly threatens to undermine the (tame) text.

---

6    Matthew Arnold, *The Study of Celtic Literature* (London: Smith & Elder, 1912), p. 149. One traveller, Robert Bell, writes in 1850 that 'at that time there were two hundred and fifty English residents in and about the town [of Dinan]'. R. Bell, *Wayside Pictures Through France, Belgium, and Holland* (London: Richard Bentley, 1850), p. 172. Martin J. Wiener, *English Culture and the Decline of the Industrial Spirit, 1850–1980* (London: Penguin, 1985), p. 49.

7    '[The] uncanny is in reality nothing new or alien, but something which is familiar and old-established in the mind and which has become alienated from it only through the process of repression.' Sigmund Freud, 'The "Uncanny"', in *Art and Literature*, The Penguin Freud Library vol. 14 (London: Penguin, 1990), pp. 363–4. For more details, see J.-Y. Le Disez, 'Un victorien au pardon: le Révérend Phillip W. de Quetteville', in *Hauts lieux du sacré en Bretagne* (Brest: CRBC-UBO, 1997), pp. 191–206.

8    Caroline Elisabeth Sarah Norton [Lady Stirling Maxwell], *The Lady of La Garaye* (London: Macmillan, 1862), p. 100, my emphasis.

### Crossing the border: Louisa Stuart Costello

In at least one narrative, Louisa Stuart Costello's *A Summer Amongst the Bocages and the Vines* (1840), this encounter coincides with the crossing of the border. The narrator and her anonymous female companion have hardly crossed the bridge into Dinan, the first Breton town, when they are threatened by a Wild man:

> and in a jargon which I supposed to be Breton, [he] offered to guide us where we could have a better view ... Through rank grass and weeds we waded on, when with a half-savage grin and bound, the guide reached a pile of broken stones and invited us to ascend.[9]

The creature insists on showing the travellers a better view of a deep abyss:

> I was weak enough to give him my hand to mount where he pointed ... but found that the only thing to see was a mass of brick and stone huddled together in what might have been a cellar, and beyond that, a deep dark abyss, which I instantly conjured into a frightful *oubliette*! ... we were two females alone in the midst of ruins and dungeons. (Vol. 1, pp. 227–8)

Of course, Costello's 'huddled mass' could stand as a metaphor for other masses,[10] allowing the whole scene to read like some sort of allegory of the impending Fall of the Bourgeoisie. This is travelling gone wild, with the guide showing the visitors what they do not want to see, as if the travelees had somehow managed to write themselves into the narrative.[11] But what makes this scene extraordinary is yet to come. Costello and her companion get rid of the guide – a piece of silver does the trick – and we learn that he is a madman from the nearby lunatic asylum of Dinan.

---

[9]　Louisa Stuart Costello, *A Summer Amongst the Bocages and the Vines*, 2 vols (London: Richard Bentley, 1840), vol. 1, pp. 226–7.

[10]　I have commented elsewhere on the fascination with menhirs and dolmens as masses of stone. (See Le Disez, *Étrange Bretagne*, pp. 95, 136.) The following passage from another traveller, T. A. Trollope, illustrates this interest. In it the mass literally stands for the masses which no amount of delegitimization can displace – hence the attention (with some revulsion) to the megaliths:

> It should seem that there could be little to gratify the eye or detain the attention in a rude unfashioned mass. And yet I continued to gaze upon the hoary stone as if it possessed the power of fascination. I could fancy it anxious but unable to communicate to the successive generations ... the facts whose memory it was intended to guard and perpetuate ... It looked so pale and mournful, too, standing alone from century to century, unaltered by the lapses of the ages, while all around had changed.

Thomas Adolphus Trollope, *A Summer in Brittany*, ed. Frances Trollope, 2 vols (London: Henry Colburn, 1840), vol. 1, p. 185.

[11]　The term 'travelees' was coined by Mary Louise Pratt to describe those who are 'traveled upon'. See Mary Louise Pratt, *Imperial Eyes: Travel Writing and Transculturation* (London: Routledge, 1992), p. 242, note 42.

The peace that money can buy, however, is short-lived:

> Our persecutor ... disappeared in the direction of the farm. We felt uneasy, for we observed a peculiar smile on his face as he passed us, and we were decided [*sic*] to retrace our steps homewards, when we were startled by the hoarse barking of a dog, and the sound of a human voice exciting him, and in a moment we beheld bounding towards us behind a rising ground an enormous brindled mastiff, growling and barking furiously. (Vol. 1, pp. 228–9)

Clearly, man and dog are one and the same creature, the materialization of thinly-disguised post-revolutionary fears. One realizes that the guide's 'ominous scowl' and 'grin' announced the mastiff's 'growling'. What would happen, the implication seems to be, if madmen were not kept behind lock and key; if the rabble were suddenly let loose? No wonder the travellers' thoughts fly *homewards*: the crossing of the border has opened one of those wounds that are not easily healed. This traumatic scene which, again, marks the entry into Brittany,[12] is the only one describing people and places in a book made up for the most part of Costello's translations of La Villemarqué's Breton ballads.[13] Because they are interested in the translations *qua* translations, most scholars have tended to overlook the link between the two apparently unrelated aspects of the book: translation and travel. Yet the rest of Costello's text is an almost desperate effort to *domesticate* the Breton wildness by translation, to dress the gaping wound. Her fluent, ethnocentric translations fulfil this desire to 'retrac[e] [her] steps homewards'.[14]

---

[12] That dog will continue to haunt Costello for the rest of her journey. At the Museum in Rennes she is fascinated with one picture in particular:

> Among the crowd of worthless paintings, I was struck with a finely executed, though hideous, representation of a large mastiff ... it has an unnatural hue, being brindled and *tacheté* with a colour more like a toad's back than anything else ... it reminds one of old stories of *loups-garoux* ... There is nothing open or honest in his bark; his face is vulgar, his manners uninteresting, and he has no friendliness in his disposition. (Vol. 1, p. 229)

Who exactly is this 'he', one wonders?

[13] Théodore Hersart de la Villemarqué's *Barzaz Breiz. Chants populaires de la Bretagne* (1839), a collection of Breton ballads and their translation into French, was known in the original across Europe before translations began to appear in most major languages. Together with Emile Souvestre's *Les derniers Bretons* (1836), it widely contributed to the vogue of Brittany both in France and in Britain.

[14] '[A] fluent strategy', writes L. Venuti, 'performs a labor of acculturation which domesticates the foreign text, making it intelligible and even familiar to the target-language reader, providing him or her with the narcissistic experience of recognizing his or her own culture in a cultural other'. Lawrence Venuti, 'Introduction', in Lawrence Venuti, ed., *Rethinking Translation. Discourse, Subjectivity, Ideology* (London: Routledge, 1992), p. 5. Just one example from Costello's text is the first stanza of her translation of La Villemarqué's 'Baron Jaouioz':

This domestication, in turn, carries huge implications not only for an understanding of her strategy as a translator and editor,[15] but, more generally, for an interpretation of Victorian discourse on Brittany as a whole. If my hypothesis is true, the writing of Brittany as wildly sweet is, like the translation of its uncouth poetry, a domestication, a movement homewards, not an instance of *de*familiarization but of *re*familiarization. The travel book, of course, is produced at home, very much with the domestic audience in mind. It is produced *after* the traveller has re-crossed the frontier. This re-crossing is not an effort to narrate an experience so much as an attempt to efface the trauma of the first crossing. That crossing is not only of the border that separates one part of France from another but of the border between self and non-self, which is also, it turns out, the border between the human and the animal.

## Calves at a market (Matilda Betham Edwards)

Costello's text exemplifies in a dramatic way the transition from self to (human) non-self to animal that takes place in most subsequent texts. Significantly, Costello never ventures far from the border. Her Brittany is a Brittany seen from the Eastern marches of the province (and from the poetry of La Villemarqué). I do not claim that animals always emerge in the text the moment the traveller enters Brittany. In later narratives, their appearance is often deferred. They do, however, manifest themselves with amazing predictability whenever the Self is threatened by a sudden invasion of Otherness, and the appearance of an animal figure invariably signals danger. But the crucial point is that danger varies from one author to the next. All animals are equal but some are more equal than others. Animals are put to different uses, depending on the interests or fears of individual authors, but they occupy the same strategic position in the general economy of their texts. In short, scenes involving animals are exactly what Antoine Berman calls 'signifying zones' (*des zones signifiantes*), those scenes where the whole work 'condenses itself, represents itself, signifies itself and symbolises itself'.[16]

---

'I stood beside the running stream
    And heard the mournful death-bird say,
'Tina – know'st thou, 'tis no dream
    Thou art bought and sold to-day?'

By making the ballad sound like an English one, Costello takes La Villemarqué's domestication of the oral tradition one step further. The two strategies are essentially similar in that they are an attempt to control by writing what was never meant to be written.

[15] As Edward Said puts it, 'It is correct to say that in Orientalizing the Orient, Lane not only defined but *edited* it.' Edward W. Said, *Orientalism* (New York: Vintage, 1979), p. 167, my emphasis.

[16] See Antoine Berman, *Pour une critique des traductions: John Donne* (Paris: Gallimard, 1995), p. 70 (my translation). Berman insists on the fact that such moments in the text are not necessarily the most 'beautiful' or even the most striking; only that they possess a very high degree of necessity ('un très haut degré de nécessité').

Such a signifying zone emerges in the market place of Plougastel in 'An Autumn Trip in Brittany' by Matilda Betham Edwards:

> Never shall I forget what a spectacle was presented in the open market-place and at the ferry. Lying on the ground like bunches of carrots, tied by the four feet in such a manner that they could not stir, tortured in a hundred ways by the boys who had charge of them, were hundreds of calves, a few days old only, half dead with hunger and ill-treatment; whilst pigs, cows, and sheep were hardly better served. 'It is only good for eating,' said the nice-looking woman who had conducted me to the bridal party when I remonstrated with her. Such brutality as I saw shown to those helpless little creatures, which were there in large numbers, I shall never remember without horror. When a market-cart came up, they were taken from the bottom and thrown out exactly as if they were bags of potatoes; it was the same at the landing-place of the ferry. So sickening was the sight that I was thankful to get away, and not a dozen weddings or calvaries would have stopped me.[17]

This may be read as a minor incident in a book that is full of praise for Brittany. But it can be no coincidence that the whole attitude of the author to her subject can be reconstructed from a passage apparently so out of tune with the rest of the book. It enables her to assert her preference for the good as opposed to the beautiful (and therefore to distinguish herself from other travellers, mere 'seekers after the picturesque'), and to indicate that although ready to observe open-mindedly, she refuses 'the mystique of reciprocity', this well-known alibi of anti-conquest, while simultaneously exposing the moral inferiority of Catholicism (which calls failure to confess a sin but allows such brutality to happen although it is forbidden by law).[18] The scene also establishes a strong if subtle link between marriage and the market place, thus conveying almost subliminally her feminist views. The calves at this one moment have brought out the best in Edwards, showing her at her most idiosyncratic, as someone with both socialist and feminist tendencies, as an anti-Catholic and anti-imperialist writer, as animal-rights campaigner and pedagogue.[19] It is no accident that she signifies her intention to leave. The animal is on the frontier

---

[17] Matilda Betham Edwards, 'An Autumn Trip in Brittany', in *A Year in Western France* (London: Longman, Green and Co., 1877), p. 276.

[18] The scene is strategically placed between one in Quimper Cathedral where she hears a sermon (pp. 265–6) and another, a pure gem of Victorian rhetorics, where she confronts the priest of Plougastel and easily wins the argument (pp. 277–8). On anti-conquest, see Pratt, *Imperial Eyes*, pp. 78–85.

[19] I have shown elsewhere (Le Disez, *Étrange Bretagne*, pp. 190–93) that Edwards constructs Brittany as a succession of female 'colonies', as she calls them, which are exactly what Mary Louise Pratt calls 'feminotopias', i.e. 'episodes that present idealized worlds of female autonomy, empowerment and pleasure' (Pratt, *Imperial Eyes*, pp. 166–7). Edwards was the author of many travel books in France and Northern Africa over almost half a century (1867–1912). She is described in the *Wellesley Index* as 'an author on French life'. She was honoured by the French Ministry of Education for her writings on education and certainly deserves more attention than she has received so far.

between Self and non-Self, between acceptance and refusal of the Other. Thus threatened, the Self can only wish to take the ferry back home.

### A dog that understands English (William Blanchard Jerrold)

William Blanchard Jerrold's section on Brittany in *On the Boulevards* (1867) purports to be a report on Breton agriculture almost a century after Arthur Young's all but flattering portrait of the state of agriculture in the province. In fact, very little in those pages is the result of direct observation and the one chapter that may qualify as such concerns not a farmer but a fisherman whom Jerrold calls his 'Ancient Mariner'. No effort is spared to present the man as a paragon of wise husbandry. 'Here is a man,' writes Jerrold, 'who could earn a dinner for his family by sea or land, and could cook it when he had earned it'.[20] His no-nonsense home reflects his virtues; the soup he makes is the result of a subtle alchemy between working-class self-reliance and bourgeois values. But the defining moment comes when his dog appears:

> The dog in question was a shaggy Scotch terrier, who had taken a great fancy to me from the moment I reached his master's fireside. It appeared that our mariner had picked the poor animal off the deserted wreck of a north country brig some years ago. Master and dog were great friends, and it struck me that the dog was attracted to me by hearing me speak English to his master when I was testing the mariner's knowledge of my native tongue. (Vol. 2, p. 311)

This dog conveniently comes out of nowhere to sum up Jerrold's whole posture. Master and dog are 'great friends' because they are one and the same character in this fiction: the scene is a confirmation of our suspicion that as a writer Jerrold relies essentially on one trope, namely metonymy (see for example the description of the house or the making of the soup, for more evidence of this). This Breton dog is in fact English – and almost speaks English – because Jerrold's Brittany is another Britain: the scene shows that as a traveller, like many of his compatriots, he considers travelling not as alienation or defamiliarization but as an exploration of familiar terrain. The dog is gentle and grateful as the working class should be: the scene shows Jerrold as a conservative, working towards the reconciliation of classes, of masters and men. (And the shipwreck itself appears as a metaphor for the French revolution and the industrial revolution, out of which would-be enemies, so Jerrold would like to think, have emerged unscathed.)

Thus has an animal once more revealed a rich and consistent subtext. Again, although the uses of animal imagery differ from text to text, its function is similar. In it most of the threads that make up the texture of the narratives are tightly interwoven to produce another 'signifying zone'. That said, although Jerrold's agenda differs

---

20   William Blanchard Jerrold, *On the Boulevards; with Trips in Normandy and Brittany*, 2 vols (London: Wm. H. Allen & Co, 1867), vol. 2, p. 311.

from Edwards', each writer uses animals to promote a gentrification of manners. The intrusion of sentimentality in this tender scene by the fireside is a reminder of the ideological function that animals were made to serve in the nineteenth century. As F. M. L. Thompson, writing about the RSPCA, has convincingly argued, 'the reformation of the lower orders, rather than the simple protection of animals, was the conscious purpose of the Society's leaders'.[21]

## A horse of great power (T. A. Trollope)

Thomas Adolphus Trollope's influential *A Summer in Brittany*, like Costello's work, also appeared in 1840. 'Domestic Manners of the Armoricans' would have been a more appropriate title as it was edited by his mother Frances Trollope, the author of the immensely successful *Domestic Manners of the Americans* (1832). It is an extremely ambitious work in two volumes running to over 800 pages. Typical of Trollope's style and manner is the following excerpt:

> My own experience of the difficulties of making my way through a Breton crowd, would lead me to think them [the Bretons] utterly destitute of the sense of feeling. The most vigorous punches in the ribs, and most determined application of the whole force of the back and shoulders against his person, will fail to make a Breton move out of your way, or even look round.
>
> I saw in the fair of Pontivy a crowd gathered in a circle around a fine spirited horse, of a much larger breed than those of the country, and of great power; he kicked out, with the whole force of both his hind-legs, and struck a man full in the ribs. I thought that his bones, of course, were shivered, and that in all probability the man was killed. But to my great surprise, one of the bystanders helped him up, and in a minute he walked away, and nobody thought any more about the matter.[22]

Trollope's obsession is to cover as much ground as possible. He sees himself, no doubt goaded on by his enterprising mother, as a pioneer,[23] literally discovering Armorica. Hence the emphasis on 'making [one's] way through the crowd'. Far from being the object of travel (despite declarations to the contrary), travelees are at best *an obstacle* to travel. They are not only written upon, but actually trampled upon.[24] More importantly, the agency of the horse is required to prove Trollope's

---

[21] F. M. L. Thompson, *The Rise of Respectable Society: A Social History of Victorian Britain, 1830–1900* (London: Fontana, 1988), p. 280.

[22] Trollope, *A Summer in Brittany*, vol. 2, pp. 373–4.

[23] After the success of *Domestic Manners of the Americans*, she went on to publish 115 books. In *The Life, Manners and Travels of Fanny Trollope* (London: Constable, 1979), Johanna Johnston has shown how Fanny used Thomas Adolphus to 'handle her administration' (p. 203), leaving to him some parts of the Continent.

[24] Travelling is often reduced to driving through the crowd; more often than not, the market crowd, since markets (the site of convenient gatherings and transactions) are the only true 'contact zone' between travellers and travelees. Here is how the Dunlop sisters,

main point: the peasant's insensibility. This anaesthetization of the Other is part of the huge enterprise to delegitimize the socially and geographically marginal that informs his text from beginning to end. The appearance of the animal signals that a climax is reached in what looks very much like a case of murder by proxy. The horse in question is the narrator's alter ego, both 'powerful' – what is at stake is not physical strength but power – *and* foreign.

Trollope's book leaves a strange impression on the reader. The heroics of conquest peter out at the end as the traveller abruptly interrupts his journey. He has come to a place largely unvisited before him, he has seen all that there is to see and he has apparently conquered, having utterly delegitimized the Other.[25] Why, then, is he in such a hurry to cross the frontier again? Probably because of a feeling of guilt and also because all these efforts at convincing himself and his readers that the male, bourgeois, metropolitan subject will triumph are proportional to his fears that things may not go that way after all. What the episode with the horse also reveals, despite the author's efforts, is the tendency of such manipulation to backfire and the ability of the colonized subject to rewrite himself into the story.

Most of the animal imagery, therefore, serves to delegitimize the Other. In George Lowth's *Wanderer in Western France* of 1863, the focus is upon a team of labouring beasts, two cows and two ponies:

> The usual team on the road consisted of two small cows at wheel and a pony in front – an incongruous union. Sometimes there were two cows at wheel and two ponies in front, all of a poor diminutive size. One man tried to get up the hill on which Hennebont is built, in front of my window, with such a team as this latter. He was a small, spare man, buried beneath his absurd and monstrous hat, and quite crippled for any energetic action by his unwieldy sabots. He had a large, long cart, heavily laden with apples. Half-way up the hill the poor half-starved cows suddenly backed out at right angles to the pole – to the end of which their heads were fastened by the horns. ... The two lean ponies in front could do nothing with the apples without the cows. The small grotesque figure of the man rolled about in the sabots, making vigorous, awkward, ill-timed efforts with a long stick ... to induce the cows to set to work in a better fashion ... By dint of much talking and poking he would after a time get them right, and then the ponies, poor little fellows, having expended their strength in spasmodic struggles while the cart was at fault, would now become sulky and take to jibbing. ... When, after much

authors of *How we Spent the Autumn* (1860), describe one of their outings: 'When we started, our driver, after *sacréing* till he was hoarse, drove on regardless of the consequences, and a woman was set to clear the way; she ran in front, calling out, and pushing people to the right and left most energetically. Those men who were too stupid to move quickly, she caught round the neck, and pitched in the ditch.' Madeline Ann Wallace Dunlop and Rosalind Harriet Maria Wallace Dunlop, *How we Spent the Autumn; or, Wanderings in Brittany* (London: Richard Bentley, 1860), p. 149.

25   One of the last scenes shows a procession of peasants following 'a cart full of human skulls' (Trollope, *A Summer in Brittany*, vol. 2, pp. 375–6). Having symbolically killed them with his pen, Trollope lets the Bretons bury their own dead.

expenditure of poking and imprecation, on the part of the buried little figure, on the cows, they would agree to try their luck once more with the apples, then would the ponies turn their heads together across the road, one way or another, in a hopeless, despairing sort of manner, evidently desponding and low in their minds about the whole proceeding.[26]

This is 'wild sweetness' made metaphor. One animal was not deemed sufficient: the incongruous combination of *two pairs* of animals reads like a picture of Breton backwardness. With the help of those animals, the Breton – in these texts any Breton stands for '*the* Breton' – is at once miniaturized, ridiculed, made to look wild, crippled and clumsy. But of course the cart is more certainly drawn by Victorian ideology. Some 'neighbours' will take pity on the poor man and rescue the apples: the peasant (and the country) may be condemned but the bourgeois (and the city) still need his produce. I am not implying here that Lowth is being more antagonistic to Breton life because he is British. Rather, he is being antagonistic to rural, self-sufficient ways of life. There are few examples of such descriptions in works by French authors because this type of travel writing was far less popular in France in the nineteenth century than in Britain, but similar tropes of delegitimization are very common in contemporary French works, notably in Balzac's *Les Chouans*.

Sometimes, however, the authors' aim is less to outlaw their wild Other than to domesticate him or her. Through animals the full range of states from wildness to tameness can be explored. But even a cursory look at texts resorting to this type of domestication shows that the concerns and the overall effect are similar.

## Mullets and sticklebacks (E. W. L. Davies)

The most obvious title to turn to for evidence of this – and indeed of the importance of animals in Victorian discourse on Brittany – is *Wolf-Hunting and Wild Sport in Lower Brittany* (1875), by the Rev. E. W. L. Davies. With one exception, all twenty-seven chapters recount the exploits of a closely-knit group of Breton aristocrats whom the author has befriended and whose lives are entirely devoted to hunting. It is easy, however, to see that the book is better described as a wild piece of fiction and a rather dubious one at that. Highly individualized dogs, wolves and wild boar are handled like characters in a novel, while the hunters are described as demigods, forming a rather unpalatable society. The text has been misread by some scholars as being entirely about hunting.[27] But there is a case for saying that the subtext has nothing to do with hunting and everything to do with ideology. The book is also about sentimentality, heroes and hero-worship, masters and servants, strategy and

---

[26]   George T. Lowth, *The Wanderer in Western France* (London: Hurst and Blackett, 1863), pp. 327–9.

[27]   For example, see J. Cornou in his preface to a recent edition of the French 1912 translation of the book (Frank [*sic*] Davies, *Chasse aux loups et autres chasses en Bretagne* (Spezed/Pont l'Abbé: Nature et Bretagne/sked, 1991).

tactics, order and rebellion, poaching and preserving. The discourse on animals is the ideal vehicle for everything that troubled travellers in Brittany. I could choose almost any hunting scene to show that the drama of hunting conceals another drama, but to make my point about animals I shall select instead an excerpt from the one chapter that is *not* about hunting.

This is how Davies describes the fish in an aquarium seen during a one-day trip to South Brittany:

> So ravenous were the mullet, and so little timid, that, before M. Coste could convey to them the food prepared for their use, they were literally jostling each other and endeavouring to snatch it from his grasp, ere his hand touched the water: moreover, they permitted him to handle and stroke them, not only without resistance on their part, but apparently with a confidence that his attentions were kindly meant, and therefore most welcome. St. Anthony himself, the patron saint of fishes, could never have had a tamer flock than this small shoal of mullet: nor were they the only subjects exhibiting the results of kind treatment in this establishment. The sticklebacks, a naturally bold, pugnacious class, were especially civilised; taking the food in his hand like a pack of pet spaniels; a little eager and jealous of one another, perhaps, but still well-behaved on the whole, and betraying no fear whatever of the hand that fed them.[28]

Marine biology, as Davies sees it, is not about breeding fish, any more than *Wolf-hunting*, as I have argued, is really about hunting. The fish are like spaniels in more than one sense: just as the mighty hunters produce through breeding fierce *but* obedient dogs by 'invigorating the race with a strain of wolf-hound' (p. 26), so is Monsieur Coste, the man in charge of the establishment, an expert at social engineering. Nor does the parallel stop there. Here is how he describes the aquariums:

> A few words more on the construction of the reservoirs. These, forming a length altogether of about 80 metres, are divided into at least 100 cells by galvanized wire-net partitions, which, while they keep the different species of fish separate, permit a free passage to the running stream; so in each compartment each kind gets the food peculiar to it, and seems to enjoy life as though unconscious of captivity. (p. 170)

This, of course, is a marine version of, and a considerable improvement on, Bentham's 'Panopticon'.[29] Translated, as it should be, into human terms, the apparatus manages a double *tour-de-force*: while keeping the classes (or races) safely apart, it permits a free passage to the running stream of ideology throughout the system; and, while keeping a tight control over its victims, it gives them the illusion of freedom.

---

[28] E. W. L. Davies, *Wolf-Hunting and Wild Sport in Lower Brittany* (London: Chapman and Hall, 1875), p. 171.

[29] See Michel Foucault, *Surveiller et punir. Naissance de la prison* (Paris: Gallimard, 1995), especially Chapter III ('le panoptisme').

Hunting as Davies describes it is just that, a game which enables a group of nostalgic aristocrats – or would-be aristocrats – to learn and teach the rules of the social game as they see it: a game that is all about dividing the participants into clear-cut roles based on social distinctions, having fun at the expense of the work or suffering of others, channelling violence for their own benefit, giving the victim the illusion of freedom while securing its ultimate death and, above all, building up a stock of countless fictional situations which are for Davies as many pretexts for venting his all but innocent ideology. In the light of all this, we understand better his motives for coming to Brittany: 'Anyone wishing to see the Celtic population of Lower Brittany in its rude simplicity – natural, wild, and unchanged as it is by the varnish of modern civilisation – should go to a wolf-hunt; the peasant's blood is then up.'[30] Brittany is like an aquarium, an ideal place not only for observation but for experimentation as well – a means for an Englishman to observe his wild (social and colonial) Other without the risks he would face at home.

### Off with their heads! (Mrs Bury Palliser)

Finally, the following excerpt from Mrs Bury Palliser's *Brittany and its Byways* (1869) is not the most typical of her rather nondescript narrative but it is certainly one of the most revealing:

> It is a pretty sight to behold the little fleet employed in the sardine fishery return in the evening, laden with the results of a day's work. The fish, when landed, are counted out into baskets, shaken in the water, and taken up to one of the curing-houses: of these there are about sixty in Concarneau. In the first shed we saw above fifty women employed in taking off their heads – 'detêter' [sic] it is called – an operation they effect with great dexterity. With one cut at the back of the neck the head is separated and the fish 'eventré' [sic] at the same time.[31]

The visit to a work display, a feature of later narratives of travel in Brittany, continues the work initiated by narratives that carefully avoided it. Nor is this the only novelty. The emphasis now is not on the clumsiness of those wild Bretons but on their dexterity. The message, I think, is clear: properly regulated, confined in a space of discipline and submitted to a protocol that divides time into clearly separate moments, the people will learn. The threat of numbers and physical strength has been diverted for the benefit of production. It is indeed a pretty sight to behold.

---

[30] Davies, *Wolf-Hunting*, p. 58.
[31] Mrs Bury Palliser, *Brittany and its Byways: Some Account of its Inhabitants and its Antiquities* (London: John Murray, 1869), p. 145.

## Conclusion

I hope to have shown that the study of Victorian travel in Brittany, despite the fact that Brittany was neither British nor a British colony, is a valuable source of information for anyone interested in the ideology behind the Victorians' relationship to their social/colonial Others. Its history is the history of the gradual domestication of Breton foreignness, of the sweetening of Breton wildness; and nowhere is this perhaps more apparent than in the handling of animal imagery.

Travelling in another part of France, Robert Louis Stevenson took care to travel with a donkey.[32] Accepting your own wildness as a travelling companion may be a means to avoid encountering it at every corner. The Victorians thought that they had had the last word on Breton wildness once they had exaggerated it, confined it within the oxymoron, and finally thus tamed it beyond recognition (the three stages correspond roughly to the early, mid- and late Victorian eras). But of course, they had only managed to deceive themselves. It occurred to none of them that Brittany, which they wrote as 'wildly sweet', was equally sweetly wild, as Wyndham Lewis was to find out at the beginning of the twentieth century when he conceived his theory of the 'Wild Body'.[33] It occurred to none of them that the crossing and recrossing of the border (which they dramatized as the crossing of the border between the animal and the human) took place within themselves.

---

[32]   Robert Louis Stevenson, *Travels with a Donkey in the Cévennes* (London: Arrow Books, 1879).

[33]   Wyndham Lewis forged his theory of the 'Wild Body' in Brittany. See W. Lewis, *The Complete Wild Body, 1907–27*, ed. Bernard Lafourcade (Santa Barbara: Black Sparrow Press, 1982).

Chapter 7

# 'The Silent Language of the Face': The Perception of Indigenous Difference in Travel Writing about the Caribbean[1]

## Peter Hulme

When Columbus instituted travel writing about the Caribbean in 1493, one of his founding gestures was to distinguish the indigenous population by colour: 'they are the color of the Canarians, neither black nor white'.[2] At the time Columbus wrote those words the only whites and blacks in the Caribbean were his own crew members, but over the next few years white Europeans flooded into the islands from Spain, and the African slave trade began, bringing whole new black populations to replace the indigenous peoples – Taino and Carib – who quickly became the victims of European genocide. Largely to replace, but not entirely. On Cuba and Hispaniola some small indigenous communities survived at least until the eighteenth and nineteenth centuries; and St Vincent and Dominica were Carib strongholds until the 1790s, with a recognized Carib Territory still existing today on Dominica. In addition, Africans, and to a smaller extent Europeans, formed mixed communities with indigenous people, allowing aspects of indigenous culture to continue in the interstices of colonial societies. Over the last century or so, as both anthropology and travel writing about the Caribbean have seen such huge growth, the perception of indigenous difference has become a significant theme. This chapter approaches that subject through analyses of texts drawn from three key moments, at roughly fifty-year intervals: 1898 and its aftermath, the 1940s, and the present day, with a focus on the two islands of Cuba and Dominica. The notion of indigenous difference in the Caribbean – seen within the dominant discourse of 1898 as slated for imminent disappearance – has shown distinct, if sometimes problematic signs of revival in recent years, complicating attempts at its intellectual and cultural placement.

---

[1]     This essay draws from two conference papers given at 'Indigenous Legacies of the Caribbean', Baracoa, Cuba (1997) and 'Borders and Crossings', Magee College, Derry (1998). Several paragraphs also appear in my book, *Remnants of Conquest: The Island Caribs and their Visitors, 1877–1998* (Oxford: Oxford University Press, 2000).

[2]     Oliver Dunn and James E. Kelley, Jr, eds, *The Diario of Christopher Columbus' First Voyage to America: 1492–1493* (Norman: University of Oklahoma Press, 1989), p. 67.

**I**

The US invasion of Cuba in 1898 changed the direction of Caribbean history. In part, the USA was able to defeat the Spanish navy and successfully invade Cuba because the rapid development of its iron industry had led to the modernizing of its ships and their weapons. Indeed one of the reasons for the USA *wanting* to invade Cuba was to enable it to control the rare sources of haematite in the eastern mountains of the island which were a necessary ingredient in modern steel-making procedures. Growing US hegemony in the Caribbean, allied to the flourishing steamship industry – an offshoot of that steel-based military marine technology – quickly led to the development of tourism in the area after 1898, with the inevitable associated growth in guidebooks and travel writing.[3]

Apart from haematite, the 'acquisition' of Caribbean islands also gave to the USA a deeper history – a connection back to 1492, to the places that Columbus had visited, to the supposed origins of civilization on the continent. Just prior to 1898 the desirability of this connection had been emphasized by the Chicago Columbian Exposition, which had gathered many of the 'relics' of Columbus into the most modern city in the USA, where they had jostled for attention with the defeated 'relics' of the country's own westward expansion, the Sioux and Cheyenne and Arapaho who were now reduced to playing earlier versions of themselves in Buffalo Bill's extravagantly staged replicas of famous battles on the western frontier.[4]

The first piece of travel writing to document the new US 'possessions' resulting from the defeat of Spain in 1898 was tellingly entitled *Our Islands and Their People as seen with Camera and Pencil*. Produced with impressive speed, its two quarto volumes contained 784 pages, with no fewer than 1200 photographs, colourtypes, and maps, all specially commissioned. The text ('special descriptive matter and narratives', as the title page puts it) was written by José de Olivares, who had made his reputation as a war correspondent during the Cuban war of independence, and whose knowledge of Spanish was an important qualification, since that language was widely spoken on three of the USA's four new islands (in fact sets of islands) – Cuba, Puerto Rico, the Philippines, and Hawaii. The proprietary nature of the project, no doubt clear enough from the phrase 'our islands', is spelled out in the gloss on the title page, which continues:

> Embracing perfect photographic and descriptive representations of the people and the islands lately acquired from Spain, including Hawaii and the Philippines; also their material resources and productions, homes of the people, their customs and general appearance, with many hundred views of the landscapes, rivers, valleys, hills and mountains, so complete

---

[3]   See Peter Hulme, *Rescuing Cuba: Adventure and Masculinity in the 1890s* (College Park, MD: Latin American Studies Center, 1996).

[4]   See Peter Hulme, 'In the Wake of Columbus: Frederick Ober's Ambulant Gloss', *Literature and History*, 6:2 (1997), pp. 18–36.

as to practically transfer the islands and their people to the pictured page. With a special consideration of the conditions that prevailed before the declaration of war, by senators Proctor, Thurston, Money, and numerous prominent writers and correspondents, and a comparison with conditions as they now exist.[5]

As backward places, largely populated by non-English-speaking inhabitants of mostly Spanish, African, and indigenous origin, the four islands obviously offered significant challenges. As far as the particular issue of indigeneity is concerned, they resolved themselves into a clear hierarchy: some of the remoter islands of the Philippines were inhabited by strange and dangerous tribes in which head-hunting and cannibalism were still practised; Hawaii also had a fairly exotic native population, though no longer dangerous; Cuba had only the smallest remnant of an indigenous community; and Puerto Rico had no remaining traces of its once extensive Taino culture.

The Caribbean sections of the book contain just one photograph with indigenous content. It shows a family of three standing by a roadside in eastern Cuba, holding bags and cases. Entitled 'Descendants of El Cobre Indians', it carries the caption:

These people are descendants of the aboriginal inhabitants of Cuba, but they are now almost extinct, and have intermarried until but little of the Indian blood remains in their veins. They lead a nomadic, Gypsy life, constantly traveling from place to place within a radius of twenty miles of El Cobre. During these migrations they carry all their worldly possessions in bundles on their heads 'from a scrap of soap to a bale of hay'.[6]

Indigenous populations often offer to travel writers a slightly distorted mirror in which travel and mobility have different origins and purposes – perhaps more intimately linked to cultural traditions or economic imperatives – from those that motivate travel writers. Here, though, the restricted migrations of the El Cobre Indians, across a meagre forty-mile range, merely provide a pathetic and pointless vestige of aboriginal roaming; a poor contrast with Olivares' own impressive travels across the many thousand miles of 'our' new islands. In any case, the Indians are 'almost extinct', almost absorbed into the larger Creole population, having no physical difference to distinguish them from the majority: by implication they therefore need not be taken with any seriousness.

This new US hegemony in the Caribbean did provide a boost for the developing discipline of anthropology, but only for its archaeological component. Before the end of 1898, Daniel Brinton was already suggesting 'promising localities for research' in the Caribbean, and Jesse Fewkes reconnoitred on behalf of the Smithsonian

---

5    William S. Bryan, ed., *Our Islands and Their People as seen with Camera and Pencil*, 2 vols (St Louis: N. D. Thompson Publishing Co., 1899), title page.
6    Bryan, ed., *Our Islands*, vol. 1, p. 239.

Figure 2. *Descendants of El Cobre Indians*. From William S. Bryan, ed., *Our Islands and Their People as seen with Camera and Pencil*, 2 vols (St Louis: N. D. Thompson Publishing Co., 1899), vol. 1, p. 239.

Institution.[7] In 1904, encouraging Fewkes to pursue a thorough ethnological study of the Caribbean, Otis Mason remarked that the region would open 'a new and rich field as a relief from the overthrashed straw of our own native tribes'.[8] The private Heye Foundation took an immediate interest in this new area: of its first set of nine 'contributions' to scholarship on the American Indian, seven related to the Caribbean,[9] and its collectors roamed the region locating interesting specimens for Heye's new Museum of the American Indian in New York. But this work had no interest in indigenous survival, indeed no interest in what had happened after 1492: Mark Harrington's important work – funded by Heye – was entitled *Cuba before Columbus*, and Fewkes' seminal articles from the early years of the century are 'Prehistoric Puerto Rico' and 'Prehistoric ... Cuba'.[10] In studies like these, the indigenous population of the Caribbean islands was removed into the dark world of 'prehistory', not only exiled into another time but put outside history altogether.

Only once did the prospect of living Indians on Cuba excite anthropological interest. Shortly after the military successes of 1898, engineers from Philadelphia working for the expanding concerns of the US mining companies reported coming across 'wild Indians' in the mountains of eastern Cuba, inciting Stewart Culin, an anthropologist based at the Free Museum of Science and Art at the University of Pennsylvania, to travel to Cuba to investigate this dramatic survival. Culin's short work is important because of its clear demonstration of the distinction between the myth of cultural survival – which brought him to Cuba – and the reality of the transcultural process which he literally faced and which was of no interest to him. As a result, the piece of writing he produced from his Cuba trip, although published in the Museum bulletin, reads more like travel writing than anthropology, and Culin took no further interest in the region.[11] Typical is his visit to the village of El Caney, about five miles east of Santiago:

> The town showed evidence of the recent conflict. The little church, its interior demolished, with altars thrown down and walls dented with bullets,

7    Daniel G. Brinton, 'The Archaeology of Cuba', *American Archaeologist*, 2: 10 (October 1898), pp. 253–6, at p. 256; Jesse W. Fewkes, 'Preliminary Report on an Archaeological Trip to the West Indies', *Smithsonian Miscellaneous Collections*, Quarterly Issue, 45 (Washington, 1903), pp. 112–33.

8    Quoted by Curtis M. Hinsley, Jr, *Savages and Scientists: The Smithsonian Institution and the Development of American Anthropology 1846–1910* (Washington, DC: Smithsonian Institution Press, 1981), p. 116.

9    Reprinted in *Contributions from the Heye Museum*, vol. 1 (New York: Heye Museum, 1913–15).

10    Mark R. Harrington, *Cuba before Columbus*, 2 vols (New York: Museum of the American Indian Heye Foundation, 1921); J. Walter Fewkes, 'Prehistoric Puerto Rico', *Proceedings of the American Association for the Advancement of Science*, LI (1902), pp. 487–512 and 'Prehistoric Culture of Cuba', *American Anthropologist*, n.s. VI:4 (1904), pp. 535–8.

11    Stewart Culin, 'The Indians of Cuba', *Bulletin of the Free Museum of Science and Arts, University of Pennsylvania, Philadelphia*, III:4 (1902), pp. 185–226.

was a sad enough spectacle. A group of rural guards was lounging in front of the police station, and a young girl held a naked baby on the porch of the adjoining house.[12]

Atmosphere is established, local colour identified. Still a young discipline, anthropology was always ready at this time to flourish its scientific credentials, so the language of travel writing gives a clear indication that Culin has not fulfilled his anthropological quest for 'wild Indians':

> We had no difficulty in securing the information we needed. There was one old Indian living in the village ... His name was José Almenares Argüello, commonly known as Almenares. He was a spare old man with iron-gray hair, and thin gray hair on his chin. He was very hale and alert for his age, which he told me was 112 years ... In his youth there were many Indians in El Caney. They were a free people wearing the same dress as their neighbors, and talking Spanish. He knew nothing of the old language.[13]

The point is emphasized by the camera: a photograph of Almenares shows a distinguished old gentleman wearing a white tunic. This is not why Culin has travelled thousands of miles at great expense.

The pattern is repeated elsewhere. Culin asks about Indians, is politely taken to see them, engages them in brief conversation, and moves on. By the end of his report he is praising the way the Americans have cleaned up Havana and bemoaning the way 'swarms of tourists have cleaned up the antiquity shops'.[14]

Culin's rejection of the idea of indigenous survival in Cuba left Dominica, and to a lesser extent St Vincent, as the only Caribbean islands with a recognized indigenous population. It had been a US travel writer, Frederick Ober, who had brought attention to the Dominica Caribs through his 1878 book, *Camps in the Caribbees*, and occasional visitors and writers made the still difficult trek across to the north-east quarter of the island where the Caribs lived.[15] US military successes in the Caribbean coincided with Britain's last – and short-lived – attempt to rescue its Caribbean islands from the trough of neglect which had followed the abolition of slavery sixty years earlier; and Joseph Chamberlain's 'new imperialism' brought younger colonial personnel to the fore, including Hesketh Bell, a new Administrator in Dominica who had a prior interest in the surviving Carib population and who was soon responsible for the formalization of the Carib Reserve where they still live.

Bell's first visit to the Carib Reserve is cast in similar – if more openly picturesque – terms to Culin's to the Indian villages of Cuba:

> At the entrance to the Reserve we were met by the old Chief of the Caribs, surrounded by about 150 of his people ... I must say that their appearance was a considerable disappointment. After all I had read about the Caribs of

---

12 Culin, 'The Indians of Cuba', p. 191.
13 Culin, 'The Indians of Cuba', pp. 191–2.
14 Culin, 'The Indians of Cuba', p. 220.
15 See Hulme, *Remnants of Conquest*, pp. 37–96.

the old days, their fine physique, their heroism in battle and their engaging cannibalistic habits, I had conjured up visions of splendid men of the Red Indian type, and half expected to see them covered with feathers and red paint.

The reality was far from my imagination. These last remnants of the magnificent savages that were once the terror of the Caribbean seas wore a distressingly dull and prosaic appearance. Auguste, the Chief, was clad in an old and dilapidated black morning-coat that shone green in the sunlight, with a pair of white cotton trousers, while, on his head, was precariously perched – as it was manifestly much too small for him – one of those flat-topped, hard felt hats beloved of churchwardens … All the rest of the Caribs were similarly dressed in ordinary European clothing, and there was nothing but their faces to show any difference between them and the ordinary Creole inhabitants of the island.[16]

Once again, the dominant note is one of loss. What is sought is difference, which for Bell is a matter of costume and demeanour. Bell's language goes one step towards suggesting that his excitable imagination might have led him into unrealistic expectations – 'engaging cannibalistic habits', 'conjured up visions' – but the brunt of his disappointment has to be borne by those he visits: 'dull and prosaic', 'ordinary European clothing', and, worst of all, the felt hat 'beloved of churchwardens', which seems to offer an insulting reminder of a provincial English village. The repeated 'ordinary' indicates just what is wrong. The faces mark difference, but that is just not enough.

## II

US academic emphasis on Caribbean 'prehistory' was confirmed by the establishment of the Caribbean Anthropological Program at Yale in 1933, which sponsored the important archaeological work carried out in Cuba by Cornelius Osgood and Irving Rouse.[17] Although this Yale and Yale-inspired archaeological work has been valuable for providing materials towards an understanding of population movements and cultural processes in the Caribbean before 1492, interpretations of the social and political dimensions of those materials have usually operated to reproduce the indigenous stereotypes that served the European colonial powers so well during the sixteenth and seventeenth centuries. In addition, for the plenary model of culture which forms the implicit template of much US research on the indigenous Caribbean, the indigenous cultures were never properly *themselves* after 1492 and therefore scientific inquiry has to end at that date. Rouse touches on the question of indigenous survival in discussing Culin's abortive pilgrimage:

16    H. Hesketh Bell, *Glimpses of a Governor's Life: From Diaries, Letters and Memoranda* (London: Sampson Low, Marston & Co., 1946), pp. 16–17, 19–21.

17    For relevant background, see Thomas C. Patterson, *Toward a Social History of Archaeology in the United States* (Fort Worth: Harcourt Brace College Publishers, 1995).

> In Cuba the aborigines gradually intermarried with their white neighbors and adopted the Spanish language and culture ... The process of acculturation is well illustrated by the archeological data to be described below ... In 1901, Stewart Culin ... searched for descendants of the aborigines in the mountains of the province of Oriente ... Everywhere the Indians were halfbreeds, who spoke Spanish and differed little from their Cuban neighbors. Only two aboriginal customs (besides those prevalent among the white population of Cuba) still survived.[18]

Rouse's use here of the accepted anthropological term 'acculturation' to describe cultural process in Cuba coincided with the coining by the Cuban anthropologist, Fernando Ortiz, of the concept of 'transculturation'. When Ortiz elaborated this concept in his major work, *Contrapunteo Cubano* (1940), he had the support, in an introduction, of Bronislaw Malinowski, the distinguished Polish anthropologist, then himself also at Yale, who had met Ortiz in Cuba in 1939, and who agreed that the term 'transculturation' was preferable to the more common 'acculturation' because it stressed the extent to which both cultures concerned were modified during contact, 'a process from which a new reality emerges, transformed and complex, a reality that is not a mechanical agglomeration of traits, nor even a mosaic, but a new phenomenon, original and independent'.[19]

This new concept did not influence Rouse. His final brackets in the extract above suggest that within his paradigm only that which is *different* from what has survived to become part of normal social or economic practice is of interest to anthropology: the term 'acculturation' simply serves to cloak what has survived *and been widely adopted*. That aboriginal customs should have survived and become prevalent among the white population of Cuba is irrelevant to Rouse – although it would be deeply important to students of transculturation. 'Survival' itself is clearly the key term here, itself a survival from the earliest anthropological theory, rich in theoretical connotations but also full of emotional resonance.[20]

Whereas Rouse knew to his own satisfaction that the processes of acculturation had removed the opportunity for indigenous encounter in Cuba, travel writers to Dominica consistently repeated Hesketh Bell's pattern of expectation and disappointment, though the quotients of each might vary. However, after the enforced hiatus in British travel writing during the Second World War, the first

---

[18]   Irving Rouse, *Archaeology of the Maniabón Hills, Cuba* (New Haven: Yale University Publications in Anthropology, no. 26, 1942), pp. 29–30.

[19]   Fernando Ortiz, *Contrapunteo cubano del tabaco y el azúcar* (Havana: Editorial de Ciencias Sociales, 1991); *Cuban Counterpoint: Tobacco and Sugar*, trans. Harriet de Onís (Durham: Duke University Press, 1995). Malinowski's words are on p. lix. Fernando Coronil's Introduction to *Cuban Counterpoint* has an excellent discussion of Ortiz and Malinowski (pp. xxx–xlvii). Ortiz had earlier offered an appreciative but subtly critical account of US archaeology in Cuba: *Historia de arqueología indocubana* (Havana: Imprenta 'Siglo XX', 1922).

[20]   Edward B. Tylor, *Anthropology: An Introduction to the Study of Man and Civilization* [1871] (London: Macmillan and Co., 1892).

major travel book to be published, Patrick Leigh Fermor's *The Traveller's Tree: A Journey through the Caribbean Islands*, strikes a slightly different note. Fermor and his companions travelled to the Carib Territory on horseback, with the (relative) arduousness of the journey becoming itself a metaphor for what was perceived as a movement back in time, which ends with a dramatic encounter:

> The road suddenly widened into a clearing, where a group of shingle huts lay back under the trees, and by the edge of the path a group of men were standing, as though they were expecting us. So sharp was the contrast of their complexion and bearing with those of the islanders, that I thought for a moment that they were white men. But they were Caribs.
>
> We dismounted and walked towards them, and, as we met, hats were raised on either side with some solemnity. We all shook hands. This meeting with the last survivors of this almost extinct race of conquerors was as stirring and impressive in its way as if the encounter had been with Etruscans or Hittites.
>
> We were now able to see that they were either ivory-coloured in complexion or a deep bronze, with features that were almost Mongolian or Esquimaux except for the well-defined noses ... They had a dignity of presence that even their hideous European rags could not stifle. A tall man in the middle, smoking a pipe and equipped with an elaborate walking-stick, took charge of us with a diffident, almost Manchu solemnity.[21]

There is no border to cross here, no documents to show, no change in the physical landscape, no sign or marker on the path to say that the travellers have reached the Carib Territory; but there is a marked 'contrast' in complexion and bearing between 'the islanders', by which Fermor means the African-descended majority on Dominica, including – although he does not say so – his guides, and this group of men standing 'as though they were expecting us', as of course they were. That sentence says a lot about the structure of expectations and identifications so frequent in travel writing about the Caribbean: Fermor almost sees his own group in a mirror, but not quite: 'they were Caribs'.

Fermor's learned comparisons – Etruscans, Hittites – show the extent to which this meeting (to use the relatively neutral term) is turned into an 'encounter', an occasion with resonance. The Caribs are representatives of their race, one of history's great conquering races, and Fermor's historical consciousness endows them with significance on this score. The Manchu reference intensifies the sense of antiquity, but also adds, alongside the Mongolian and Esquimaux, to the particular history of American Indian groups, lending them the dignity of their own historical connections back to the Old World, retracing the supposed migratory paths. Ultimately Fermor sees no future for the Caribs – he speaks later of how they will doubtless be swept away by 'the black tide of history' – but they are allowed to retain their solemnity, although arguably it is the writer rather than his subject

---

[21] Patrick Leigh Fermor, *The Traveller's Tree: A Journey through the Caribbean Islands* [1950] (Harmondsworth: Penguin, 1984), p. 108.

that is aggrandized by the comparisons *he* is able to make, and which would mean nothing to *them*. The Carib present is once again only seen in the 'hideous European rags' they wear, although Fermor's tone and language allows the Carib faces and bearing to push costume into the background.[22]

## III

The whole question of indigenous survival in the Caribbean is highly complicated and increasingly fraught. In Cuba the official position has followed the line laid down by Rouse in the 1940s: in an article in *Granma* at the end of the 1980s, the Cuban archaeologist Dr Estrella Rey – seemingly responding to the work of Oscar Tejedor Alvarez – was quoted as saying that, because of the history of mixing, 'there are no absolutely legitimate Indians left in our country'.[23] The term 'legitimate' helps indicate some of the complexities. Does this statement imply that there are 'illegitimate' Indians left in Cuba? Who gets to decide what counts as legitimate? When the term 'legitimate' is employed, it usually means that the state has taken an interest. There might be a parallel here with an opinion expressed in a report produced in 1823 by the US House of Representatives Committee on Indian Affairs about the Florida Seminoles:

> The Seminole Indians are not a *'legitimate'* tribe of *native* Americans. They are an association of desperados, who have been banished from other tribes, and who have drawn into their confederacy, many runaway negroes, whose African sullenness, has been aroused to indiscriminate vengeance, by the frantic fury of the American natives.[24]

Often, as in the US case, the state arrogates the power to define who is and who is not a 'legitimate' Indian, a definition that is not easily challenged and which anyway serves to define those who seek to challenge it. Often, historians seeking to count Indian populations, in the Caribbean and elsewhere, have relied on censuses in which state officials have taken decisions based purely on the presence or absence of what they take to be significant markers of 'Indianness', often long, black hair.

---

[22]   For a fuller discussion of Fermor's book, see Wayne Burke, 'Double G(l)azing: Regarding a Colonial Imagination in Patrick Fermor's *The Traveller's Tree*', *Caribbean Quarterly*, 46:2 (2000), pp. 67–84.

[23]   Gladys Blanco, 'Indians of Cuba', *Granma Weekly Review*, International Edition, no. 25 (18 June 1989), p. 4; cf. Pedro Juan Gutiérrez, 'Have Cuban aborigines really disappeared?', *Granma Weekly Review*, International Edition, no. 20 (24 May 1987), p. 12.

[24]   'Report of the House Committee on Indian Affairs' (21 February 1823), *American State Papers, Indian Affairs* (Washington, DC: US Congress, 1834), vol. 2, pp. 411–12; quoted in Michael Paul Rogin, *Fathers and Children: Andrew Jackson and the Subjugation of the American Indian* [1975] (New Brunswick: Transaction Publishers, 1991), p. 197.

The language of 'legitimacy' can be challenged in two ways. The dangerous route goes into scientific discourse to demonstrate that those deemed 'illegitimate' are *really*, *authentically*, on some level Indians. There are twin dangers here. Scientific observation has not progressed beyond the deeply subjective analysis offered by Culin at the beginning of the century, analysis rooted in the presence or absence of certain physical features. For example, Ruggles Gates' 1954 study of the eastern Cuba area is based purely on physical features, with a pseudo-scientific codification of skin colour and a set of tabular remarks such as 'Indian features', 'Looks Indian', or 'Nose depressed (Negro)'.[25] The study is also marked by a tendency to read off the supposed inheritance of supposed psychological characteristics ('in all these mixed families where there is considerable Indian ancestry the quiet temperament of the Indian makes itself apparent').[26] The subjective nature of these exercises is not disguised by the tables of measurement. Identity is a social category. Its somatic component is undeniable, but the complexities of identity are never resolvable by quantification. In these circumstances, a more significant yardstick may well be self-perception, what José Barreiro, in a felicitous phrase, calls quite simply 'a casual sense of Indian identity'.[27] The historical irony here is that just as more sophisticated notions of identity seem to offer the prospect of a break with the blood quantum obsession that has been the constant companion and weapon of colonial categorization, there appears on the horizon, in the shape of the Human Genome Diversity Project, the 'promise' (better 'illusion') of a supposedly conclusive and scientifically objective index of ethnic identity through genetic analysis.[28] There are temptations in this game from an indigenous perspective: if the one-drop rule which raised the black population of the United States were applied to Indians, indigenous numbers would instantly increase a hundred-fold. But such fantasies only demonstrate in the long run the *reductio ad absurdum* involved in all racial calculus.

The ideal of cultural plenitude usually demands a narrative of loss and therefore inevitably a narrative of death, which means that the appropriate genre for visiting writers to adopt is often that of the elegy, as is apparent in some of the passages already considered. However, where identity is troped as *visible* – through physical characteristics like straight black hair – then survival is possible beyond cultural death, as trace. Maurice Barbotin, the curé of Grand-Bourg, on the small French island of Marie-Galante, ends his discussion of the history of the indigenous settlements on that island with these words: 'In our time there is no longer a single

---

[25] R. Ruggles Gates, 'Studies in Race Crossing: VI. The Indians of Eastern Cuba', *Genetica*, XXVII (1954), pp. 65–96, at pp. 80–81.

[26] Gates, 'Studies in Race Crossing', p. 93.

[27] José Barreiro, 'Indians in Cuba', *Cultural Survival Quarterly*, 13:3 (1989), pp. 56–60, at p. 58.

[28] See Tom Wilkie, *Perilous Knowledge: The Human Genome Project and Its Implications* (Berkeley: University of California Press, 1993).

Carib of pure race on Marie-Galante, but in several families of the region where they had their last carbet you can still find undoubted traces of their mixed race, traces that are getting weaker more and more quickly',[29] an idea the French travel writer, Jean Raspail, glosses as '[t]he silent language of the face ... When memory has died, at least that language remains.'[30]

Raspail's words mark a further shift in the reading of Carib faces. For Bell there was 'nothing but their faces' to indicate Carib indigeneity, with the clear implication that faces are insufficient. For Fermor, Carib features mark a clear boundary with 'the islanders', and give the informed traveller an impression of a deep history, sharpened by the sense of their imminent demise. For Raspail, finally, the face is enough: it speaks its own truth, its own 'silent language'. That haunting phrase is unwittingly eloquent about travel writing to the indigenous Caribbean. The natives may have forgotten their language and history, and their blood might be mixed, but the face has its own language – in the slant of an eye or the raising of a cheekbone – which the perceptive traveller can read. But that 'language', it should be noted, is silent: the natives must not spoil the moment by opening their mouths and letting spill the concerns of the present.

Three final pieces of writing can stand as oblique commentaries on these issues:

> The old Indian woman, a descendant of Cuba's Taino-Arawak people, bent over and touched the leaves of a small tree. Her open-palmed hand lifted the round, green leaves in a light handshake. 'These are good for inflammations of the ovaries,' she said. 'I gave them to all my young women.' 'She knows a lot,' her daughter, Marta, said. 'She doesn't need a pharmacy. You have something wrong with your body, she can make you a tea – *un cocimiento* – and fix you up.'
>
> The mother and two sisters, part of a large extended family known in this town for its Indian ancestry, continued to show me their patio. Around an old well, where they wash their laundry, they pointed out more than a dozen herbs and other useful plants. The Cobas Hernandez clan, from which Maria and her several daughters, her son, Pedro, and his brothers spring, counts several living generations of families from here to the city of Baracoa, about 120 km west from Los Arados on Cuba's southern coast. They are not the only such extended family and they are not the only people of clear Indian ancestry in Cuba still living in their aboriginal areas.[31]

Despite Culin's negative report, there has been a persistent strain of Cuban anthropologists who have taken an interest in Indian survival in Cuba, however

---

[29] Père Maurice Barbotin, 'Arawaks et Caraïbes à Marie-Galante', *Bulletin de la Société d'histoire de la Guadeloupe*, 11–12 (1976), pp. 77–118, at p. 118 (my translation).

[30] Jean Raspail, *Bleu Caraïbe et Citrons Verts: Mes Derniers Voyages aux Antilles* (Paris: Éditions Robert Laffont, 1980), p. 83 (my translation of 'Le langage muet des visages ... Quand de la mémoire tout est perdu, il reste au moins ce-langage-là').

[31] Barreiro, 'Indians in Cuba', p. 56.

defined.[32] José Barreiro, a US academic of Cuban descent, went back to eastern Cuba in 1989 and wrote this travel account, which eventually served as a kind of manifesto for a series of conferences which have taken place in Baracoa annually since 1997, serving to bring the issue of indigenous survival in Cuba back onto an international agenda.[33] Barreiro's interest came from a combination of current activism within the American Indian community in the USA (he edits the journal *Native Americas*) and the memory of stories told by elder Cuban relatives about the Indian origins of Cuban peasant lifeways. Barreiro is not much interested in physical appearance. Rather, he speaks to people and listens to what they have to say:

> My questions concentrated on a person's basis or rationale for claiming an Indian identity. All pointed to family history: 'We are an Indian family. It has been always that way.' 'We do Indian things, like my mother, she drinks from a *jicara*, nothing else, she won't use a glass or cup.' 'We know the wilderness [*manigua*].'[34]

The second piece is by Amryl Johnson, a Trinidadian who lived in England from the age of eleven until her death in 2001, and who also returned to the Caribbean, this time in 1983 and 1984, in order, in her own words, to appease the ghosts that haunted her. So her book belongs to that sub-genre of travel writing that involves a return to a place of origin – which, as always, turns out not to be quite the place of memory:

> Visitors come to the reserve specifically to see the Caribs. What must it feel like to be gawked at all the time? Theirs was the last bastion. This is their last bastion. They fought the white man for the right to remain in their own lands ... I could not say how many of the people in the reserve were of pure Carib descent. Many had intermarried with other peoples. ... Inscrutable faces which did not budge when cars slowed down to scrutinize them. They looked so placid going about their work like anyone else. Were these the warlike people who raised a fearless spear to destroy the enemy? I searched faces and hands weatherworn from fishing, looking for a throb from the pulse which sang of warriorhood ...[35]

---

[32]   For example, Felipe Pichardo Moya, *Los indios de Cuba en su tiempos históricos* (Havana: Academia de la Historia de Cuba, 1945), Antonio Nuñéz Jiménez, *Geografía de Cuba: Adaptada al Nuevo Programa Revolucionario de Bachillerato* (Havana: Editorial Lex, 1959), pp. 174, 176, 562, Manuel Rivero de la Calle, 'Los indios cubanos de Yateras', *Santiago*, 10 (1973), pp. 151–74.

[33]   The question of Taíno identity is also a lively issue within Puerto Rico and the North American Puerto Rican community: see Gabriel Haslip-Viera, ed., *Taíno Revival: Critical Perspectives on Puerto Rican Identity and Cultural Politics* (New York: Centro de Estudios Puertorriqueños, 1999), and Richard Kearns, 'The Return of the Taínos: Our Own "Lost Tribe"', *Issues in Caribbean Amerindian Studies*, II (October 1999–October 2000) (http://www.centrelink.org/KearnsA.html).

[34]   Barreiro, 'Indians in Cuba', p. 59.

[35]   Amryl Johnson, *Sequins for a Ragged Hem* (London: Virago, 1988), pp. 237–40.

Like many others, Johnson's visit to the Carib Territory is brief, but the tone of her writing is particularly anxious and awkward, with some efforts at empathy – 'What must it feel like to be gawked at all the time?'; an unusual confession of ignorance – 'I could not say how many of the people in the reserve were of pure Carib descent'; and some of the usual search for traces of the 'pulse which sang of warriorhood', as if the response to invasion of one's lands somehow defined the entry for ever more in the great encyclopaedia of nations. But then something different does begin to happen:

> We drove slowly through the Carib Reserve. I was like a tightrope walker edging my way along one of those eroded, rusty spokes. Blindfolded. If I fell, I would do my best to hang on. I had not set out to look for anything more profound than a basic understanding. Almost by accident, somehow, I could feel myself close to the hub. I was arriving. I was getting there. History had come alive, been lifted off the page into the shape of a reality. The spectres had been given some form of substance.[36]

There is no attempt at conversation, no pretence at anything other than a slow drive through the Carib Reserve. Yet there is a disturbance to the narrating self, which feels on edge, on the edge, close to the hub. It is never clear quite what this hub is. Perhaps some of the unease comes from the fact that the writer might have expected the spectres to be the ghosts of slavery, but actually finds a *different* history which lifts off the page to become reality.

Unusually for a travel writer, Johnson is openly puzzled by what she finds, and conveys her puzzlement in her writing. It is striking, however, that, like many travellers – though not the three earlier discussed here – she seeks no elucidation from the Caribs themselves. At least since the 1930s Carib chiefs have been eloquent spokesmen for their people, and their words – or at least reports of their words – are represented in dozens of travel books. However, not until very recently has any publication offered a directly Carib viewpoint on any of the issues which travel writers address.[37] Towards the end of 2000 the Dominica-based NGO, SPAT (Small Projects Alternative Technology), dedicated an issue of its journal, *Koudmen: Issues in Development*, to the topic of 'Carib Identity in the New Millenium'.[38] This issue was partly written by a Carib employee of SPAT, Julius Green, in consultation with the Carib Chief, Garnette Joseph, and members of the Carib community. It offers a number of articles on different aspects of Carib identity, including a surprisingly open discussion of internal conflicts. Most strikingly, however, it demonstrates that Carib faces are not going to remain content to speak the 'silent language' that visitors see in their features.

---

[36] Johnson, *Sequins for a Ragged Hem*, p. 240.
[37] A partial exception is *The Caribs and their Colonizers* (London: EAFORD, 1983), published under the name of the then Carib chief, Hilary Frederick, but prepared by Yusuf M. Hamid.
[38] 'Carib Identity in the New Millenium', *Koudmen: Issues in Development*, 9:2 (2000).

Chapter 8

# Night Train to Belo Horizonte: South American Travels

## Erdmute Wenzel White

Fundamentally, Japan and China are not the Far East, but the far West: they are further West than London and Paris. (Osip Mandelstam)[1]

For the fashionably active, and those longing for the unknown, travel is the perfect medium of transformation. Travel has exerted the most powerful pull on writers and artists seeking new territories of the imagination. The reasons why artists travel are as varied as their passions. For the French poet Gérard de Nerval, who suffered from deteriorating mental health, the ideal destination was Germany. There, the poet noticed, he was of sane mind ('On ne me trouve pas fou en Allemagne').[2] Arthur Rimbaud left for Ethiopia, Henri Matisse went to Morocco, and Henri Michaux explored Ecuador. For most people, the desire to travel derives from the feeling that there is something lacking in their own experience. Others, who perceive society as restrictive and unpleasurable, find in travel an escape from the controlling gaze. Yet, for the modern tourist who seems to want everything, all the time, elsewhere no longer exists. The allure of travel encourages and at the same time avoids a new mobility of the spirit. Instead of changing the nature of reality, travel serves as a stand-in, perpetuating an illusion of unfolding reality. It is a means to insert oneself in the guise of orthodoxy, without resolving alienation from the conventional world. Travel accentuates culturally induced notions of taboo, while deflecting the promise of fulfilment into an experience of imaginary plenitude.

This essay examines how space and imagination are carved up simultaneously. It frames the experience of travel, its ethics, illusions and sensual pleasures, by tracking the real and imaginary travels of a group of twentieth-century Brazilian artists against the backdrop of early European discoveries.[3] What these radical artists hoped to explore was not only geographical distance, but an alertness implicit in all travel dreams: an almost hallucinatory clarity that feels like ground zero, if only in fantasy.

---

[1]    Cited in David Kelley and Jean Khalfa, *The New French Poetry* (Newcastle upon Tyne: Bloodaxe, 1996), p. 187.
[2]    'In Germany, people don't think I am insane' (my translation). Gérard de Nerval, *Œuvres*, vol. 1 (Paris: Garnier, 1958), p. 864.
[3]    The original editions of the discoveries are located in the Bernardo Mendel and Charles R. Boxer collection, Lilly Library, Indiana University, USA. The author thanks the Lilly Library for permission to consult these rare documents.

The issue raised in these pages concerns the reversal and transcendence of an alien past, the predicament of artists attempting to craft a cultural flowering from the ruins of a tradition unknown to them except by testimony of those who deprived them of their identity. How to coax strength from a stolen past seems a dubious, if not utopian, scheme. The works of art examined here are crossing-points between reality and myth. They are much like transparent, interlocking planes designed to reconcile past and future by virtue of actual and imaginary transport. The Brazilian artists who reacted to the European Conquest responded with two successive, remarkably different, and even conflicting cultural considerations. What began as a struggle over images ended in disdain for the paradigm of European navigations. Brazilians learned to consume, vandalize, and shock with zany confidence, creating their own 'travel fiction'. They did not change history, but they changed the feeling that we bring to it.

The first news from Brazil to King Manoel of Portugal dates from 1 May 1500. A few days earlier, at Easter, Admiral Pedro Álvares Cabral had made his accidental landfall on Brazilian shores, a land baptized 'Ilha da Santa Cruz' (Vera Cruz Island or Island of the True Cross). Drafted by the scribe Pero Vaz de Caminha, the letter relates how for eight days the sailors explored the coast, celebrated mass, played and danced, performed on instruments akin to bagpipes, and coiffed natives in red caps.[4] While Columbus's First Letter from America (1493)[5] was widely distributed throughout Europe and printed in various languages and editions, the earliest Brazilian travel report received scant publicity. The Portuguese king ordered follow-up descriptions and scientific evidence to back the drafting of legal documents, but the original letter by Vaz de Caminha was soon lost in the Lisbon maritime archives.

How strange Brazil looks to the European eye! The first travelogues traffic in delightfully improbable things, 'choses singulieres & du tout incognues par deça'.[6] Its people are like none that had ever been seen before. The earliest manuscripts evoke a cabinet of wonders set within nature's plentiful gifts. Maps, engravings, and written sources survey an antiworld of hybrid animals, plumed natives, and plants to heal all suffering.

---

[4]    Pero Vaz de Caminha, 'Letter to King Manoel', 1 May 1500, trans. William Brooks Greenlee, *The Voyages of Pedro Álvarez Cabral to Brazil and India*, 2nd ser., 81 (London: Hakluyt Society, 1937), pp. 3–33. For the history of the letter, see Jaime Cortesão, *A carta de Pero Vaz de Caminha* (Lisbon: Livros de Portugal, 1943).

[5]    Cristoforo Colombo, *Epistola Christofori Colom: cui etas nostra multum debet: de insulis Indie supra Gangem nuper inventis* (Rome: Stephan Plannck, 1493). The letter was widely distributed by Spanish royalty, Fernando V (1452–1516) and Isabel I (1451–1504), and went through nine editions.

[6]    'Uncommon things and things totally unknown in our part of the world' (my translation). Jean de Léry, *Histoire d'vn voyage fait en la terre dv Brésil* (La Rochelle: Antoine Chuppin, 1578), p. 3.

Figure 3. *Lisbon in the Time of the Voyages of Discoveries*. Engraving (1592).

In his book *Les singularités de la France Antarctique autrement nommée Amerique*,[7] the Franciscan monk André Thevet (1502–90) displays a four-legged creature with a human face that 'lives off air',[8] demons, dragons, and porpoises surpassing the size of ships. Sixteenth-century engravings depict unicorns, one-eyed populations, and flying fish swirling high above the sails, an event accompanied by a sailor's spontaneous bursts of celebration. The treasure of native birds soon enraptured travellers and scientists alike. Jean de Léry (1534–1611), one of the first Protestant missionaries in the New World, devotes a chapter to the bird population of Brazil. Under the title 'Índios', the reader finds in Léry an image of Tupinambá in dance costumes, a small monkey at their feet, and, sitting on the perch above, a parrot. Even the Indians resemble birds. Dancers have donned feathered headdresses and display a splendid tail of feathers. The author describes native regalia with precise elegance: 'When these feathers have been mixed and combined, and neatly bound to each other with very small pieces of cane and cotton thread (there is no featherworker in France who could handle them better, nor arrange them more skillfully), you would judge that the clothes made of them were of a deep-napped velvet.'[9]

Birds represent the longing for freedom, and they soon reflect the very identity of the continent. The famous world maps of Alberto Cantino (1502) and Nicolau Canério (1505) illustrate the virgin territories with a series of large-beaked birds flitting about or arranged in clusters of spatial whorls.[10] The painter Albert Eckhout, who travelled with Franz Post on behalf of Moritz von Nassau-Siegen during the Dutch occupation of northern Brazil (1637–44), recorded an unparalleled number of birds and beasts, all of them unknown in Europe at the time. On his return to Germany, in the salon of the small hunting lodge at castle Hoflössnitz, near Dresden, Eckhout painted eighty tropical birds.[11] Seduced by the abundance of birds, he adds to the avian population his own shimmering bird dreams. Who could blame him? What he had seen during his journey was the fantastic made literal. This odd

---

[7]     André Thevet, *Les singularités de la France Antarctique autrement nommée Amerique* (Anvers: Christophle Plantin, 1557). The publication date is often given as 1558. However, Suzanne Lussagnet cites 1557 as the probable date of publication. See Suzanne Lussagnet, *Le Brésil et les Brésiliens*, vol. II (Paris: PUF, 1953), p. 241, n. 1.

[8]     Lussagnet, *Le Brésil et les Brésiliens*, vol. II, p. 175.

[9]     Jean de Léry, *History of a Voyage to the Land of Brazil, Otherwise Called America*, trans. Janet Whatley (Berkeley: University of California Press, 1990), p. 60. The first Portuguese version of Léry's book was published by Tristão de Alencar Aripe (1889). A second edition, by Monteiro Lobato (1926), appeared at the time when Brazilian artists showed keen interest in early European travel writing.

[10]    Scholars of critical cartography – among these David Harvey, J. B. Harley, and David Woodward – argue that maps make geographic constructs possible and are necessarily suffused with agendas. Jeremy Black writes: 'the map is constitutive of a certain form of reality, not merely representative of it'. *Maps and Politics* (Chicago: University of Chicago Press, 1997), p. 21.

[11]    Albert Eckhout, *Pássaros do Brasil* (Rio de Janeiro: Agir, 1970).

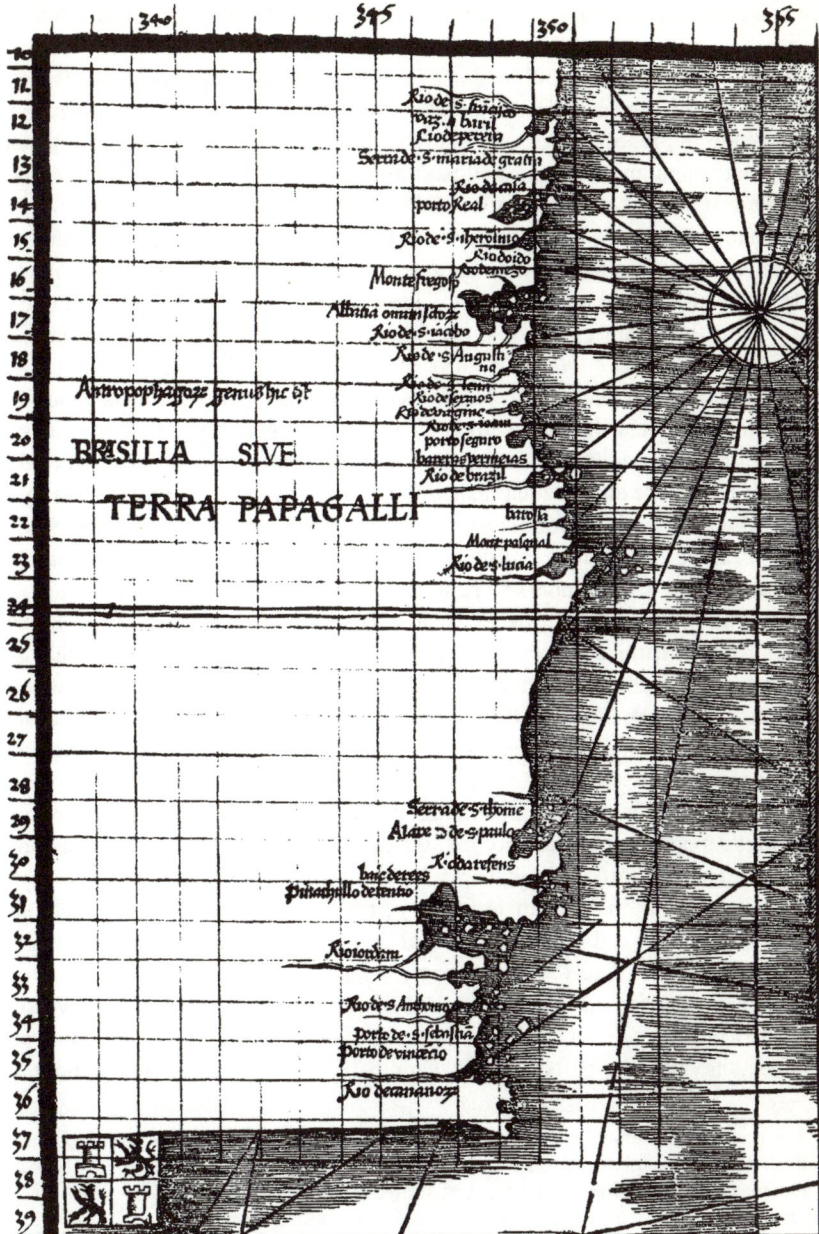

Figure 4. *Brazil*. Early maritime map. From Martin Waldseemüller (1470–1521),
*Cosmographiae introductio cum quibusdam geometriae ac astronomiae principiis ad eam
rem necessariis ...* (Saint-Dié, 1507). In this volume, Waldseemüller named the New World
'Amerigo' or 'America', falsely attributing the discovery of the New World to Vespucci.

betrayal of the senses was to characterize both visitor and host. In Chinese Macao, for example, portrayals of Portuguese navigators exhibit distinctly Asiatic features. A European image of Indians found in Léry's *Historia navigationis in Brasiliam ...* (1594) transmutes the natives into Greek gods.[12] Publishers of early travel accounts continued to use woodblocks left over from previous publishing ventures instead of commissioning more accurate illustrations.

But the new land was not only exotic, it was also deeply menacing. In 1516 the humanist Martin Waldseemüller compiled a world atlas based on Ptolemy's *Geography*. In it, the mapmaker identifies Brazil as the country of cannibals and 'terra papagalli' ('land of parrots').[13] These two emblems, man-eater and exotic bird, would for centuries to come provide the code for selective representations of the New World.

The crucial image of distant inhabitants was created by the account of a German sailor, Hans Staden's *Warhaftig Historia un Beschreibung eyner Landtschafft der Wilden* (*True History and Description of the Landscape of Savages*), published in 1557.[14] Like no one else, Staden shaped Western fantasy, and thereby the history of what was then thought to be a new continent, Brazil. A native of Hamburg, Staden signed on as a gunner with a Portuguese ship and was captured by the Tupinambá. How his fellow crew members were seized and eaten by cannibals constitutes the main narrative of the book. Staden relates that even sporadic visits from French traders offered little comfort: they were perfectly willing to confirm that the captive was Portuguese and therefore an enemy of the Tupinambá. Extravagantly illustrated, the book includes violent renditions of ritual cannibalism that turned Staden's travel writing into a sensation. The resourceful author, clearly, had made it home safely.

Besides chronicles of monks, adventurers, and bureaucrats, the history of the new territories remains largely unrecorded. Whether well-intentioned or not, travellers were the sponsors of the visible world. Mild-mannered or barbarian, the hosts did not register their thoughts. For residents of the 'discovered' areas, the encounter with Europeans proved fatal. In a cultural divide of unequal cunning, the decline began almost immediately. The creature's nakedness created a perfect excuse for exclusionary practices. The native way of life was repudiated either as perversion or as innocence in need of salvation. Although Europeans accepted mutilation and violence, they were horrified by tribal cannibalism. Historically accurate but rare,

---

[12]   Jean de Léry, *Historia navigationis in Brasiliam quae et America dicitur* (Geneva: Heirs of Eustache Vignon, 1594). There were numerous attempts to link Indian languages to ancient Greek, including suggestions of similarity by Montaigne. See Léry, *History of a Voyage to the Land of Brazil*, p. 253, n. 7.

[13]   Martin Waldseemüller (1470–1521), *Cosmographiae introductio cum quibusdam geometriae ac astronomiae principiis ad eam rem necessariis ...* (Saint-Dié: Gautier Lud, 1507).

[14]   Hans Staden, *Warhaftig Historia un Beschreibung eyner Landtschafft der Wilden ...* (Marburg: Andreas Kolbe, 1557).

the practice was based on a food taboo. The cannibal connotes limitless appetite and insecurity to the traveller. He also gives new meaning to the age-old legend of the man-eating foreigner. Henceforth, he symbolizes depravity and macabre ugliness, yielding high-minded reasons for strategies of intolerance and death.

Early travel writers reveal deep ambivalence, mingling expectation and observation, legend and speculation. For Thevet and other French explorers, the New World could rightfully be called 'Antarctic France'. Through a network of new printing presses, Brazil turned into an incongruous land of paradox, at once lush paradise and realm of irrational hostility. The tourism of the caravels and transatlantic ocean liners continued, despite expressions of displeasure by native inhabitants. Braving 'that abyss of water that is the Western Sea', travellers were inspired by science, religion, and greed.[15] Those whose lives were disrupted by unwanted visitors could only hasten their own decline. Scorn trails off into wistfulness.

It falls to the artist to make accessible what is missing and to reinvent 'difference'. In Brazil, the desire for wild beauty finds expression in Italian-inspired opera and lofty Romantic texts, stylizing isolation and flight beyond the linear flow of language and time. From earliest literature to the beginning of the twentieth century, the national repertoire of music, literature, and painting demonstrates, above all, that whatever was there, was asserting its power. The issue for Brazilian artists was not simply authenticity or dissimilarity from European art: writers and artists recognized that when the Portuguese made their landfall, they mapped the Brazilian world in the language of duality, christening mountain and river, measuring thunder and tree. The real conquest was not geographical; it was the colonizing of reality.

Although Brazil gained independence from Portugal in 1822, the literature of Brazil continued to reflect the European canon. By the second decade of the twentieth century the concept of Brazilian identity had acquired new urgency. No longer willing to confine themselves to a culture of credentials, poets and painters began to define a truly Brazilian consciousness, one that was breathing the atmosphere of their birthplace. Under the auspices of modernism, a new resolve took hold among artists, deepening gradually into extreme worldviews and subsequent intensely charged works of art. The raw feelings behind this search for identity are expressed in a poem by the prolific Brazilian poet and musicologist Mário Raúl de Morais Andrade (1893–1945), entitled 'Ode to the Bourgeois':

> I revile the bourgeois! Those paltry bourgeois!
> The bourgeois-bourgeoisie!
> Products of São-Paulo gluttony!
> Hunched-over types! Fat-buttocked fellows!
> French, Brazilian or Italian,
> Crawling cautiously inch by inch!

---

[15]  Léry, *History of a Voyage to the Land of Brazil*, p. 8.

I revile these penny-pinching aristocracies!
Fly-by-night barons! Small-time counts! Braying dukes!
Lying inside their unassailable walls;
Sweating blood for a few measly cents
To be able to say that their daughters speak French
And play 'Printemps' with the tips of their polished nails![16]

The poet captures the life of the wealthy and fashionable, the 'grã-finos', who lived along the Avenida Paulista and in the residential districts of the Gardens, in extravagant palaces of unabashedly pompous taste, monuments to new-found luxuries of the coffee boom. The poet undertook expeditions to the Amazon and collected tales, dances, and songs. He published, among other folklore, *Música de feitiçana no Brasil* (*Music of magic ceremonies in Brazil*) and *O samba rural Paulista* (*The samba of rural São Paulo*). Brazilian modernist artists were in contact with the European avant-garde. Even Mário,[17] who never travelled abroad, corresponded with European writers and subscribed to influential magazines. The French composer Darius Milhaud and the writer Paul Claudel lived until 1917 in Rio de Janeiro. The Italian futurist Filippo Marinetti visited repeatedly, and there were other, direct ties to French surrealists, as well as to the sculptor Constantin Brancusi.

The journey beyond Western tradition coincides with the arrival in Santos, Brazil, of a world traveller, the French-Swiss iconoclast Blaise Cendrars. In 1924, at the request of yet another poet, Oswald de Andrade, and Oswald's painter friend and future wife, Tarsila do Amaral, Cendrars spent several months in South America. He was met by local artists with grace and calculated drama. He adored Brazil, his second spiritual country, as he fondly called it so many times. The absurd, delirious, and marvellous became tangible: 'Past and future are always part of the present', he writes, 'but nowhere except in Brazil may we actually touch it.'[18]

During Holy Week, Cendrars organized a trip to the eighteenth-century mining towns of the state of Minas Gerais. A cast of young Brazilian artists participated, including Mário and Oswald de Andrade, as well as Tarsila. This journey into non-coastal regions, the first for artists who travelled so frequently to Europe, momentously shifted the art of the country. Participants set out to discover their heritage precisely on Easter, Semana Santa, the date of the discovery of Brazil. And they were enchanted by what they saw: ornate interiors and religious vestments, open-air galleries and sculptures carved from soap stone, the rare mixture of naïve style and abstract aerial views. They admired, above all, the perfect integration of space and architecture. Bathed in golden light, the outlines of baroque churches

---

[16]    Paulo Mendes de Almeida, ed., *Semana de 22*, catalogue, trans. Edwina Jackson (São Paulo: Museo de Arte de São Paulo, 1972), n. p.
[17]    I follow the Brazilian custom and refer to some of these writers by their first names. This procedure avoids any confusion created by identical family names.
[18]    Blaise Cendrars, *Trop c'est trop. Œuvres complètes* (Paris: Denoël, 1960–65), vol. 8, p. 185; my translation.

created spare, rhythmic lines, embedded in brightly nuanced tones of habitations and delicate palm trees, suggestive of the aesthetics of calligraphy.

While the architecture and its splendid settings were enough to hold the attention of the visitors, it was the emotional content of the historic past that seemed nothing short of miraculous. During the journey, the poets read their latest work to each other, and it was during the long train ride, the land hurtling past him, that Mário composed his pathbreaking ode 'Noturno de Belo Horizonte' ('Night train to Belo Horizonte'):

> The miracle of thousands of glimmering glass beads
> Calm of the night train to Belo Horizonte
> Crisp cold falls leaf-like from trees
> And bedews the lonely garden.
> Broad sweeping strokes of darkness.
> Policemen between roses ...
> Present where they are not needed, as usual ...

Abrupt scenic shifts convey hallucinatory disorientation. Out of silence, sonorous surfaces appear and dissolve into pure chromatic effects:

> The costumed samba school of Minas history
> Moves along the avenue of six-rowed trees.
> The sun explodes in fireworks
> The day is cold without clouds, like glimmering glass beads.
> But it is not day! There is no Sun exploding in the sky!
> This is the nocturnal hallucination of Belo Horizonte ...
> Let's not forget the local color:
> Itacolomi ... *The Daily Minas Newspaper* ... the little train of Calafete ...
> And that silence ... sio ... sio ... quiriri ... [19]

During the journey, Oswald took notes for his collection of poems entitled *Pau Brasil* (*brazilwood*),[20] and his wife, Tarsila, sketched her delicate still-lifes and domestic scenes. Shortly thereafter, Oswald issued his first literary manifesto, also entitled *Pau Brasil*. His poems, *Poesias reunidas*, bear the subtitle: *Por ocasião da descoberta do Brasil* (*On the occasion of the discovery of Brazil*).[21] The introductory poems of the collection, 'História do Brasil', are based entirely on texts written by clerics and colonists from different centuries of the Conquest. The poems are quite literally stolen from sources collected by Paulo Prado and other researchers during the 1920s. They derive from Portuguese and Spanish manuscripts as well as from writings of a seventeenth-century French Capuchin monk, Claude d'Abbeville.

---

[19]   Mário de Andrade, *Poesias completas* (São Paulo: Editôra Itatiaia, 1987), pp. 178–89; my translation.
[20]   *Pau Brasil* (brazilwood, *Caesalpinia echinata*) refers to the native tree that yields precious red dyes. It was the first commercial export of the country. The designation 'Terra do Brasil' was eventually transferred to the nation itself.
[21]   José Oswald de Sousa Andrade, *Pau Brasil: Cancioneiro de Oswald de Andrade* (Paris: Au Sans Pareil, 1924); my translation.

Oswald's cutout poems combine modern aesthetic procedures with the symbolic acts of demarcation and appropriation. The first poem, 'Pero Vaz de Caminha', is broken into fragments entitled 'A descoberta' ('Discovery'), 'Os selvagens' ('The savages'), 'Primeiro chá' ('First tea', here: 'High tea'), and 'As meninas da gare' ('Young women at the train station'). The poet compresses Renaissance writing into granular, firm lines:

> Discovery
>
> We followed our path along this sea
> Until Easter week
> We discovered birds
> And land came into view.[22]

Not much is left of Vaz de Caminha's letter from which the poem derives. The selected segments shatter the source text and its meaning, reintroducing ambiguity. Yet the minimalist poem shows pinpoint control. The poem evolves from the eventless passage of a first, long line of sensory anticipation, interrupted by a brief assertion of time. Birds signal the discovery. They seem to fall into the world, their sudden appearance echoed by the utopian coming into view of visible objects. As our gaze comes to a swift halt at each line, there seems to be no sense in seeking anything deeper than the facts. The violence works on the procedural level: the poet stakes out a territory. He carves his poem from the original material, much like a navigator or mapmaker carves topography from alien space, forcing reconsideration of all that went before. In the austere space of four lines, the Brazilian artist reflects and refracts the birth of his nation. The diminutive space of his poem embodies new territorial integrity.

'Os selvagens' recalls natives frightened by a chicken, while 'Primeiro chá' ('High tea') records a single acrobatic leap: 'Depois de dançarem/Diogo Dias/Fês o salto real' ('At the end of the dance/Diogo Dias/performed a regal somersault'). The last poem, 'As meninas da gare', suggests that the Indian women, in innocent stages of undress, are prostitutes of urban train stations. Isolated from the original context, we perceive an entire history of prejudice. Each separate poem is a scene of life that illustrates our tendency to confirm our own convictions. Only when expectation is broken is discovery again possible.

While Oswald pulverizes the texture of travel writing, the poet Raúl Bopp creates utopias of sound, evoking a malleable world, at once childlike and threatening. His epic poem, *Cobra Norato* (1931), is a most compelling work anchored in the movement for renewal.[23] Like other artists, the poet travelled extensively throughout the country. Stark rhythms and freely introduced tonal textures recall 'naïve' traditions of rural Brazil. His poem narrates the adventures of a snake,

---

[22] Oswald de Sousa Andrade, *Pau Brasil*, p. 72.
[23] Raúl Bopp, *Cobra Norato e outros poemas* (Rio de Janeiro: Block Editôres, 1951).

Cobra Norato, on its way to the heart of the Amazon region, the murky, mucky land without end, the place where earth itself is fabricated. Cobra Norato assumes different guises, takes human form, or takes flight by attaching himself to the tail of the great, talismanic armadillo.

Cobra Norato is the poet himself, wrapped in the silken skin of the snake, as he glides into the realm of 'mussangulá', a state of erotic yearning that allows him to see and feel things with brutal purity. In his quest for the daughter of Queen Luzia, whom he must marry, Cobra Norato proves his capacity for suffering, and endures extreme trials of body and soul. He obtains the woman he loves not by acts of patience or courage, but by a perilous gesture of compassion. When he comes upon Cobra Grande in its glistening silver helmet, Cobra Norato interrupts his own quest to free the hostage of the Great Snake, who turns out to be the beautiful beloved of his dreams, his future bride, the light of day, the graceful, restorative power of faith and love.

While the poem speaks of truth and goodness, its art derives from cumulative effects of polyrhythmic speech. Surging verses, drunk with mesmerizing waves of cascading sound, seem to press beyond ample lines, much like the river displacing the forest in its waters. Then again, the metre is sharp, fresh, imitating dance movement, rumbling, rattling wind instruments and strings, or the raspy sounds of animals crying out, cut off by long, virtuosic bird trills. Sounds not only dwell in space but exhale it. Colloquial voices mingle with choirs, lullabies, spells, and plaintive song. Bopp defines his work as a 'zoofonia', a noise concert that generates charmed musical effects, suggesting that the life of language holds the key to the secrets of life.

If the epic poem *Cobra Norato* can be defined as a soundscape, namely words hovering between pure sound and semantic meaning, then the music of Heitor Villa-Lobos might be understood as *Tonmalerei* (painting with sound). The composer studied pseudo-ethnographic texts and Indian melodies. Like his friend Oswald, he returns to the moment of the first arrival of travellers on Brazilian shores. The ballet *A descoberta do Brasil* (1937) is based on the first letter of Pero Vaz de Caminha.

Villa-Lobos's compositions derive from the sound of native instruments, among these *agogô* (bells), *apito* (whistle), *chocalho* (rattle), *atabaque* (drum, also *lê*), and *buzina* (horn). Birds are prevalent throughout. *Uirapurú, saracurinha*, and *irerê* are some of the birds that inspire swirling chromatic motifs, crystallizing emotions of a fleeting moment, as in 'aria' and 'dansa' of the *Bachianas Brasileiras Nr. 5*. The composer listened to early phonographic recordings collected by Edgar Roquette Pinto of the National Museum of Rio de Janeiro. Based on his ethnographic research, Villa-Lobos incorporates melodies of the Pareci Indians ('Nozani-ná') in his *Chôro Nr. 3*. Other musical works feature Afro-Brazilian ceremonial chants:

> Xangô! Olê gondilê. Olalá!
> Gon gon gon gond-dilá!

Xangô! Olê gondilê. Olalá!
Gon gon gon gond-dilá!
(Xangô)[24]

Villa-Lobos's composition *Jurupary* (*Creation*) depicts the creation myths of the Tupi-Guarani. Serge Lifar danced in a ballet with the same title at the Paris Opera. In this work the composer makes use of collaged elements taken from Johann Baptist von Spix, who published a scientific travel report entitled *Reise in Brasilien: 1817–1820*.[25] This last book comprises a number of notations and dances of the Camacan Indians. Like Oswald, who takes possession of the earliest known document of the Conquest, Villa-Lobos pays tribute to the first known ethno-musicological notation of his country. He encountered five melodies of the Tupinambá in Léry's *Histoire d'un voyage fait en la terre du Brésil*. Léry records a melody devoted to the yellow canindé bird, entitled 'Canidé [*sic*]-Ioune-sabath' (canindé = yellow bird, sabath = elegy). Léry was stunned by the colours of the canindé,[26] a stately bird featured among Eckhout's eighteenth-century inventory of Brazilian birds. Although the particular melody varies, or is missing in different editions, one of these simple tunes provides the source for Villa-Lobos's *Três poemas indígenas* (*Three native poems*):[27]

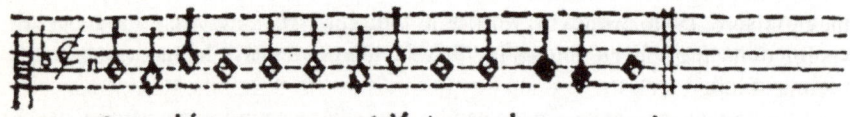

*Canidé-ioune, canidé-ioune heura-oueh*

Brazilian artists perceive early travel accounts as 'still-lifes' of sheer inventiveness, invitations to their own highly metaphorical spatial and ethical explorations. Travel writing constitutes a place of metamorphoses and ambivalence

---

[24] Lisa M. Peppercorn, *The World of Villa-Lobos in Pictures and Documents* (Aldershot: Scolar Press, 1996), p. 137.

[25] Johann Baptist von Spix, *Reise in Brasilien: 1817–1820* (Munich: M. Lindauer, 1830).

[26] The canindé 'has all the plumage under the belly and around the neck as yellow as fine gold; the upper part of the back, the wings and the tail are of a blue as clear as can be. You would think that he was dressed in golden cloth below, and clad in a mantle of violet damask above; one is enraptured by his beauty.' Léry, *History of a Voyage to the Land of Brazil*, p. 88.

[27] For the history of this tune in different editions of Léry, see Peppercorn, *The World of Villa-Lobos*, pp. 101–3. The musical motif cited here is found in the fourth edition (not counting a third 'false' edition), published in 1599–1600 by Eustache Vignon (*Histoire d'vn voyage fait en la terre dv Brésil* [Geneva]), p. 173.

of the senses. Artists valued manuscripts as catalysts for the ambitious task of creating modern, fetishlike objects. Their reading of early manuscripts, however, was purely artistic. That the tiny *uirapurú* is a divine bird for the Tupi, or that unauthorized telling of sacred legends is done by the intrinsically untrustworthy, all this would not have entered the artistic programme of the era. The art of the modernists was at once dream travel and elegy. While the rescue of ethnographic sources opened a new world of feeling and art making, Brazilian modernist works derive from the science that imparted legitimacy to colonialism. Their original sources, much like pinned butterflies, were reminders of what no longer existed, or perhaps never was.

Indeed, one of the first artists to admit that the movement had failed to pierce the surface of Brazilian life was Oswald, the impresario of the *Pau Brasil* movement. Realizing that the Conquest had trespassed on the purity of the place, he came to regard the imposition of an alien language as a fall from grace. Anthropology and Western science in general, he felt, were offspring of colonialism. Brazilian art, the poet conceded, subtly continued to reinforce the bond between colonizer and colonized. 'Serve me', it whispers, 'turn into me, and I will see you.' Cendrars's admiration of Brazilian life was such a love. Far from having created a native consciousness, his own *Pau Brasil* is another, purely aesthetic alignment, one that directly or indirectly gratifies Western notions of culture. A truly new art must seek the formation of a new human being: 'all of our reactions generally take place within the confines of the tramway carrying an imported civilization. We have to jump off, set fire to it', the poet concluded.[28] The disillusionment of Brazilian intellectuals became focused after their contact with subversive forces of the European avant-garde. Acutely aware that even transgression pays homage to the foreign patron, Oswald proceeded to reverse the argument. Cultural radicalism, he proposed, was not only a method for deciphering and recapturing a past long believed inaccessible, it *was* the authentic voice of pre-colonial times.

A tactic as well as a distinctive style, *antropofagia* (cannibalism) was founded by Oswald in the spring of 1928. Its aim was to provoke and threaten 'civilized' people. The movement touched upon philosophy, art and politics, economics and sociology, science, history, and myth. It called for unbridled psychic cannibalism to purge the country of foreign intrusion, 'the truth of missionary people'.[29] Its underpinning was egoism, 'the only law of the world',[30] but a legitimate egoism founded in self-respect and the love for a people who during four hundred years of colonialism complied so completely that they bankrupted their civilization. Behind

---

[28]   José Oswald de Sousa Andrade, 'Contra os emboabas', *O Minas Gerais*, 13 May 1928, p. 5.

[29]   José Oswald de Andrade, 'Manifesto antropófago', *Revista de Antropofagia*, 1 May 1928, pp. 1–3; rpt. *Obras completas*, 11 vols (Rio de Janeiro: Editôra Civilização Brasileira, 1971), vol. 6, p. 17; English trans. Leslie Bary as 'Cannibalist Manifesto', *Latin American Literary Review*, XXXVIII (July–December 1991), pp. 35–47.

[30]   Oswald de Andrade, 'Manifesto antropófago', *Obras completas*, vol. 6, p. 13.

Figure 5. *Flying fish*. Engraving, sixteenth century. From Carlos Malheiro Dias, ed., *História da colonização portuguesa do Brasil*. Vol. II (Porto: Litografia Nacional, 1923), p. 120.

the mask of morality, man was an animal in carnival costume, a notion that recalled Tristan Tzara's cynical assessment of humanity as 'animals in costumes'.[31]

The 'manifesto antropófago' was signed at Piratininga, the place name for São Paulo in the Indian language Tupi, in the year 374, year of the deglutination of the aptly named bishop Dom Pedro Fernandes Sardinha, assassinated and eaten by cannibals in 1556. This act of vengeance was commemorated by a new calendar. The manifesto proclaimed the advent of the Caraïbe Revolution:[32]

> Against dressed man ... against Father Vieira, author of our first loan ... the reversible world and objectified ideas, cadaverized, against the individual as victim of the system ... against all histories that take their beginning at Cape Finisterre ... the truth of missionary people ... against memory as source of tradition ... against social reality, dressed up and oppressive, mapped out by Freud.[33]

The main organ of the group was the *Revista de Antropofagia*, which, during its first run, existed from May 1928 to February 1929, and during its 'second teething' appeared as a weekly page in the newspaper *Diário de São Paulo*, from March until August of the same year. All in all, there were twenty-six numbers. Its cast of editors – 'butchers', as they preferred to call themselves – published cannibalistic news from all over. Articles, art, parodies, and malapropisms appear from known and invented sources:

> Destroy: all creation is born from destruction. (Marcel Schwob)[34]

> Where there are two people, one stronger than the other, one devouring the other, we find universal harmony,[35] signed Oswaldo Costa.

> A madman is not a man who has lost his mind, but a man who has lost everything but his mind. (Chesterton)[36]

> The gentle approach: from these Indians we have learned that they are more likely to be converted because of fear rather than because of love. (Father José de Anchieta)[37]

---

[31] Tristan Tzara, 'Dada Manifesto 1918'; see Lucy Lippard, *Dadas on Art* (Englewood Cliffs, NJ: Prentice Hall, 1971), p. 16.

[32] 'The term Caraïbe was applied to men who claimed and to whom were attributed prophetic powers, [André] Thevet uses caraïbe in speaking of the culture heroes of Tupi mythology. Early Jesuit writers say that caraïbe meant "the sacred"' (Léry, *History of a Voyage to the Land of Brazil*, p. 248, n. 12).

[33] Oswald de Andrade, 'Manifesto antropófago', *Obras completas*, vol. 6, pp. 13–19.

[34] Oswald de Andrade, *Diário de São Paulo*, 31 March 1929, insert; my translation.

[35] Oswald de Andrade, *Diário de São Paulo*, 17 March 1929, insert; my translation.

[36] Oswald de Andrade, *Diário de São Paulo*, 11 July 1929, insert; my translation.

[37] Oswald de Andrade, *Diário de São Paulo*, 1 May 1929, insert; my translation.

> What all these gentlemen seek is a god, a religion, an ideology of some kind, which will give them peace of mind while they exploit the lower classes.[38]

Riding high on the new riches of their export economy, artists and intellectuals argued that only a prosperous society remains autonomous. Instead of denouncing capitalism, they praised it for exhibiting all the virtues of cannibalism. They admired the aggressive will of capitalists to consume and destroy their competitors. However, Oswald, in a typically provocative manner, diverged from orthodox capitalist ideology. He did not wish to place the profits of Brazil's economy at the free disposition of a self-perpetuating élite. His goal was to eradicate inequalities by abolishing inheritance. The *antropófago* would establish a modern matriarchal society to be known as the Indian Republic of Pindorama. There would be no notion of sin, and capitalism would flourish in an egalitarian society where everything would eventually belong to everyone. He called upon poets to give voice to intrinsically 'magic' dimensions. New artists, he declared, would live *within* art, an art based upon undivided space: 'Cosmos, parte do eu' ('The Cosmos inhabits me').[39]

The principles of *antropofagia* were incoherent, an amalgam of the kind of fanciful thinking the movement genuinely welcomed. The group placed the spirit of provocation above any social, political, or aesthetic purpose. There was only the infinite state of flux. Creation was perpetual revolt in a world of energy and irradiation. Oswald warned that the enemies of intolerance could become intolerant themselves: 'for the *antropófago* all legislation is dangerous, much like our own prejudices'.[40] An abrasive nature and non-conformism would protect the *antropófago* from stagnation of thought and new subservience. The very notion of relativity, as members of the group pointed out, originated in the essay 'Des cannibales' by Michel de Montaigne, who in 1550 interviewed some of the fifty Brazilian Tupinambá Indians brought to Rouen harbour to celebrate a visit by Henry II. Montaigne also seems to have studied Léry's account of Brazil. Inspired by Montaigne's discussion of communal property, Rousseau formulated the incendiary ideas that would shape the French Revolution. The Caraïbe Revolution was yet another stage of permanent revolutionary and artistic renewal.

*Antropofagia* enjoyed a brief, rambunctious reign and became stranded in the sands of political life. In Brazil, the revolution was made by the military, not the intellectuals. The movement was brought to an abrupt halt when the economy collapsed. By 1931 its few festive seasons seemed irrevocably to belong to the past. What *antropófagos* hoped for was the revolutionary life; what they got was

---

[38] Odjaun (pseudonym for Oswald de Andrade), 'Revistofagia, comendo estrêlas', *Diário de São Paulo*, 1 May 1929, insert; my translation.

[39] Oswald de Andrade, 'Manifesto antropófago', *Obras completas*, vol. 6, p. 15; my translation.

[40] Freuderico (pseudonym for Oswald de Andrade), 'De Antropofogia', *Diário de São Paulo*, 17 March 1929, insert; my translation.

modern capitalism and attendant consumerism. Oswald turned to Communism, and Tarsila travelled to Moscow instead of Paris. Cendrars, never an *antropófago*, lost contact with his Paulista friends. The society that *antropófagos* vowed to devour had reversed the process.

While *Pau Brasil* artists watch a flickering past through the keyhole of travel writing, precariously balancing optical and *trompe-l'œil* effects, *antropófagos* pursue a different art of distinctly harsh improvisation. Their art evokes the journey of the shaman peering beyond the horizon, creating characters capable of inhabiting entirely invented planes. Two novels are examples of *antropofagia*: *Macunaíma* by Mário de Andrade,[41] and *Serafim Ponte Grande* by Oswald de Andrade.[42] Directly related to the movement are works belonging to the surrealist phase of the painter Tarsila do Amaral.

Mário's *Macunaíma*, completed in December 1926, before the appearance of the 'manifesto antropófago', was published only in 1928. *Antropófagos* immediately recognized it as the kind of work they advocated. The experimental novel draws on Indian legends, establishing the unusual texture for the loosely woven adventures of a picaresque protagonist, Macunaíma, and his two brothers. All three leave the jungle to live in São Paulo, hoping to regain the *muiriquitã*, a legendary green stone that brings happiness to its owner. Macunaíma's quest for the amulet represents the quest of all Brazilians for their lost purity. The hero lives in a world of make-believe where contradictory things are happening at once. He uses his imagination to make reality conform to his desire. Ironically he is the only one able to make sense out of an otherwise incomprehensible world. Macunaíma is the 'hero without character', a 'primitive' man who just happens to live in a modern world. Amoral and unpredictable, motivated by intuition, unhampered by external evidence, he devotes most of his time to magic herbs and erotic impulse. With freedom from logic comes overwhelming joy in existence. Even violence and pain seem to induce childlike delight. Death is not finite in Macunaíma's cosmography; it is a metamorphosis that only affects exterior shape. Both Ci, Macunaíma's love and 'mother of the jungle', and the hero himself become stars when they pass from one existence into the other. Nothing prevents Macunaíma from reversing even this last transformation. Vocabulary and syntax rely on dialects from the four corners of the nation, creating a mixture of style and grammar spoken nowhere in Brazil. *Macunaíma* has since become the most popular Brazilian novel of the 1920s.

*Serafim Ponte Grande* by Oswald was privately published in 1933. In place of the usual copyright, the reader finds an announcement: 'Right to be translated, reproduced and distorted in all languages.'[43] The note sets the tone for one of the most disconcerting works written in South America. Institutions, social conventions,

---

[41]   Mário Raúl de Morais Andrade, *Macunaíma, o Herói sem nenhum caráter* (São Paulo: Livraria Editôra Martins, 1965).

[42]   Oswald de Andrade, *Serafim Ponte Grande* (Rio de Janeiro: Ariel, 1933).

[43]   Oswald de Andrade, *Serafim Ponte Grande*, p. 97; my translation.

values a Brazilian might hold sacred, are shown to be based on truculent self-interest. There is no use to think of reform, the author notes; what the world needs is a total demolition job. The representative of all evil is the semi-educated, mediocre Benedito Pereira Carlindonga. As head of an administrative division, he spends his time lamenting the absence of 'culture', and dreaming of the strong man who will lead the unruly flock of citizens to permanent law and order. A small-time tyrant, he dies, like Marat, in his bathtub, killed by Serafim Ponte Grande, a once mild-mannered bureaucrat turned anarchist. Serafim is the *antropófago* as exterminator, a hero-clown who worships hypocrisy and forever abhors 'good taste'. Although ordinary and mean, he saves himself in the revolutionary act.

Deliberate scandal is not confined to the content of the book. Oswald calls his work an 'invention', a genre intended to combat the concept of literature as entertainment for cultivated people.[44] The author applies the same process of negation to the art of fiction, cultivating formal awkwardness, systematically discrediting sentiment, and enticing the reader to become interested in a variety of plots that break off at the peak of interest, never to be resumed. He skilfully imitates different genres, ranging from diary to detective story, from love story to farce. The novel overlaps cryptic meaning with a blend of deliberately unemotive or high-pitched sensibility. Disoriented readers who stay long enough with it finally watch protagonists fight over their future role in the book.

The apotheosis of the novel takes place on board a luxury ocean liner sheltering the permissive happiness of a freethinking community. Its members sail between Europe and Brazil, escaping old and new worlds in oceanic bliss. Suspended between dream and life, and experiencing fluctuating worldviews, they are in permanent exodus from the diaspora. The floating *antropófago* stakes his life on the wide open spaces of experiment. He refuses *terra firma*, but he does so in bad faith or in naïveté, since his dissidence and aristocratic tourism are redolent of the most ancient purveyor of freedom: money.[45]

Oswald's desire for revolt did not abate after the demise of *antropofagia*, but he never got over a profound sense of having wasted the moment. He left the revolution of the spirit to join the Communist party, the other social force that promised to create the alternative form of society he dreamed about. The Brazilian movement was at heart no more subversive than the ascendant European surrealism of the time. And yet *antropofagia* marks the beginning of a new political consciousness, transcending the colonial code and initiating the history of militant dissidence. Its ideals shaped a complex and formally authentic shift in modern creativity.

---

[44] Haroldo de Campos, 'Serafim: Um grande não-livro'. See Oswald de Andrade, *Obras completas*, vol. 2, p. 102.

[45] The New Utopia on board freedom ships is no longer a fantasy. The *World Residensea*, built by the Norwegian architect Petter Yran, contains 110 luxury apartments. Another vessel, *Freedom Ship*, is under construction in La Ceiba (Honduras). The ship, which is a mile long, will evade control by staying in international waters. Thomas Fischermann, 'Flucht in den Cyberspace', 19 April 2001, < www.zeit.de/2001/17/staatenlose>.

The man-eater has since turned cult figure. As glorified outcast and resistance fighter, he assumes the essentially critical function of postcolonial revisionism, giving rise to the realm of cultural anthropophagy. The discipline rejects any notion that progress is the result of race, culture, or climate. Racism is but the instrument of power. Similar reflections define the search for new cultural-historical meaning initiated by native associations, among these the North American Alcatraz group (1970), the liberation theology of the Brazilian Leonardo Boff, as well as the activism of the Tupac Katari, a group that confronted the Pope on his 1985 Bolivian trip. Demands for Indian rights by Mexican Zapatistas[46] – who appeal simultaneously for assistance to global trade unions and US punk rock-bands – despite temperamental differences, hark back to the Caraïbe quest. The mostly unreported protest meetings and declarations opposed to the Spanish and Portuguese quincentennial celebrations may also be linked to the usefully angry, cannibalist revisionism. Recent agit-prop and even urban terrorist activities belong to the fabric of resistance conceived in the 1928 manifesto.

Not surprisingly, *antropofagia* forms a vital topos in contemporary Brazilian life and letters. The 'manifesto antropófago' is vested with totemic meaning. The filmmaker Nelson Pereira dos Santos directed *How Tasty Was My Little Frenchman* (1971), filmed mostly in the Tupi language. The film features ordinary male and female nudity throughout and eschews classical cinematic technique. Dos Santos interrupts the narrative with excerpts from Staden, Léry, and vintage citations that may well have been lifted from the *Revista de Antropofagia*. Another filmmaker, Joaquim Pedro de Andrade, pays tribute to the artists of the twenties. In his introduction to the cinematic version of *Macunaíma* (1969), the filmmaker argues that ideologies continue to colonize the world:

> Today we can clearly note that nothing has changed. The traditionally dominant, conservative social classes continue their control of the power structure – and we rediscover cannibalism.
>
> Every consumer is reducible, in the last analysis, to cannibalism. The present work relationships, as well as the relationships between people – social, political, and economic – are still, basically cannibalistic.
>
> …
>
> Those who can, 'eat' others through their consumption of products, or even more directly as in sexual relationships. Cannibalism has merely institutionalized itself.
>
> … Meanwhile, voraciously, nations devour their people.[47]

The filmmaker goes beyond the anarchic posturing and strategic games of his 1928 predecessors. He acknowledges the mechanisms of pure power. In the realm

---

[46] Subcomandante Insurgente Marcos, *Our Word Is Our Weapon* (New York: Seven Stories Press, 2001), includes extensive documents pertaining to the supranational Indigenous Resistance Movement.

[47] Joaquim Pedro de Andrade, 'New Line Cinema Corporation', broadsheet; circa 1978, three pages.

of ethics, the artist argues, we have scarcely moved beyond the intelligence of voracious exploration. While we yearn for bursts of rapture, in practice, cultural difference is either lost or ends with a crash of violence.

As the history of the discoveries demonstrates, the wayward cannibal has served an odd mixture of cynicism and idealism. He is part of a peculiarly equivocal system, one that informs both the exclusionary tradition of colonialism and the desire to escape from the perspectival prison to which we are confined. It is probably fair to speculate that in his many transgressions, he acts as key protagonist for a journey through nightmares and the outer limits of travel imaginings. *Antropófago* artists created a paradigm for appropriate and imaginative resistance to the colonizing appetite of the first European explorers. Indeed, the *antropófago* embodies a transformational force that the early European travellers were seeking and could not fulfil. Warrior of hope and vigilance, he is the electrifying image for the innovator and for experimental space itself, the world at its beginnings. But there is, of course, a warning attached to such unimpeded views. Calling attention to distinctly aberrant and violent realms, the atavistic figure arouses suspicions of heresy. Like travellers discovering that the possession of space is only illusory, antropofagic strategists find that imaginary and ideologic spheres are sealed into the system they seek to transform. For those in search of a different life beyond the fallen world, for the hidden and the sacred, for the spark that cannot be absorbed, the mythologized, man-eating misfit serves as a reminder that deeply dissident ideas are in themselves criminal. We have invested the very figure of the antiworld with supreme purpose to propitiate the powers we cannot control.

Figure 6. *Canindé* (*ara ararauna*, Linnaeus, 1758). Albert Eckhout, *Pássaros do Brasil* (Rio de Janeiro, 1970). Original size: 90 × 90 cm. The editors and author thank Agir Editôra Ltda, Rio de Janeiro, Brazil, for permission to reproduce this image.

1925 - jubileu de "pau brasil" - 1950

no 396° ano da de-
glutição do bispo sar-
dinha, aos vinte e
cinco vindos de mar-
ço.

são paulo de pirati-
ninga ao mais jovem
dos seus escritores.

Figure 7. *Jubilee*: Invitation card, 25th anniversary celebrations of the foundation of *Pau Brasil*. Private collection. Real and imaginary travel merge in this illustration (the sixteenth-century engraving is from Hans Staden). Distinctions between *Pau Brasil* and *antropofagia* have thus dissolved.

Chapter 9

# Between Gender and Genre: The Travels of Estella Canziani

## Loredana Polezzi

### Genre connections

There are both historical and formal links between travel writing and autobiography, and scholars of the two genres are increasingly, though not always explicitly, interested in their common features, their overlapping boundaries and their often similar reception. Drawing links, however, is a risky business. Both autobiography and travel writing are notoriously fuzzy, hybrid, complex genres, which tend to resist simple definition – and drawing them together may create further difficulties of interpretation. This is probably why we tend to stick to a single-genre assignation, even when the same work has clearly been read, and different critics may have discussed it, as both a travelogue and an autobiography.

Even when the link between two genres is explicitly made, the tendency is usually for the more 'prestigious' text-type to dominate the other. This is to a large extent the case of traditional interpretations of travel writing as a minor genre whose importance is mainly to be found in the instrumental role it played in the development of the novel.[1] Yet recent trends which tend to read travel accounts as the expression and testimony of historically located discourses could also be accused of reducing the genre to a sub-set of the increasingly large pool of documents which form the basis of (new) historicist analysis.[2] The connection between travel writing and autobiography does not escape such risks. It is in fact

I would like to thank Tessa Sidey, of the Birmingham Museums and Art Gallery, for drawing my attention to Estella Canziani in the first place, and for her help with my research. Thanks also go to the Birmingham Museums and Art Gallery for allowing the reproduction of two of the works by Canziani held in their collections. Finally, I am grateful to colleagues at the Università degli studi 'G. d'Annunzio' in Pescara for their interest and support.

[1] See, for example, Percy G. Adams, *Travel Literature and the Evolution of the Novel* (Lexington: University Press of Kentucky, 1983); and for volumes directly relating to Italy, Roderick Marshall, *Italy in English Literature, 1755–1815: Origins of the Romantic Interest in Italy* (New York: Columbia University Press, 1934); C. P. Brand, *Italy and the English Romantics: The Italianate Fashion in Early Nineteenth-Century England* (Cambridge: Cambridge University Press, 1957); Kenneth Churchill, *Italy and English Literature, 1764–1930* (London: Macmillan, 1980).

[2] The area in which this trend is most in evidence is possibly that of colonial and postcolonial studies. See, for instance, Stephen Greenblatt, *Marvelous Possessions: The Wonder of the New World* (Oxford: Clarendon Press, 1988).

not at all uncommon for travel accounts to be read primarily – or exclusively – as autobiographical documents, not necessarily 'important' in their own right, but capable of offering us a key to other, usually more prestigious works by the same author, or of clarifying the intricacies of his or her personality. And even when the travel book is the central object of analysis, an autobiographical reading may be used to 'explain away' its distinctive features, possibly by invoking an overriding psychological, or psychoanalytical interpretation.[3]

In the case of women travel writers – though one could probably say the same of other women writers too – the tendency to privilege the autobiographical reading of their work is even more predominant. As noted by Sara Mills, this kind of 'labelling' can be the result of 'an attempt to deny women the status of creators of cultural artefacts': by confining women's writing to the private, or even the 'confessional' sphere, this reception 'has two effects: firstly, the downgrading of the value of the text (if the text is simply an overflow of emotions, then it is not an artistic production); and secondly, the text is read as only relating to the individual concerned', thus denying its scope and significance.[4]

While the tendency to read travel writing as autobiography may entail such critical difficulties and lead to misreadings, the two genres clearly share some of their defining conventions. Adrien Pasquali, following De Certeau, has remarked that 'par généralisation de la notion de déplacement du personnage, "tout récit est un récit de voyage", qu'il soit factuel ou fictionnel', while on the other hand 'tout voyage est une machine à produire du récit'.[5] If we restrict the field to autobiography and travel writing, we find that the central overlap is to be located in the way in which both genres construct their subject and object positions: in both cases conventions lead the reader to expect author, narrator and protagonist to coincide, while the object of the narration is assumed to be truthful and factual.[6] What is essential to both autobiography and travel writing is the centrality of the 'I', its gaze and

---

[3]   See Dennis Porter, *Haunted Journeys: Desire and Transgression in European Travel Writing* (New Jersey: Princeton University Press, 1991), or, more cogently, Mark Cocker, *Loneliness and Time: British Travel Writing in the Twentieth Century* (London: Secker & Warburg, 1992).

[4]   Sara Mills, *Discourses of Difference: An Analysis of Women's Travel Writing and Colonialism* (London: Routledge, 1991), pp. 12, 109.

[5]   'If we generalize the notion of displacement of the character, "any kind of récit is récit de voyage", whether it is factual or fictional'; 'any kind of travel is a mechanism for the production of récit' (my translation). Adrien Pasquali, 'Récit de voyage et autobiographie', in *L'odeporica/Hodoeporics: On Travel Literature*, ed. Luigi Monga, special issue of *Annali d'italianistica*, 14 (1996), pp. 71–88, quotation at p. 71.

[6]   This is not to say that all travel writing or autobiography follows this pattern: as noted by Pasquali (p. 72), we should never forget that even when author, narrator and main character do coincide, in narrative terms they remain functionally distinct; at a more radical level, famous fakes, parodies, or ghost-written texts are all suitable examples of texts which deviate from the convention, yet still acknowledge it in doing so.

its voice, as well as its authoritative stance as guarantor of the authenticity and accuracy of the narration.[7]

Precisely because of their 'factual' nature and their supposed adherence to 'reality', both types of text are traditionally classified as minor or marginal genres, and accused of lacking the invention, creativity, and imagination which characterize highly 'literary' genres such as fiction. Yet both are also perfect candidates for the category of minor literature that Deleuze and Guattari have described as the only type of literature worth writing, due to the freedom it affords from canons, schools and similarly binding constraints.[8] If we take this line of thought, the fact that both travel writing and autobiography have been among the genres in which women writers first found their space can be seen not just as an instrument for the marginalization of their work, but also as an indication of the greater freedom and flexibility allowed by these genres.

The analysis of women's travel books and autobiographies, and of the links between them, may then allow for a closer look at the way in which women have constructed and performed their identity, firstly as individuals, and secondly as 'women writers'. Both genres are recognized, crucial locations for the formation of identity, whether we think of the identity of places (what used to be called the *genius loci*, but which we now tend to think of as the result of the relationship between observer and observed, between the traveller and his or her mapped territory), or the identity of people (which includes the individual self, as well as cultures and their collective formations). The way in which identity is constructed, modified, reproduced, inherited, and so on, is repeatedly re-enacted in the narrative representation of encounters, conflicts and transformations which lies at the core of travel writing and autobiography. This also means that such writings constitute a fertile ground for the exploration of contemporary identity theory, from the binary model of Self versus Other, to notions of nomadism, mestizaje or hybridity. The temptation in the case of 'minority writing' (as women's writing is often classed) is to imagine that, of necessity, all such work will be innovative, resistant, progressive in its ideological stance and its identity formations. Yet freedom to roam the world and meet 'the Other', minority status, or, indeed, female gender are not guarantees of innovative and progressive thinking – and a lot of travel writing is remarkably conservative, in terms both of its politics and its discourse. This is not so surprising if we think of who travels, and, most of all, who writes about travel and for whom. As pointed out by Sara Mills, women, too, bought into (or were brought into) the discourse of colonialism. Yet this simply amounts to a reminder that we cannot but

---

[7] Another genre which shares this focus is constituted by ethnographies; on this subject see Mary Louise Pratt, 'Fieldwork in Common Places', in *Writing Culture: The Poetics and Politics of Ethnography*, ed. James Clifford and George E. Marcus (Berkeley: University of California Press, 1986), pp. 27–50.

[8] See, in particular, Gilles Deleuze and Félix Guattari, 'Qu'est-ce qu'une littérature mineure?', in *Kafka: Pour une littérature mineure* (Paris: Minuit, 1975), pp. 29–50.

read women's texts, like all others, whether factual or fictional, within their context. In doing so we may well discover that, even in works which appear to conform to dominant discourses and traditional identity models, 'it is possible to trace the instability of individual statements'[9] – that is to say, the instability of discourses, and the instability of collective or personal identities.

Estella Canziani seems a particularly appropriate character to introduce at this point, because hers is a case in which traditional categories are constantly evoked only to be immediately challenged. She is eminently English, yet identifies with Italians and explains the 'peculiar traits' of her own life through her American ancestry. She is partly an explorer and a scientist, but also an artist, an inveterate traveller, and yet a recluse. Additionally, all we have in the case of Canziani are her self-portraits: no coherent contemporary account was left of her, no comprehensive study has been produced, and what little information there is about her turns out, on inspection, to be almost exclusively derived from her own writings.[10] This raises a series of questions relating to the truthfulness and reliability of travel accounts and autobiographies, to the faithfulness of representation and self-representation, and to the related questions of reticence and narrative construction. After all it is obvious – but easy to forget – that there is a difference between travelling and writing about travelling, just as there is a difference between living and writing one's autobiography. Both types of narrative are, among other things, retrospective summaries – what Pasquali has called an 'archéologie intime' – requiring a reorganization and reorientation of experience.[11] So when faced with Estella Canziani's accounts of her life and Self we need to decide, among other things, whether we trust her or not, whether we believe she is a faithful witness (of herself and others) or a liar. Yet her self-portraits are multiple, expressed in different forms, or even in different media – and it is in comparing these portraits, as well as in discovering the gaps they leave unfilled, that we may find a key to interpret Estella's reconstruction of herself.

---

[9]    Mills, *Discourses of Difference*, p. 197.

[10]    See, for instance: E. F. Coote Lake, 'Obituary: Estella Canziani', *Folklore*, 75 (1964), pp. 206–8; D. Zwar, 'Wanted: A Buyer for the House that Died with Miss Canziani', *The Evening Standard* (15 November 1967), p. 5; Marilena Cotellessa, 'Il paesaggio abruzzese agli inizi del secolo XX, secondo Estella Canziani: *Through the Apennines and the Lands of Abruzzo. Landscape and Peasant Life*', degree thesis, Università degli Studi 'G. d'Annunzio', Chieti (1998); Piercarlo Grimaldi, 'Piemonte, cent'anni dopo', in Estella Canziani, *Piemonte* (n.p.: Omega Edizioni, 1993), pp. iii–xvi; Andrea Livi, 'Introduzione', in Estella Canziani, *Attraverso gli Appennini e le terre degli Abruzzi*, trans. Alessandra Iommi (Fermo: Andrea Livi, 1996), pp. 5–8; Linda Strain, 'Louisa Starr and Estella Canziani: Mother and Daughter – The Lives of Two Women Artists', student project, University of Wolverhampton (1995).

[11]    An 'archaeology of the self' (my translation). Pasquali, 'Récit de voyage et autobiographie', p. 79.

## Female genealogies

Estella Canziani's autobiography, *Round About Three Palace Green* (1939), takes its title from the address of the London house, on the grounds of Kensington Palace, where Estella was born on 12 January 1887, lived for her entire life, and died on 23 August 1964. The title of the book, its dedication (to 'my parents', 'other kind friends', 'my maids' and 'animals and birds')[12] and the motivation given by Estella for writing it ('friends have pressed me to write some of my reminiscences, and to tell of this house', p. vii), seem to point to a still, motionless life, lived in the aura of the *genius loci* of the family home, and marked by sheltered privilege and eccentricity. Yet this is only part of the picture and, indeed, the other clear indication given in the preface of the volume points to the incomplete nature of the author's memories ('I regretfully had to decide: "No room: the book is already too large"', p. viii).

The entire volume is what the Italian writer Natalia Ginzburg would have called a *lessico famigliare*: a glossary of family words, life, things, people and memories.[13] The two main features of Canziani's narrative of her own life are its polyphony and its coverage – or lack of it. The text is a collage of family voices and images, both in the sense that much of the volume is devoted to Estella's family history and family life, and, more poignantly, because she intersperses her text with pages of her parents' letters to each other and to her, of their diaries, of their public speeches, and of letters and poems sent by friends to both her parents and herself. The voices at times become so overlapping that it is virtually impossible to tell whose words we are reading.

This is particularly true in the case of Estella and her mother, Louisa Starr, a painter from an American family who lived all her life in Britain and who was the first young girl to be admitted to the Royal Academy School of Art, to which Estella herself would later gain access. According to Estella's narration, Louisa was highly independent, and her radically modern attitude to women's education and work (which Louisa in turn is alleged to have inherited from her American mother) is a trait that Estella makes much of throughout her own autobiography. The picture we get of Louisa is that of a woman determined to be an artist first, and then, possibly, a wife (p. 29) and a mother (p. 73).

The identification with the mother and, in particular, with her career as an artist, is foregrounded by Estella from the very first chapter, 'Introducing the Family'. Describing Louisa, Estella notes that:

> She was nearly always called Stella, and seldom Louisa, which was her
> real name, and because of this, and because of her other name of Starr, she

---

[12]  Estella Canziani, 'Dedication', *Round About Three Palace Green* (London: Methuen, 1939), p. 5.

[13]  See Natalia Ginzburg, *Lessico famigliare* (1963), now in *Opere*, 2 vols (Milan: Mondadori, 1995), vol. 1, pp. 897–1134.

signed her pictures with a five-pointed star intertwined with an L for Louisa.
I was called Estella after my Italian grandmother, but this also included
Stella, after my mother. My own device is a star and a crescent for the C
of Canziani. (p. 3)

The parallels between the artistic education and career of mother and daughter are
drawn out in detail, from their early display of talent, to their unusual acceptance into
some of the best Art Schools in London, or, later, to their professional recognition
by the British arts establishment. In some instances, the parallels between the two
women and their experiences are so tightly narrated, and the two voices so closely
interwoven, that the reader could easily confuse the one with the other.

Louisa Starr married an Italian cousin, Francesco Canziani, who was a successful
engineer. Having left Italy to live in London with his wife, Francesco opened an
office in Lombard Street and became one of the most prominent figures in the
Italian colony in London between the end of the nineteenth century and his death
in 1931. He held positions as President of the Italian Chambers of Commerce and
of the Dante Alighieri Society in London, as well as being Italian Director of the
Society of Friends of Foreigners in Distress, and President of the Italian Benevolent
Society.[14] Francesco Canziani clearly never considered himself anything but Italian,
and although the Canzianis developed numerous connections in London, including
a number of famous artists such as Lawrence Alma-Tadema and Lord Leighton,
his elective circle was that of the Italian expatriates.

The fact that her father followed his wife to London is narrated by Estella as
another marker of the strength of character and modernity of her mother, and is
explicitly associated with Louisa's artistic profession. Yet the 'Italianness' of the
family and the importance of the 'Italian connection', both in London and in Italy
itself, are constantly underlined in *Round About Three Palace Green*, as is the
bilingual and bicultural education of the author. In the autobiography, Estella's
portrayal of her own identity shifts continuously between the various poles of her
origins and upbringing. Not only does she hold dual nationality all her life, but
'home' is 3 Palace Green in London, as well as 'my Italian home' or 'our Italian
village'. She even records an occasion in which, while travelling in the Swiss
Alps with her father, she was asked whether they were Italian or English: Estella's
answer was 'We are both' (p. 117). This kind of ambiguity is also reflected in the
way Estella is perceived – or sees herself as being perceived – by different social
groups. In her book, for instance, she is clearly English in the eyes of her British
artist friends; but when recalling a reception held at the Italian Embassy during
a visit to London by the Queen and Crown Prince of Italy, she notes that at the
moment of introductions 'I heard myself being announced as "our artist and writer,
of the Italian colony in London"' (p. 11).

---

[14]   See also Raffaello Piccoli, ed., *The Book of Italy* (London: Fisher Unwin,
1916).

Leaving aside the issue of nationality, the self-images which emerge from Estella's autobiography are, in succession: the ailing child who cannot undergo a proper school education because of her poor health and spends her time drawing and reading at home; the dutiful daughter who devotes her existence to fulfilling the dreams and expectations of her parents; the talented artist who is repeatedly told by famous friends how she has justified her presence in this world by painting beautiful pictures; the animal lover who communicates with birds of all species; the accidental expert, called to become a member of the Folk-Lore Society and other organizations but maintaining an air of naiveté throughout the process; the indefatigable worker performing charity and hospital duties during the First World War, and so on. Estella's travel experiences (especially those linked to Italy and to her identity as a travel writer) are, on the other hand, strictly contained, taking up a limited number of pages and consisting of often extremely sketchy accounts. In the autobiography the persona of the artist clearly dominates that of the traveller, even though Estella's reticence is thinly disguised by the repeated claim that many of the places she had visited had become, by the time she was writing *Round About Three Palace Green*, too well known to deserve full descriptions.[15]

Once both her parents were dead, Estella disappeared from her own canvas: she apparently 'lost her voice', and abandoned her writing, never to return to it. Louisa Starr died in 1909, Enrico Canziani in 1931, and Estella's autobiography (published in 1939) ends with the re-enactment of her father's death and the image of the two tombs on which Estella has arranged for bird-baths to be kept constantly filled with fresh water (p. 370). All that follows is a farewell to the readers, accompanied by the usual disclaimers – about her book being merely 'rambling', about not having consciously told any lies in it – but also by two revealing pieces of information: that the volume was written partly as 'the fulfilment of a resolve made in student days that I would write my mother's life'; and that the composite nature of the text was the result of her condensation of a 'tremendous collection' of 'family documents, notes, cuttings, letters and sketches' (pp. 370–1). To the question 'Shall I ever write another book?', Estella answers with an Italian '*Chi lo sa*?' ('who knows?', p. 371). In fact, she went on to live until 1964, but never wrote again for any public.

The plates included in the volume offer a similar kind of narrative, but also highlight further aspects of Estella's life and her relationship with others. She includes images of her house and of some of the collected treasures it contained; a mixture of her own and her mother's artwork, as well as a painting by her father; and photos of herself (mostly as a child) and of her parents, as well as of dear (and famous) friends. The choice of photos, in particular, points to an idyllic upper-middle-class family life at 3 Palace Green, in the shadow of Kensington Palace: they depict the family

---

[15] Estella's autobiography also contains a brief mention of her first trip abroad, to Holland, with her parents (pp. 112–13), and fuller accounts of a brief trip to Sweden (pp. 212–20), of repeated visits to Morocco (pp. 221–42) and of a journey to the Balearic Islands (pp. 339–68).

under the tree from which Queen Victoria was supposed to have picked mulberries (p. 50), or on their way to a fancy dress ball at the Walter Cranes', where they would be among prestigious friends (p. 160).[16] There are no photos, on the other hand, of Estella's travels, or, indeed, any images of Estella outside her house.

Significantly, while the final event in Estella's autobiography is her father's death, the last words in the book are left to her mother, in an appendix which reproduces extracts from a paper on 'Women's Work in Art' given by Louisa Starr in Chicago in 1893. The essay traces a genealogy of women artists, from ancient Egypt to Angelica Kauffmann, ending with an appeal to 'the women of my own nation' to 'rouse [...] to the fullness of your vocation as artists!'[17] This closing statement highlights the dominant image Estella selects for her autobiographical self: among the many facets she presents to the readers of *Round About Three Palace Green*, she foregrounds that of the modern woman artist, fully committed to her work as a painter and determined to be perceived as part of a (small) lineage of women who have adopted art as a fully fledged profession. It is this double marker, pointing to a modernity firmly rooted in established tradition, which is highlighted by Estella's identification with her mother. Louisa provided her daughter with a double female genealogy: via her own American parents (and, especially, her forward thinking and energetic mother) Louisa represented a direct link to the States, seen as the land of progress and of progressive thinking, not least in the area of gender; but Louisa's painting career also allowed her daughter to position herself within an uninterrupted lineage of women artists, guaranteeing Estella both symbolic stability and social acceptability within that most traditional of old European establishments, the English élite.

**Travels in fatherland**

Estella's travels tell a different story, they adopt different modes of representation, draw different connections, and present the reader with a different portrait of their author/narrator. Estella published three travel books: *Costumes, Traditions and Songs of Savoy* (1911), *Piedmont* (1913),[18] and *Through the Apennines and*

---

[16]  Next to the photo of Estella and her parents in disguise, there are images of Millais dressed as Dante, and of Eleanour Rohde (Estella's history teacher, friend and fellow traveller on her trip to the Balearic Islands) as a Roman peasant girl in traditional costume (p. 160).

[17]  'Appendix II', p. 396.

[18]  The English edition of *Piedmont* gives two authors, Estella Canziani and Eleanour Rohde, but when the book was translated into Italian in 1917, the name of Eleanour Rohde disappeared; see Estella Canziani, *Piemonte*, introd. Paolo Boselli, trans. E. Sacchi (Milan: Hoepli, 1917). In *Round About Three Palace Green* Canziani does not explain this change, noting only that because of the rush to get the book to the publishers, Rohde helped her to arrange some of the collected material and translated from the French some of the legends included in the volume (p. 190). *Through the Apennines and the Land of the Abruzzi* (Cambridge: W. Heffer and Sons, 1928).

*the Lands of the Abruzzi* (1928). Her first volume was successful enough for her publishers to put pressure on Canziani to write another one very quickly (and in fact the third book, devoted to the Abruzzi, would have been published much earlier than 1928 had the First World War not intervened). Her travel writing also gained Estella membership of the Royal Geographical Society, as well as a place on the council of the Folk-Lore Society, in whose journal she published a number of articles.[19]

All three travel books, and their genesis, have a number of characteristics in common. Estella travelled with her father, and to the land of her father (or, at most, to its borders: as if to reinforce the message, the Savoy book bears a dedication 'To their Majesties the King and Queen of Italy').[20] In her travels she also spoke mostly the language of her father (or some variation on it). Moreover, Enrico Canziani not only accompanied his daughter on her Italian journeys, but directly helped in gathering material and information for her volumes, and also in editing and revising them.[21] Father and daughter visited remote mountain areas, avoiding the traditional Grand Tour destinations, and *Piedmont*, for instance, opens with a double statement of Estella's ability to go beyond the beaten track. First, sketching a distant view of her destination, she observes that:

> Most people know the beautiful view one gets of the range of the Alps
> from Turin, but perhaps comparatively few have seen from the top of Milan
> cathedral, at sunrise, the plains of Lombardy and Piedmont, half veiled in
> mist, stretching away to the mountains. (p. 1)

Then, approaching her final target, Estella pointedly observes that 'every train on the Simplon line into Italy stops at Domodossola, and yet very few passengers alight there. But it is well worth doing so' (p. 3).

Her travel books represent Estella eschewing comfort and undergoing hardship, as well as undertaking strenuous exercise, while living in poor hygienic conditions among the local peasants. While all three books are written in the first person – alternating 'I' and 'we' – and offer a more or less chronological account of the Canzianis' journeys, Estella consciously avoids writing in diary style, or concentrating on her interior experience of places. Instead, she chooses to highlight the systematic nature of her work as a collector of folklore and ethnographic data,

---

[19] See *Round About Three Palace Green*, pp. 207–8; and Strain, 'Louisa Starr and Estella Canziani'. Details of Estella's articles in *Folk-lore* can be found in Grimaldi, 'Piemonte, cent'anni dopo'.

[20] *Piedmont* and *Through the Apennines and the Lands of the Abruzzi* also bear dedications, the first 'To her Majesty the Queen Mother of Italy, Margherita di Savoia', and the second to Estella's father 'untiring in his search everywhere for anything and everything which was of value for my purpose'. It is significant that Estella chose to write travel books only on Italy and the nearby Savoy, although she also travelled to Holland, Sweden, Morocco and the Balearic Islands, and left some traces of these trips in her autobiography (see note 15 above).

[21] See *Round About Three Palace Green*, pp. 189–90, and Grimaldi, 'Piemonte, cent'anni dopo'.

Figure 8. Estella Canziani, *Return from the Mountains*, watercolour and gouache on paper laid down on board, 203 mm × 150 mm, Birmingham Museums and Art Gallery (as published in *Piedmont*, facing p. 6).

often interrupting the narration to reproduce entire folk-songs and sequences of local legends and superstitions, all accompanied by, or rendered in, her own translation. The volumes are meant to offer a first-hand account of unknown, and fast-disappearing ways of life,[22] and the narrative sections of the books are often used to explain how Estella managed to gain the confidence of the locals and obtain detailed information about their habits and beliefs. In keeping with her character and her stated objectives, Estella was also an inveterate collector: she gathered hundreds of local artefacts and traditional costumes, which she dutifully carried back to England and stored for future memory.[23]

The same mechanisms are at work in the drawings and paintings which constitute an important part of each volume. All three travel books have subtitles which highlight the presence of illustrations,[24] and while this is far from being unusual in travel writing of this period, it is clear that the author's artistic qualifications are perceived as a selling point. However, the contrast between the pictures published in her travel books and Estella's British production is staggering. Her most famous commercial work, a watercolour entitled 'The Piper of Dreams' which was first exhibited at the Royal Academy in 1915, depicted an idyllic, imaginary fairyland, and went on to become one of the most consistent best-sellers in the Medici Society series.[25] Estella's travel sketches have very little in common with the rarefied atmosphere of 'The Piper', nor do they share the orientalizing narrative style of her mother's Italian sketches, such as 'The Eternal Door'.[26] In fact, in the travel books, Estella's sketches are not accompanied by Louisa's work, but are rather mixed (at times beyond recognition) with drawings produced by her father during

---

[22]   In the introduction to *Through the Apennines and the Lands of the Abruzzi*, for instance, Estella stresses the lack of previous studies devoted to the area: 'few travellers go to the Abruzzi, for they are wild in every sense of the word' (p. v). This was not, in fact, entirely true: a number of French, German and British travellers had not only visited the region but written about it; English visitors included W. Hamilton, Edward Lear, Keppel Craven, and Anne Macdonell. On travellers and travel writing in the Abruzzi see Franco Cercone and Maria Concetta Nicolai, eds, *English Travellers in Abruzzo, 1838–1914*, special issue of *D'Abruzzo* (Ortona: Regione Abruzzo Regional Tourist Authority, 1995); and Attilio Brilli, ed., *Abruzzo pittoresco: Viaggi dalla Marsica a Pescara, 1876–1918* (Città di Castello: Edimond, 1997).

[23]   A large part of her collection was later donated to the Birmingham Museums and Art Gallery, where it is still preserved. As I write, an exhibition is being planned for 2003–2004.

[24]   The extended titles are: *Costumes, Traditions and Songs of Savoy, Illustrated with Fifty Reproductions of Pictures by the Author and Many Line Drawings*; *Piedmont, with Fifty Reproductions of Pictures & Many Line Drawings by Estella Canziani*; *Through the Apennines and the Lands of the Abruzzi: Landscape and Peasant Life, described and drawn by Estella Canziani*.

[25]   See *Round About Three Palace Green*, pp. 203–20, and Strain, 'Louisa Starr and Estella Canziani'.

[26]   The painting is reproduced in *Round About Three Palace Green*, p. 268, and is part of the collection donated by Estella to the Birmingham Museums and Art Gallery.

their joint trips. Enrico's and Estella's sketches do include some landscapes, but the vast majority consists either of detailed depictions of minute aspects of everyday life, or of extremely colourful images of women, men and children in traditional regional costume, portrayed inside, or on the doorstep of, their homes, while going about their daily tasks, or engaged in preparations for religious celebrations. The style is reminiscent of the pre-Raphaelites, and of that Arts and Crafts movement of which Estella was an admirer and supporter. Her travel sketches strive for detail, characterization and realism – although the accompanying narrative makes it quite clear that Estella carefully staged every aspect of the scene, selecting or rejecting models in accordance with her own aesthetic criteria, dictating their attire, arranging posture and setting. Estella often describes the difficulties she had to overcome in order to find suitable models and convince them to sit for her; and she strives to impress upon the reader the fact that she would spare no energy in order to obtain what she felt was the best possible picture (or the best possible story).

The overall image which emerges from the three travel books is that of Estella Canziani as a strong, determined and experienced traveller, ready to take on any obstacle which stood between her and the 'reality' of a place. Her no-nonsense approach leaves no room for romantic stereotypes. In the preface to *Through the Apennines and the Lands of the Abruzzi*, for instance, she notes:

> Before setting out with my father I was warned that it was 'not safe' …
> it was 'all brigands', but I hope that the contents of my book will show
> that, however primitive and at times emotional the peasants may be, true
> kindliness, and not seldom unusual courtesy, are shown to sympathetic
> strangers. (p. 5)

Estella depicts herself as an acute observer whose scientific accuracy is, however, matched by an unusual ability to empathize with her objects. She presents herself as a serious student (if not a full blown scholar) of folklore, determined to use her artistic training for the benefit of her scientific goals, and to subject her inspiration to the rigid discipline of faithful and intricately detailed testimony. Yet in all her travel books this dedicated 'scientist' and professional artist portrays herself travelling with her father – and his benign figure looms large over everything she does: he incites her, accompanies her, supervises her, sits down to sketch side by side with her, even edits her books for her. Whenever Estella travelled without him, it was to places other than Italy, and she did not produce any extensive accounts of her trips.

Estella's travel books enact a complex performance of identity.[27] She is Italian, and hence an insider, when she needs to impress upon the locals (or, indeed, upon the reader) her ability to empathize with and understand her objects of study. She makes the most of her fluency in Italian, constantly reminding the reader of the advantage

---

[27]  On travel as performance see, in particular, Judith Adler, 'Travel as Performed Art', *American Journal of Sociology*, 84 (1989), pp. 1366–91; and Jill Steward, 'The Adventures of Miss Brown, Miss Jones and Miss Robinson: Tourist Writing and Tourist Performance from 1860 to 1914', *Journeys*, 1 (2000), pp. 36–58.

she has over other travellers, whose limited ability to communicate with local informers calls into question their thoroughness and reliability. She also scatters handfuls of Italian and dialectal expressions throughout her books, and frequently uses English archaisms such as 'thou' and 'thee' in the attempt to reproduce the original feeling of conversations with Italian peasants.[28] In practice, however, Estella seems to have had little real feeling for the complexity of local identities across the peninsula, and her grasp of dialect, when not of Italian itself, appears to have been erratic (her father, in fact, may have had an even greater role than Estella was prepared to admit in gathering and preparing material for her books).[29] Gender also becomes part of the traveller's performance: Estella foregrounds her female identity in order to gain access to women and to the sphere of private life; but she also strives to project a masculine persona, marked by endurance of hardship and professional determination. Whenever needed, she does not hesitate to revert to her English identity, and even to the established stereotype of the 'English woman-traveller', in order to explain her 'odd' habits (such as sleeping with the windows open, or wearing strange hats) and her 'scandalous' behaviour (travelling alone, approaching and talking to strangers, and so on), which clearly mark her as an outsider. Significantly, this tough, unfussy and daring self-image re-surfaces in Estella's autobiography when she deals with two areas traditionally associated with the breakdown of social conventions: travel (in particular to Morocco and the Balearic Islands) and war.[30] In all other cases, *Round About Three Palace Green* depicts her life as safely contained within the boundaries (both spatial and social) of domesticity and of the London art world.

## Conclusions: Estella and her matrix

If we take a final look at the profile of Estella's individual and cultural identity as it is performed in all her interconnected self-portraits, what we find is a multiple formation, which refuses to remain constrained into fixed categories. She is English: an upper-middle-class girl/woman who moves in artistic circles, carries

---

[28]   On this subject see Cotellessa, 'Il paesaggio abruzzese agli inizi del secolo XX, secondo Estella Canziani'.

[29]   Estella's mistakes in the transcription of dialect are noted, for instance, by the translator in a recent edition of *Through the Apennines and the Lands of the Abruzzi*; see E. Canziani, *Attraverso gli Appennini e le terre degli Abruzzi*, p. 4. Estella describes her transcription technique in her preface (p. vi), where she illustrates her attempts to approximate dialect through the use of spelling and accents. On the same page she explains that her translations were 'as literal as possible' since 'literalness will give a true impression of the atmosphere and naïveté of the original'.

[30]   For details of sections of *Round About Three Palace Green* devoted to Morocco and the Balearic Islands see note 15 above; on Estella's experiences during the war see pp. 263–71 and pp. 295–312.

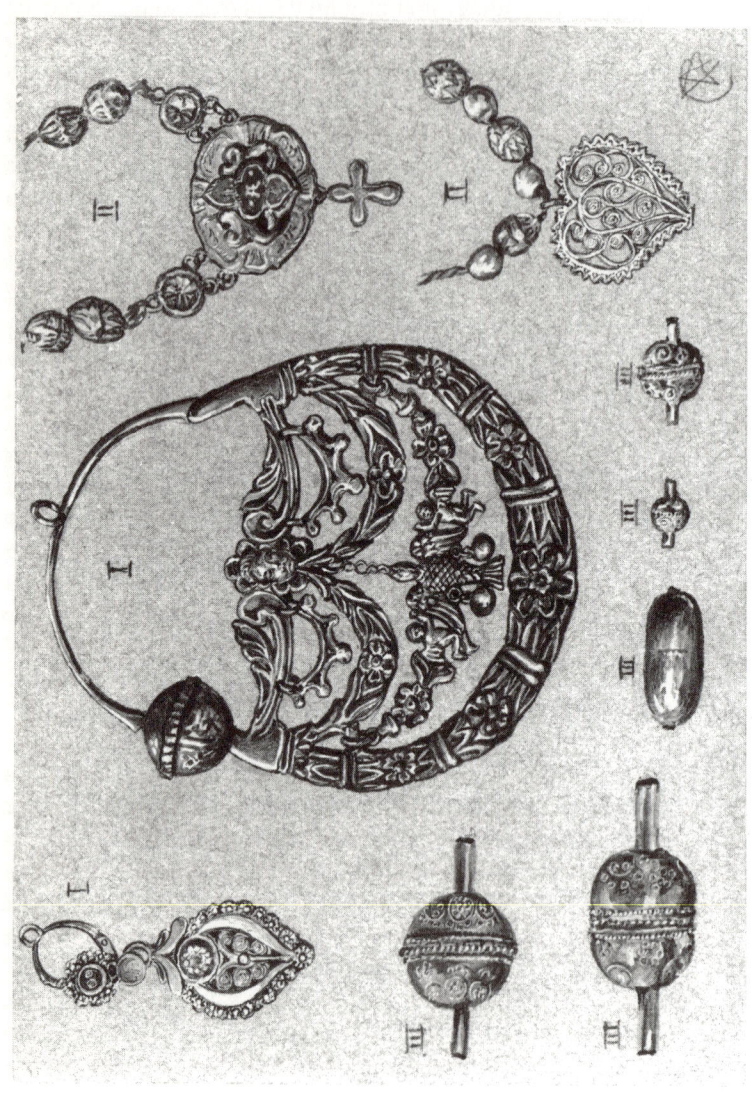

Figure 9. Estella Canziani, *Gold Jewellery*, pencil, watercolour and gouache on blue paper, 126 mm × 177 mm, Birmingham Museums and Art Gallery (as published in *Through the Apennines and the Lands of the Abruzzi*, facing p. 100).

out charitable work, has a disproportionate love of animals and an obsession with the royals (she would even have us believe that her first conscious memory as a child was of being held up by her nurse to see Queen Victoria during the Jubilee show of 1887 – aged 6 months).[31] The image of the ailing child and debilitated young woman who turns into a stubborn mountain traveller also fits with this English image of Estella, providing a suitable mix of conservative respectability and endearing eccentricity.

Yet Estella is also partly American. Through her mother, she appropriates the image of 'modern' woman, intent on maintaining her independence and establishing her professional reputation. And it is useful to remember that it is precisely when Estella is telling this kind of story about herself or her mother that the two voices mix, becoming virtually indistinguishable. Modernity, innovation, freedom and emancipation, all point to the well-established (if partial) image of the American – and of the American traveller to Europe – as the bearer of the new, at once dazzled by the wealth of history which Europe carries within itself and revolting against it in the name of modernity.[32]

Finally, Estella is also Italian: she repeatedly asserts her familiarity with the language, her appropriation of local customs and traditions, her knowledge and commitment to Italian history and politics. Yet Italy is definitely the land of the father, and as such a mixture of freedom, security, danger and constraints; a place where more is possible and yet less is permitted, which is also a good description of the space of travel. In Italy Estella can trek to remote villages, speak to strangers, befriend members of all social groups. Yet it is clear that her father protects (and controls) her movements, and that both her mother and Estella herself never really thought of living there, because they could not have coped with the strict rules regulating family life and the role of women within it.

England then comes to represent the symbolic locus of stability and reconciliation, of friendship, enclosed and intimate spaces, emancipation controlled by strict social convention, and self-contained professional personae. It is a space dominated by a matrilineal genealogy which finds its expression mainly in the retrospective self-construction of Estella's autobiography. Italy, on the other hand, is the space of travel, at once liberating and threatening, as becomes the land of the father (and it is worth remembering that Estella never travelled, or planned to travel, to the States). Estella journeyed to other destinations, at times on her own, but it was Italy that became the subject of her travel books, while significantly remaining marginal in her autobiography.

These portraits are clearly distinct, only partially overlapping, and not always easy to reconcile. We should not be tempted, however, to 'explain Estella away' by

---

[31]   The episode is recorded at the very start of *Round About Three Palace Green* (p. 1).

[32]   On such ambiguous attitudes see Susan Stewart, *Crimes of Writing: Problems in the Containment of Representation* (Oxford: Oxford University Press, 1991), pp. 173–205.

labelling her as 'hybrid', 'nomadic', or perhaps as an example of one of the many Freudian 'types' often associated with travellers.[33] Perhaps what could be applied to her is the idea of a matrix of identity: a composite network in which her various 'I's can find a disposition which does not exasperate internal contradictions.[34] Estella's travel books and autobiography represent her as essentially good at one thing: communicating – with her family, her friends, artists of all nationalities, the Italians in London and the Italians in Italy, the villagers of Piedmont and of the Abruzzi, her animals, and so on. And while some travellers appear to use travel (and travel writing) in order to shed their luggage and find themselves, Estella endlessly accumulates, annotates, and generally piles things precariously on top of each other, to try and reach the same goal. There is identity by depletion and identity by accretion, and Estella Canziani definitely belonged to the second category: to the collectors, the hoarders, the witnesses and ventriloquists of life. She attempted to construct, or maybe only to re-construct, her own identity through mechanisms of condensation and polyphony, and did so by performing a series of personae marked by often distinct gender, national and personality traits.

The two genres she selected for her writings, autobiography and travel books, allowed Estella to keep her different personae and their respective territories at least partly distinct. It was the shared formal features of these genres – their retrospective quality, their factual presuppositions and the centrality of the author's/ narrator's voice within them – which meant that Estella could offer multiple parallel performances of herself, hoping to achieve complementarity rather than mere repetition or glaring contradiction. The final paradox in her performance is to be found, fittingly, in the response of her audiences: while in Britain any interest in Estella has concentrated on her career as an artist and, consequently, on her autobiography as a source of information about her and her milieu, in Italy it is her travel books which receive attention, usually at regional level, in the areas which she elected as the object of her books. There, she has become 'just another foreign writer', whose work can be searched for clues to a pre-industrial past now often constructed as idyllic, exhibited in the struggle for local prestige and tourist income, or, lately, even brandished as a weapon in support of nostalgic regionalist

---

[33] The temptation is there, and although Freudian interpretations seem to be more popular when dealing with male travellers, Susan Stewart's connection of travel with the incest prohibition could easily be applied to Estella's case; see Stewart, *Crimes of Writing*, pp. 173–84.

[34] This type of identity formation has been described as feminine (though not only applicable to women) and as 'an encounter in which partial subjects co-emerge and co-fade', characterized by elements which precede the formation of subjectivity, the establishment of the ego in Freudian terms: 'if the *matrix* points to *what is not reducible to one* and what does not "yearn" for the *one*, then this is because it never was One'; see Bracha Lichtenberg-Ettinger, 'The Becoming Threshold of Matrixial Borderlines', in George Robertson *et al.*, eds, *Travellers' Tales: Narratives of Home and Displacement* (London: Routledge, 1994), pp. 41, 49.

discourses. The introductions to recent Italian editions of *Piedmont* and *Through the Apennines and the Lands of the Abruzzi* are a case in point: in 'Piemonte, cent'anni dopo', Grimaldi calls Canziani's book a pioneering study and identifies it as an important contribution to contemporary attempts to revive local culture (and politics) as a form of resistance to the pressures of globalization;[35] while in his 'Introduzione' to *Attraverso gli Appennini e le terre degli Abruzzi*,[36] Livi goes as far as connecting the relevance of Canziani's book for today's Abruzzesi to the need for lasting physical contact between culturally homogeneous groups and their territory, as embodied in the call for administrative autonomy raised by regionalist political movements across Europe. A few decades after her death, Canziani, her genre-shifting tales, her complex and carefully constructed identities have thus been appropriated and simplified by new audiences, whose rigid application of the travel writing label and dominant local interest may well end up erasing Estella from her own pages.

---

[35]  Grimaldi, 'Piemonte, cent'anni dopo', p. v.
[36]  Livi, 'Introduzione', pp. 7–8.

Chapter 10

# Varieties of Nostalgia in Contemporary Travel Writing

## Patrick Holland and Graham Huggan

It is a truism to say that travel writing, like travel itself, is generated by nostalgia. As Paul Fussell says in his study *Abroad* (1980) – himself succumbing to nostalgia – '[a] travel book, at its purest, is addressed to those who do not plan to follow the traveler at all, but who require the exotic anomalies, wonders, and scandals of the literary form *romance* which their own place or time cannot entirely supply'.[1] Contemporary travel writers, it might be argued, are well aware of their nostalgic leanings and ironize these in 'belated' narratives that undercut the very anachronisms they cultivate.[2] It might equally be argued, though, that such writers' self-ironization provides an alibi for their own indulgences and for the recuperation of a genre that capitalizes on being defiantly out of date.[3] The nostalgic urge of travel writing derives in part from its reaction against those modernizing forces that are felt to compromise the specificity and/or authenticity of the world's different cultures. Travel writing serves, in this sense, to protect the idea of cultural diversity from the threat of homogenization and the undifferentiated sweep of 'global culture'. Paradoxically, globalization, mediated through the latest communications technologies, has helped create *new* forms of nostalgia, not so much for the past as for the present and the future.[4] A further paradox is that the cultural diversity so much loved and celebrated by Western travel writers tends to be relayed through

---

[1] Paul Fussell, *Abroad: British Literary Traveling Between the Wars* (New York: Oxford University Press, 1980), p. 203 (Fussell's italics). Fussell's point is of course debatable. It could be argued, on the contrary, that the current boom in travel writing is a function of the expansion of the tourist industry, and that the reason several people read travel books is to compare the writer's experiences with their own. Fussell's own nostalgic tendencies are reconfirmed in the distinction – much loved by travel writers themselves – between the 'traditional' adventure-seeking traveller and the lazy modern tourist. The distinction is, at best, specious, although ironically it still proves useful for a tourist industry that takes full advantage of such nostalgic travel myths. For a detailed treatment of the links between nostalgia and tourism, see John Frow, 'Tourism and the Semiotics of Nostalgia', *October* (Fall 1990), pp. 127–54.

[2] See Ali Behdad, *Belated Travelers: Orientalism in the Age of Colonial Dissolution* (Durham: Duke University Press, 1994).

[3] See Patrick Holland and Graham Huggan, *Tourists with Typewriters: Critical Reflections on Contemporary Travel Writing* (Ann Arbor: University of Michigan Press, 1998), especially chapter 1.

[4] See Fredric Jameson, *Postmodernism, or, the Cultural Logic of Late Capitalism* (Durham: Duke University Press, 1991) for different forms of 'postmodern nostalgia'.

a shared vocabulary of cliché and stereotype that freezes 'other' (non-Western) cultures in time and place. The nostalgia for more exciting times when the world was 'truly different' might thus be seen as a function of the desire to keep it more or less the same. Nostalgia is the mark of travel writing's cultural complacency and of the power differentials that have historically enabled travel, and the writing that follows upon it, to take place. Yet it is also the mark of a genre that acknowledges the impossibility of its own controlling gestures, that ironically seeks reassurance through the appeal to an invented past. Travel writers' reminiscences are often, though by no means always, wilfully fabricated, put into the service of times and places that are brought alive through narrative – *that never existed*. As Susan Stewart, among others, has recognized, nostalgia has an anti-referential function; it engenders a process that is always ideological insofar as

> the past it seeks has never existed except as narrative, and hence, always absent, that past continually threatens to reproduce itself as a felt lack. Hostile to history and its invisible longings, and yet longing for an impossibly pure context of lived experience at a place of origin, nostalgia wears a distinctly utopian face, a face that turns toward a future past, a past which has only ideological reality.[5]

Hence the irony of a genre that seeks to persuade us of its referential validity while simultaneously relying on a mode – nostalgia – that turns its back on the referentiality of the experienced past.

This essay seeks to probe these ironies by looking at some different forms of nostalgia that circulate in contemporary travel writing, from the end of the Second World War to the present day. All of these forms are related, directly or indirectly, to what the anthropologist Renato Rosaldo has called 'imperialist nostalgia'. Imperialist nostalgia, for Rosaldo, is not the same as the commemorative mourning of Empire, even though such mourning rituals – albeit in self-parodic form – are much in evidence in the work of several contemporary British travel writers. Rather, it describes the variety of elegiac modes of perception through which the West mourns the passing of a world that it itself has irrevocably altered.[6] As Rosaldo explains sardonically:

> Imperialist nostalgia revolves around a paradox: A person kills somebody, and then mourns the victim. In more attenuated form, someone deliberately alters a form of life, and then regrets that things have not remained as they were prior to the intervention. At one more remove, people destroy their environment, and then they worship nature. In any of its versions, imperialist nostalgia uses the pose of 'innocent yearning' both to capture people's imaginations and to conceal its complicity with often brutal domination.[7]

---

5    Susan Stewart, *On Longing: Narratives of the Miniature, the Gigantic, the Souvenir, the Collection* (Baltimore: Johns Hopkins University Press, 1984), p. 136.
6    See Holland and Huggan, *Tourists with Typewriters*, p. 29.
7    Renato Rosaldo, *Culture and Truth: The Remaking of Social Analysis* [1989] (London: Routledge, 1993), pp. 69–70.

Imperialist nostalgia is a staple of contemporary travel writing, whether in blatantly colonial forms such as 'Conradian atavism' or 'Raj revival' or in displaced, often pastoral, forms such as the type of environmentally-conscious travelogue that wishes to distinguish itself from invasive tourism.[8] This suggests the view of travel writing, articulated by several critics, as a vehicle for the transmission and consolidation of 'colonial discourse'.[9] As these critics recognize, however, travel writing remains a useful medium for the interrogation of ethnocentric arrogance and for the displacement or estrangement of received ideas and wisdoms about 'other' cultures. Nostalgia holds the balance between these conflicting ideological purposes: first, by displacing the desire for domination and conquest onto 'benign' mythologies of loss or remembered pleasure; and second, by allowing for a critical reading of these self-serving mythologies and mechanisms of displacement.

One of the tropes through which nostalgia is filtered in contemporary – especially British – travel writing is the self-ironic figure of 'the English gentleman'. Hopelessly behind the times, perversely guarding a code of honourable conduct long since superseded, the latter-day English gentleman-explorer becomes the figure for a genre itself outmoded, a genre of adventure writing that simultaneously laments and celebrates its own imagined obsolescence.[10] A good example of the trope in action is in the narratives of the popular English travel writer Eric Newby, one of an older generation of postwar writers whose work clearly harks back to Evelyn Waugh and Robert Byron.[11] Newby, the author of more than a dozen commercially

---

[8]    On 'Conradian atavism', see Rob Nixon, 'Preparations for Travel: The Naipaul Brothers' Conradian Atavism', *Research in African Literatures*, 22 (1991), pp. 177–90; on 'Raj revival' see Salman Rushdie, 'Outside the Whale', in his *Imaginary Homelands: Essays and Criticism 1981–1991* (London: Granta, 1991), pp. 87–101; on the environmentally-conscious travelogue and its intersections with pastoral and nature writing, see Holland and Huggan, *Tourists with Typewriters*, chapter 4.

[9]    See Dennis Porter, *Haunted Journeys: Desire and Transgression in European Travel Writing* (New Jersey: Princeton University Press, 1991); Sara Mills, *Discourses of Difference: An Analysis of Women's Travel Writing and Colonialism* (New York: Routledge, 1991); Mary Louise Pratt, *Imperial Eyes: Travel Writing and Transculturation* (London: Routledge, 1992); David Spurr, *The Rhetoric of Empire: Colonial Discourse in Journalism, Travel Writing, and Imperial Administration* (Durham: Duke University Press, 1993); Inderpal Grewal, *Home and Harem: Nation, Gender, Empire, and the Cultures of Travel* (Durham: Duke University Press, 1996); and Steve Clark, ed., *Travel Writing and Empire: Postcolonial Theory in Transit* (London: Zed, 1999).

[10]   For a more detailed treatment of the Englishman gentleman-adventurer and his reincarnation in contemporary travel writing, see Holland and Huggan, *Tourists with Typewriters*, chapter 1.

[11]   In the Preface to Eric Newby's *A Short Walk in the Hindu Kush* (London: Penguin, 1958), Evelyn Waugh locates him fairly and squarely within a 'whimsical tradition' of British (specifically, English) travel writing which takes delight in 'the foreignness of Foreigners', and which has little truck with the new breed of English travellers or, as Waugh describes them, '(dammit) lower types' (Newby, *A Short Walk*, p. 12). Nostalgia is allied here, as it is in Newby's work, with a thoroughgoing class consciousness.

successful travelogues, likes to style himself as a latter-day gentleman in an era when gentlemanliness has obviously lost both its political effectiveness and its moral force.[12] Simon Raven sums up the plight of the anachronistic gentleman: 'Gentlemen can only now behave as such, or be tolerated as such, in circumstances that are manifestly contrived or unreal.'[13] This atmosphere of enhanced affectation is exploited to maximum comic effect in narratives such as Newby's *A Short Walk in the Hindu Kush* (1958), an acclaimed post-Byronic escapade in which gentlemanly theatrics come to assume the proportions of full-blown farce. *A Short Walk*, the ironically-titled rendering of Newby's strenuous expedition into Kipling country (any resemblance between Newby's Nuristan and Carnehan and Dravot's mountain kingdom being, however, entirely intentional), is an example of what might facetiously be called 'the 100-years-too-late' school of travel writing.[14] For it is not just that Newby is indebted to Kipling, among other late nineteenth-century adventure writers, but that he actively seeks to emulate the self-defeating heroics of Kipling's characters – with similarly disastrous results. In works like this, travel writing's more-or-less plausible 'factual' record of personal experience is assimilated to the contrivances of nostalgic literary myth. Nostalgia, in Newby's text, involves the longing for a *literary* fantasy embodied in Kipling's honorifics and self-aggrandizing, if also potentially self-destructive, imperial capers. The feebly comic rehearsal of Kipling's already self-parodic imperial adventures merely reconfirms the sense of the text's, as of its author's, belatedness. *A Short Walk* inhabits the ruins of Kipling's self-consciously juvenile fantasies of the British Orient: ruins literalized in the description of the consulate building at Meshed, which was

> lost and forgotten; arcades of Corinthian columns supported an upper balcony, itself collapsing. The house was shaded by great trees, planted perhaps a century ago, now at their most magnificent. Behind barred windows were the big green safes with combination locks in the confidential registry.[15]

---

[12]   See David Castronovo, *The English Gentleman: Images and Ideals in Literature and Society* (New York: Ungar, 1987), p. 144.

[13]   Quoted in Castronovo, *The English Gentleman*, p. 144; see also Holland and Huggan, *Tourists with Typewriters*, p. 29.

[14]   See Eric Newby, *A Traveller's Life* (London: Pan, 1982), pp. 161–2, where a moment serves to cement this membership. On a visit to the rapidly modernizing city of Istanbul in the fifties, Newby casts his thoughts back to the grandeur of nineteenth-century Constantinople. The comparison is, as one might expect, weighed in favour of the latter; Newby is left to mourn the fact that he has been born 'a hundred years too late'. (See also Holland and Huggan, *Tourists with Typewriters*, p. 34.) Other active members of the school might include Redmond O'Hanlon and several other writers for *Granta* magazine; see Charles Sugnet, 'Vile Bodies, Vile Places: Travelling with *Granta*', *Transition*, 51 (1991), pp. 70–85.

[15]   Eric Newby, *A Short Walk*, p. 57.

Newby asks his pukka companion Carless how the consulate's former occupants might have managed to get the massive safes into the building; to which Carless replies: 'In the days of the Raj you could do anything.'[16]

This tongue-in-cheek Orientalism is typical of Newby's travelogue, which oscillates between the pre-emptive gesture toward ironic self-entrapment and the traveller-writer's notorious propensity to self-exoneration – to 'escape'. Nowhere is this clearer than in an incident in Tehran when Newby and Carless, after having accidentally run over and killed an unidentified peasant, are hauled before the local judiciary and ominously charged with murder. However, they are eventually acquitted, the Prosecutor deciding that because '[they had] all been so gentlemanly … he [would] not proceed'.[17] So the joke, it appears, is on us: gentlemanliness, for much of the text a source of self-inflicted ridicule, turns out in the end to be a godsend, as nostalgia's victims become its beneficiaries. Whimsy such as this no doubt appeals to Newby's (mostly white middle-class) readers while deflecting attention away from the larger, less savoury implications of his work. The heady days of the Raj might be over but, as self-consciously anachronistic travelogues such as *A Short Walk* indicate, the conventions of travel narrative may be deployed to pretend *as if they had never ended*.

A similar point is made in Charles Sugnet's diatribe against the *Granta* school of travel writers, whose numbers include Eric Newby's younger compatriots Redmond O'Hanlon and the late Bruce Chatwin. As Sugnet suggests, the demise of the British Empire has spawned a plethora of travel narratives that trade in colonial nostalgia; not, however, as a means of transporting their writers and, by extension, their readers back into the past – real or imagined – but rather as a means by which they might absolve themselves of the consequences of the present. The end of Empire, argues Sugnet, has actually made things easier for travel writers, allowing them to 'suppress the sense that [they] are connected by lines of responsibility to the events they report'.[18] This point is debatable insofar as it ignores the work of self-irony in contemporary travel writing. Self-irony, as previously mentioned, functions as critique but also as alibi, just as the parody of earlier, now apparently vitiated, forms of travel and travelogue may provide a tacit rationale for their self-perpetuation. To suggest, however, that travel writers – as they no doubt sometimes are – are wilfully irresponsible in their behaviour may be to underestimate their capacity to test the limits of responsibility in their work. For example, Newby's writing, for all its self-indulgent high jinks and good-ol'-boy frivolity, might be seen among other things as a 'serious' examination of the double-edged nature of nostalgia: its capacity to reveal, not just fantasies of 'historical' retrieval, but also traces of the ideological processes through which such fantasies are invoked and expressed.

---

[16] Newby, *A Short Walk*, p. 57; see also Holland and Huggan, *Tourists with Typewriters*, p. 34.

[17] Newby, *A Short Walk*, p. 86.

[18] Sugnet, 'Vile Bodies, Vile Places', p. 85.

These traces persist in the work of O'Hanlon and the more sophisticated Chatwin, among other contemporary travel writers. Travel writing, it bears reminding, is both an agent of deception and a means by which deception – of which nostalgia is just one form – may be analysed and reassessed. Even so, it is difficult not to agree with Sugnet that there is indeed a 'curious fusion of the 1880s and 1980s [that keeps the *Granta* writers, and before them Newby] afloat over the … globe, their luggage filled with portable shards of colonial discourse'.[19]

Bruce Chatwin is arguably the writer who connects Newby to the *Granta* crowd, certainly packing his luggage with more than a few 'portable shards of colonial discourse', but with a flair and style that make it seem wrong to align Chatwin with Newby. Nevertheless, on occasion he can perform with equal crudity. For example, at least twice he uses the informal imperial argot, referring on one occasion to 'the Beja in the Eastern Sudan, the Fuzzy-Wuzzies of Kipling', and on another to 'the country of the Danakils, first cousins of Kipling's fuzzy-wuzzies'.[20] Tellingly, the second usage occurs in an article, 'Abel the Nomad', reviewing Wilfred Thesiger's memoir *Desert, Marsh and Mountains*.[21] In the review Chatwin affiliates himself with an already legendary figure who indexed a number of constituent features making up that well-worn nostalgic tradition, including Eastern nomadism, veneration of the eccentric British adventurer-writer, and amateur – if not dilettantish – learning. Chatwin, though, certainly differs from Newby in largely staying away from self-irony, at least in its more obvious forms. No less at work, however, is the large fantasy of threatened wandering societies to which Chatwin devoted many pages, published and unpublished, which romantically motivated his own 'anatomy of restlessness', and which he finally embodied in that wandering discourse *The Songlines* (1987).[22] Anti-imperial, at least on the surface, *The Songlines* has fuelled a not insignificant fad for nomadism, inviting readers now to enter nostalgically into yet another vanishing world, now to romanticize – and perhaps enact – the individual nomadic tour.[23]

---

[19]  Sugnet, 'Vile Bodies, Vile Places', p. 85.

[20]  Bruce Chatwin, 'Letter to Tom Maschler', in *Anatomy of Restlessness: Uncollected Writings*, ed. Jan Borm and Matthew Graves (London: Picador, 1997), p. 80; and 'Abel the Nomad', *Anatomy of Restlessness*, p. 110.

[21]  Wilfred Thesiger, *Desert, Marsh and Mountains* (London: Collins, 1979).

[22]  *Anatomy of Restlessness*, the title of Chatwin's posthumously edited writings, comes from a phrase in a memoir in that collection, 'I Always Wanted to Go to Patagonia', p. 12. Two pieces in *Anatomy of Restlessness* relate directly to Chatwin's plan to write a treatise on nomadism: the 'Letter to Tom Maschler' dated 29 February 1969, pp. 75–84, and 'The Nomadic Alternative', a contribution to the catalogue for an exhibition of nomad artwork held in New York in 1970, pp. 85–99. While *The Songlines* (New York: Viking Penguin, 1987) established Chatwin's popularity as a travel writer and as an 'authority' on nomadism, leading more than one travel writer to invoke the nomad figure as self-identity, the earlier essays on nomadism clearly indicate a very different project from that executed in *The Songlines*.

[23]  Some recent writers have begun to express scepticism about the cult of nomadism, which is still flourishing. See, for example, Rebecca Solnit, *A Book of Migrations: Some Passages in Ireland* (London: Verso, 1997). Not mentioning Chatwin, Solnit comments on an

In his review of the Thesiger memoir, Chatwin profiles a figure he both admires and distances himself from. Chatwin praises his style, that of one who 'has so absorbed the temper of the heroic world that his descriptions of raids, blood-feuds and reconciliations give his prose the character of an ancient epic or saga'.[24] He admires Thesiger's many expeditions in Sudan, in the Empty Quarter, in the marshes of southern Iraq and with the Bakhtiari, Kurds, and Kaffirs. He sympathizes with Thesiger's distress at 'find[ing] his old Bedu friends driving around in cars and seduced' by the West.[25] He summarizes the eccentric imperial boyhood of one who 'was born to travel', whose favourite reading was *Jock of the Bushveld*, 'that child's bible of the British Empire',[26] and whose father was British Minister in Addis Ababa. He praises Thesiger for not being 'an armchair anthropologist' but a man who 'knows what he is talking about' from experience.[27] Yet, retaining his own authority over the nomadic experience, Chatwin concludes that Thesiger was traveller, not nomad, as he defines the 'nomad proper':

> a herdsman who moves his property through a sequence of pastures. He is tied to a most rigorous time-table and committed to the increase of his herds and his sons. It is no accident that such words as 'stock,' 'capital,' 'pecuniary,' and even 'stealing' come from the pastoral world.[28]

Here, even as Chatwin rightly – if not characteristically – insists on the materiality of the life of nomadic cultures, he prepares a space for nostalgia: the accumulative pressures of nomadic life will, sooner or later, seduce its practitioners into settled society.

Granted Chatwin's concessions to a historicized, material reckoning of nomadic practices, ultimately his own work foregrounds the romance of individual wanderers whether, like Wilfred Thesiger, belated imperialists or, like his hero Robert Byron, dilettante cultural and aesthetic rebels.[29] Chatwin, astutely noting Thesiger's status as traveller rather than nomad, is measured in his appreciation of the English Arabist. His appreciation of the ill-fated Byron, by contrast, is beyond measure. In his Byron essay, Chatwin adroitly claims the earlier traveller as his own precursor, in discursive moves that suggest connections between the nomad persona, the

---

'enormous contemporary enthusiasm for nomads', but regards the 'idea that nomads embody on a mass scale the freedom of the solitary traveler, that romantic figure silhouetted against an exotic landscape like the individualist tree' as 'dubious' (p. 159). To be fair, Chatwin's earlier work on nomadism is serious, complex and occasionally learned.

24 Chatwin, *Anatomy of Restlessness*, p. 111.
25 Chatwin, *Anatomy of Restlessness*, p. 110.
26 Chatwin, *Anatomy of Restlessness*, p. 109.
27 Chatwin, *Anatomy of Restlessness*, p. 110.
28 Chatwin, *Anatomy of Restlessness*, p. 113.
29 See Bruce Chatwin, Introduction to Robert Byron, *The Road to Oxiana* [1937] (London: Picador, 1994), pp. xi–xx. 'Among the targets of Byron's abuse', declares Chatwin, 'were the Catholic (as opposed to the Orthodox) Church; the art of Classical Greece; the paintings of Rembrandt; [and] Shakespeare' (p. xi).

aesthete-dandy and the dilettante.[30] Anyone who reads around the travel books of
the 1930s must, in the end,

> conclude that Byron's *The Road to Oxiana* is the masterpiece. Byron was a
> gentleman, a scholar and an aesthete, who drowned in 1941 when his ship
> to West Africa was torpedoed. (p. xi)

Incorporating such personae, Chatwin establishes Byron as the nonpareil of
privileged British traveller-writers of the interwar years and, by extension, himself as
the nonpareil postwar traveller. In his Introduction to *The Road to Oxiana*, Chatwin
candidly invites his readers to admire his own admiring parody of Byron's style,
offering his own notebook entry for 5 July 1962 for comparison with Byron's entry
of 21 September 1933.[31] Offering the entry for inspection, Chatwin highlights the
traveller's double – and contradictory – warrant of spontaneity and imitation. It
comes as no surprise, then, that Chatwin writes 'as a partisan, not as a critic'; nor
that he will 'raise [*The Road to Oxiana*] to the status of "sacred text"'.[32]

In the concluding paragraph of his 'Introduction', Chatwin – in a move that
capitalizes on Evelyn Waugh's notorious 'ubi sunt' gesture[33] – again assimilates
Byron to his own project, while also sweeping their shared terrain into an
extraordinary nostalgic peroration:

> We shall not lie on our backs at the Red Castle and watch the vultures
> wheeling over the valley where they killed the grandson of Ghenghiz. We
> will not read Babur's Memoirs in his garden at Istalif and see the blind
> man smelling his way around the rose bushes. Or sit in the Peace of Islam
> with the beggars of Gazar Gagh. We will not stand on the Buddha's head at
> Bamiyam, upright in his niche like a whale in a dry-dock. We will not sleep
> in the nomad tent, or scale the Minaret of Jam. And we shall lose the tastes
> – the hot, coarse, bitter bread; the green tea flavoured with cardomoms; the
> grapes we cooled in the snow-melt; and the nuts and dried mulberries we
> munched for altitude sickness.[34]

Surely an audacious rhetorical gesture, but one that has apparently proven successful
in lodging both Byron and Chatwin in a 'pantheon' of the foremost (Western)
travel writers.

---

[30]   See, for example, the first paragraph of his Introduction.

[31]   In Afghanistan, Chatwin followed Byron's footsteps, and imitates his diary
entries. The chief feature of the two entries Chatwin invites his readers to compare is a list
of objects located in the rooms of their (different) hosts. Chatwin, however, unhesitatingly
declares most of the items of his visited room fakes – something he was noted for at
Sotheby's – while Byron was less certainly dismissive. See Robert Byron, *The Road to
Oxiana*, Chatwin's Introduction, p. xiii and Byron's text, p. 39.

[32]   Chatwin, Introduction to Byron, *Road*, p. xi.

[33]   See Evelyn Waugh, *When the Going Was Good* (London: Duckworth, 1946), p.
11: 'Never again shall we land on foreign soil with letter of credit and passport ... and feel the
world wide open to us'; and Holland and Huggan, *Tourists with Typewriters*, Introduction.

[34]   Chatwin, Introduction to Byron, *Road*, p. xx.

Chatwin's Byron 'Introduction' confirms that, in his writing, nostalgia becomes the lens through which different places and people acquire *aesthetic* value: either as 'historical' curios, dislodged from their material cultural context, or as collector's items, treasured less for their beauty than for their capacity to generate a seemingly endless supply of legends and myths.[35] Nostalgia, in Chatwin's narratives, often co-exists with a kind of mysticism, a sentimental belief that the world, for all its eye-catching diversity, is somehow united – or was once united – in the spiritual kinship of different things. The idea of purity, so central to nostalgia, appears in a variety of contemporary 'shamanic' travelogues which, less playful than Chatwin's, attempt to distil the disparateness of experience into a unified body of spiritual myths. These travelogues – and they are legion – are variants on the paradigm of the travel narrative as surrogate pilgrimage, a paradigm that has unsurprisingly reappeared with renewed vigour at the millennial turn.[36] One form the paradigm takes is the New Age narrative of spiritual reawakening; another, the ecological parable on the need to 'reconnect' with threatened nature. These forms are brought together in mass-market travelogues such as Marlo Morgan's *Mutant Message Down Under* (1994),[37] which tap into a vaguely intuited, but astutely commodified, 'indigenous spirituality' by co-opting elements of indigenous beliefs and value-systems into the author's personal quest. What often emerges in vehicles like these is a kind of bargain-basement mysticism that capitalizes on the nostalgia for a 'primitive' civilization, of great spiritual worth, perceived as standing on the brink of 'extinction'. Needless to say, such nostalgic yearning tends to fly in the face of historical realities; rather, the invocation of loss or disappearance, often touched by romantic liberal-humanist sympathies, tends to mask the historical role played by (Western) agents of destruction – a classic case, in other words, of Rosaldo's imperialist nostalgia.[38]

An earlier and more sophisticated example of this type of 'narrative of disappearance' is Laurens Van der Post's acclaimed *The Lost World of the Kalahari* (1958).[39] The narrative takes its author, a prototypical New Age guru-figure, into the South African Kalahari desert in search of the Bushmen (the ethnic term now used is Khoi-san), whose endangered status acts as a collective symbol for a decline in Western civilization. The following passage gives an indication of

---

[35] On Chatwin as traveller-collector, see Holland and Huggan, *Tourists with Typewriters*, chapter 1.

[36] On the travelogue as surrogate pilgrimage, see Eric Leed, *The Mind of the Traveler: From Gilgamesh to Global Tourism* (New York: Basic Books, 1991); on some (post)modern variants, see Holland and Huggan, *Tourists with Typewriters*, chapter 4.

[37] Marlo Morgan, *Mutant Message Down Under* (New York: HarperCollins, 1994).

[38] For a fuller discussion of 'narratives of disappearance', see Holland and Huggan, *Tourists with Typewriters*, chapter 4.

[39] Laurens Van der Post, *The Lost World of the Kalahari* (New York: Morrow, 1958).

the narrative's misplaced nostalgic fervour, which uses the romantic vision of a putatively 'vanishing' people to wax philosophical on the degeneration of spiritual values in Western culture:

> With our twentieth-century selves we have forgotten the importance of being truly and openly primitive. We have forgotten the art of our legitimate beginnings. We no longer know how to close the gap between the far past and the immediate present in ourselves, it seems, as the lungs need air and the body food and water; yet we can only achieve it by a slinking, often back-door entrance. I thought finally that of all the nostalgias that haunt the human heart the greatest of them all, for me, is an everlasting longing to bring what is youngest home to what is oldest, in us all.[40]

The language here is achingly condescending and anachronistic, merely advertising the contradictions in Van der Post's portrayal of the Bushmen as, on the one hand, 'survivor-victims of European imperialism' and, on the other, 'primal beings virtually untouched by history'.[41] What is interesting in works such as *The Lost World of the Kalahari*, however, is the enduring usefulness for travel writing of patently outdated modes of ethnographic inquiry and analysis (the idea of 'primitive' culture; the trope of 'disappearance'; the notion that Western writer-observers, in salvaging the values of 'other' cultures, might somehow rescue their own; and so on).[42] These modes have long since been recognized by anthropologists themselves as tacitly imperialist. Why then do they re-emerge in ecologically-conscious forms of travel writing? In part, this has to do with a coming together in the genre as a whole of amateur and romantic sensibilities. Amateurism and anachronism are the twin prongs of a genre that frequently capitalizes on the fear of its own obsolescence; and which is given to project this fear onto societies, cultures, 'worlds' that, seen from the untutored outsider's perspective, are no longer 'the way they once were' and thus confirm that the world itself is in – possibly terminal – decline.[43] Travel writing, in this sense, performs the work of what, adapting James Clifford's phrase, we might call *pseudo*-ethnographic salvage; it makes, through writing, as if to retrieve the world from the clutches of imminent destruction, but the world that it fears losing is one that no longer conforms to the dominant culture's myths. Hence the contradictory temporalities of much travel writing, its tendency to bypass history in search of (spurious) universals and

---

[40]   Van der Post, *The Lost World of the Kalahari*, p. 163.

[41]   Mary Louise Pratt, 'Fieldwork in Common Places', in James Clifford and George Marcus, eds, *Writing Culture: The Poetics and Politics of Ethnography* (Berkeley: University of California Press, 1986), p. 48.

[42]   See Holland and Huggan, *Tourists with Typewriters*, p. 181.

[43]   Travel writing's ubiquitous predictions of its own demise might be seen, paradoxically, as a means of ensuring its perpetuation. On the end-of-travel-writing trope, see the Postscript to Holland and Huggan, *Tourists with Typewriters*; also see the Postscript for a discussion of the interrelation between rhetorical and material forms of exhaustion ('the end of travel writing' meets 'the end of the world').

'timeless' truths. In this context, while it would be churlish to suggest that Van der Post is being insincere in his wider liberal-humanist agenda (despoliation of the environment; wastage of natural resources; continuing mistreatment of indigenous peoples; and so on), the nostalgia he invokes is, by definition, *antithetical* to historical change.

Perhaps his 'romance' with the USA as promising a utopic ahistorical permanence beyond the real – the *hyper*real – accounts for Baudrillard's treatment of nostalgia in *America*.[44] It's certainly strange, at first blush, to find Baudrillard invoking the concept at all, given his refusal to wax sentimental about, say, the extermination of American indigenous peoples, but on reflection the term's semantic displacement becomes clear enough. The journey through the American desert – and for Baudrillard it is America as totality, as well as specific regions, that *is* the desert – is itself, he claims, an abstraction: a fantastic virtual trajectory through a pre-cultural and post-cultural landscape.[45] Baudrillard's nostalgia is something like the romantic poet Wordsworth's, for 'the light that never was, on sea or land';[46] 'never was' because it precedes and supersedes culture. His hyper-speedy trajectory through the actual desert spaces cannot, according to Baudrillard, be *verbally* represented: since it is experience of the simulacrum in, apparently, purity and ecstasy, there is no adequate cultural form for its representation except that of a pure virtuality that endlessly repeats it. When Baudrillard, then, writes that 'this stay [in Santa Barbara] has become a sojourn in a previous existence', it is hardly a case of the achieved 'longing to bring what is youngest home to what is oldest' – as it is for Van der Post – but a feeling of Santa Barbara 'as the predestined site of an eternal return',[47] an ahistorical, anti-cultural simulacrum. If nature in the American desert has a 'magical presence', that presence is not one that still somehow contains ancient, 'primitive' wisdom, but one constituted by massive – if transcendent – geophysicalities that intimidatingly predated the indigenous peoples and that now entrance the European visitor. *America*, recording in postmodernist fashion a journey across a country, is less a sentimental travelogue than a poetics of nostalgia for both the absolutely pre-cultural and for the utopic future.[48]

Baudrillard's repetitive reduction of America to virtuality, even as it rules out the in-between of the cultural, indulging its own 'nostalgic desire for forms to revert to immobility',[49] nevertheless casually adverts to the victims of Western colonization, but in the most flagrant erasure of history. Early massacres of the

---

[44]   Jean Baudrillard, *America*, trans. Chris Turner (London: Verso, 1988).
[45]   See Nick Perry, *Hyperreality and Global Culture* (London: Routledge, 1998), pp. 78–80.
[46]   William Wordsworth, 'Elegiac Stanzas', *Poetical Works* (London: Moxon, 1847), p. 434.
[47]   Baudrillard, *America*, p. 72.
[48]   For a brief chapter on nostalgia and cybernetic futurism, see Svetlana Boym, *The Future of Nostalgia* (New York: Basic Books, 2001), pp. 345–55.
[49]   Baudrillard, *America*, p. 7.

colonial era, it seems, become fortunate falls, enabling the deserts to gain sublimity from the cruel evacuation of human beings. With 'the Indians [*sic*]' out of the way, anthropology lost its point, even as a host of (pre-cultural) 'signs' came to visibility: 'a mineralogy, a geology, a sidereality, an inhuman facticity, an aridity … , a silence that exists nowhere else'.[50] In rejecting anthropological nostalgia, Baudrillard displaces it onto the American Puritans, citing

> [a] Puritan obsession with origins in the very place where the ground itself has already gone. An obsession with finding a niche, a contact, precisely at the point where everything unfolds in an astral indifference.[51]

Apart from that last phrase about 'astral indifference', the sentence might well be read as a critique – or the germ of one – of Van der Post; but with that last phrase, Baudrillard destroys his own ground, at least for those resistant to being rapt by *America*'s dense, poetic, metaphysical prose.

For all its poetic utopianism, indeed, there is another side to Baudrillard's *America*, one that reveals its status as nostalgic European fantasy, in which 'Baudrillard's voice [is] … a Swiftian persona spinning out modest proposals whose absurdities point towards truths'.[52] Thus, while Europeans 'possess the art of thinking, of analysing things and reflecting on them', Americans inhabit 'a world completely rotten with wealth, power, senility, indifference, puritanism, and mental hygiene, poverty and waste, technological futility and aimless violence'; in spite of – or because of – which, Baudrillard 'cannot help but feel it has about it something of the dawning of the universe'.[53] This turns out to be the contradiction at the heart of Baudrillard's project: America both already *is* an achieved hyperreality and *points towards* an as yet unachieved (geopolitical) form.

Baudrillard's own nostalgia, it turns out, is finally for the Europe he has temporarily escaped. The nostalgic privileging of Europe shines through those sections of the book in which Baudrillard turns from desert fantasies to generalized and comparative cultural critique, where he – again, nostalgically – invokes the nineteenth-century writer Tocqueville as his precursor.[54] Using Tocqueville's analysis of American manners, democracy and governance in 1831–32, Baudrillard swerves from his hyperrealist, futurist, utopian fantasy of Reagan's America to refigure that geopolitical space back into an eighteenth-century frame where it looks more like a historical anachronism than an embodiment – or precursor – of a virtual, global order.[55]

---

[50]   Baudrillard, *America*, p. 6.

[51]   Baudrillard, *America*, p. 8.

[52]   James Berger, *After the End: Representations of Post-Apocalypse* (Minneapolis: University of Minnesota Press, 1999), p. 236, n. 6.

[53]   Baudrillard, *America*, p. 23.

[54]   Alexis de Tocqueville, *Democracy in America* [1831–32] (Garden City, NY: Anchor Books, 1969).

[55]   Although Tocqueville's tour took place in the nineteenth century, Baudrillard regards the America Tocqueville toured as an eighteenth-century society.

Ultimately, then, Baudrillard's heady but confusing work of travel communicates a plangent nostalgia for high European culture.

Even Baudrillard's apparently unsentimental and celebratory tour through the desert of America turns out to be not so much a foray into a different place or space as an ironic alibi for the evocation of a Europe that may well be an illusion. It points to the possibility that, in the words of Svetlana Boym:

> At first glance, nostalgia is a longing for a place, but actually it is a yearning for a different time – the time of our childhood, the slower rhythms of our dreams. In a broader sense, nostalgia is a rebellion against the modern idea of time, the time of history and progress. The nostalgic desires to obliterate history and turn it into private or collective mythology, to revisit time like space, refusing to surrender to the irreversibility of time that plagues the human condition.[56]

The transformation of 'history' into 'private or collective mythology' suggests the presence of powerful fantasy elements in travel writing, and indeed the close relationship between travel writing and the remembered and regretted exercise of power.

Nostalgia is unlikely to disappear as one very strong constituent of travel writing, particularly given its force as an engine of the commodity economy and consumer culture, under the guise of commemoration.[57] But while nostalgia has a bad name – as travel writing does for some people – it is nonetheless a contradictory, even paradoxical process, veering from illusion to strenuous exercise of memory, from cultural self-congratulation to self-critique, from blatant acquisition to property divestiture. Clearly, then, close attention to travel writing – and not only modern and contemporary and postmodern travel writing – can lead to interrogation of the phenomenon of nostalgia itself, in its several varieties. And no doubt such interrogation will lead to more travel – and many more travel books.

---

[56] Boym, *The Future of Nostalgia*, p. xv. Boym's recent narrative (rather than study) of a form of nostalgia focuses on nostalgia as commemoration, in the historical context of postwar European (particularly central and eastern European) exile and migration. Regrettably, Boym has nothing to say about travel and migrancy outside her Eurocentric context.

[57] See Boym, *The Future of Nostalgia*, pp. 38–9.

Chapter 11

# Mediaeval Travel in Postcolonial Times: Amitav Ghosh's *In an Antique Land*

## Padmini Mongia

Described on its book jacket as 'the story of two Indians in Egypt', Amitav Ghosh's *In an Antique Land* is the story of Bomma, an Indian slave, and of Ghosh himself, the student anthropologist and writer who traces the story of Bomma some eight hundred years after it occurred. At its most simple, *In an Antique Land* is the story of two Indians in Egypt, but even the jacket blurb complicates the simplicity of this description by going on to label the book as 'subversive history in the guise of a traveler's tale'. *In an Antique Land*, published in 1992, is in part based on research that Ghosh conducted for a D. Phil. in social anthropology, but manages to appear as travel narrative, ethnography, history, and fiction all at once. It casts a wide net. Bomma's story is set in the twelfth century, in a world of flourishing trade on the Indian Ocean between Masr (Egypt) and Mangalore in south-western India, although he only exists as a shadowy presence in a few letters to and from his master, the Tunisian, Abraham Ben Yiju. As Ghosh attempts to create Bomma's tale, he interweaves his process of doing so into it. The story of the second Indian, Ghosh, is presented to us at several different chronological moments: the time of his fieldwork in 1980, his return to Egypt in 1988, and finally the Gulf War in 1990.

Covering the encounter between Indians and Egyptians at different times over an eight-hundred-year span, *In an Antique Land* melds many genres. The modes of intellectual or narrative expression that Ghosh deploys produce a work that challenges the categories he explores and forces a contemplation of form, the shapes and contours usually associated with distinct genres. By doing so, and indeed through the means that Ghosh uses to stretch the boundaries of genre, he poses many of the questions that have come to be associated with postcolonial writing. Amongst these is the question of how the post-structuralist, postcolonial anthropologist negotiates his/her location to produce an ethnography that does not replicate the disturbing structure of knowledge as power, or the tension between centre and periphery, and between metropolitan anthropologists and their 'primitive' objects of study. The question I want to ask is whether there is a postcolonial travel writing. If there is, can Ghosh's *In an Antique Land* be regarded from this perspective?

### Postcoloniality, anthropology, travel writing

In the introductory essay to the inaugural issue of the journal, *Studies in Travel Writing*, Peter Hulme remarks on the vigorous interest recently accorded to travel writing. While the globe is supposed to have shrunk in these last decades, Hulme points out that travel writing is enjoying the kind of popularity it did in the 1920s.[1] Travel writing is also entering academic domains, as witnessed by the formation of at least two new journals devoted to it.[2] In part, this academic interest can be explained by the cross-disciplinary nature of travel writing itself. In the new academic environments of the late-twentieth and early twenty-first centuries, travel writing is ideally poised for receiving interest from a variety of disciplines interested in contact zones and culture.

James Clifford, in his 'Notes on Travel and Theory', describes travel as 'a figure for different modes of dwelling and displacement, for trajectories and identities, for storytelling and theorizing in a postcolonial world of global contacts'.[3] Travel, he further suggests, is 'a range of practices for situating the self in a space or spaces grown too large, a form both of exploration and discipline'.[4] Clifford's suggestions remove travel from the interplay between home and abroad and remind us that increasingly – especially over the last fifty years – one must recognize that 'every center or home is someone else's periphery and diaspora'.[5] The geographical places to which one travels by traversing space are peopled already with lives and histories more textured than one could imagine. Syed Islam, in a similar vein, makes a distinction between the sedentary and the nomadic traveller. Sedentary travel and travel writing are rigid; sedentary travellers need to 'establish essential difference on a binary frame' and although they may traverse vast distances, no travel need have been undertaken at all.[6] Only nomadic travel, Islam argues, deserves the name of travel in an ethical sense, since it deals with 'encounters with otherness that fracture both a boundary and an apparatus of representation'. In nomadic travel, 'dwelling and travelling merge into one another'.[7] Travel, then, is not so much about physical movement and the journey from here to there as it is a figure for different modes of stasis, movement, and knowledge. If travel is indeed about situating the self in spaces grown too large, travel demands as much attention on the position taken by the writer as it demands attention on the locations it addresses. To consider travel

---

[1]    Peter Hulme, 'Introduction', *Studies in Travel Writing*, 1 (Spring 1997), p. 1.

[2]    *Studies in Travel Writing* is devoted to travel writing, while *Journeys* focuses on travel culture more generally.

[3]    James Clifford, 'Notes on Travel and Theory', *Traveling Theory, Traveling Theorists*, *Inscriptions*, 5 (1989), p. 177.

[4]    Clifford, 'Notes', p. 177.

[5]    Clifford, 'Notes', p. 179.

[6]    Syed Manzurul Islam, *The Ethics of Travel: From Marco Polo to Kafka* (Manchester: Manchester University Press, 1996), p. viii.

[7]    Islam, *The Ethics of Travel*, p. vii.

as a form of situating the self focuses attention on the traveller as well as on the places and geographies to which s/he travels.

This shift in understanding travel is similar to a shift that has marked anthropology and other human sciences in the last two decades. The linguistic turn taken by various humanistic disciplines demands a renewed focus be paid to the ethnographer/historian as well as to the sites of academic and/or literary production. In the last twenty years, the ethnographic mode has been subjected to severe scrutiny, resulting in anthropology acknowledging 'the constructed, artificial nature of cultural accounts'.[8] The older ethnographic model, which erased the specificity of the participant/observer, has been replaced by ethnographies where acute attention is paid to the observer as well as to the object of study. Both have been complicated as a result. Recent ethnographic accounts draw self-conscious attention to the anthropologist as well as to the scene of writing that is an equal partner in the ethnography produced.

This focus on location challenges the intellectual boundaries associated with fields such as anthropology and history. That travel writing reflects the same shifts we find in anthropological writing is no surprise, since the former might be regarded as the poor cousin of the latter. Most European travel and travel writing of the last five hundred years took place under the rubric of the colonial relationship, even as anthropology emerged out of that relationship.[9] Not surprisingly, the new space in which travel writing finds an academic home is the same one that has produced what has become known as postcolonial theory. Indeed, travel and its related conditions – migrancy and exile – are recurrent concerns in the work of many postcolonial writers. Definitions of the postcolonial vary greatly and have been subjected to scathing scrutiny over the last few years.[10] However, one of the most compelling ways of understanding the postcolonial challenge is via the rethinking of structures of knowledge and power it demands. As a chronological marker, postcolonial is a troubling nomenclature since arguably the era of colonization has yet to end. As a theoretical approach, though, the postcolonial project critiques the terms whereby knowledge has been produced in the post-Enlightenment era.

Gyan Prakash describes postcolonial criticism as critiquing the 'historicism that projected the West as History', where Europe is its theoretical subject.[11] The work of the Subaltern Studies Collective, for example, intervenes in the production of academic history by attempting a historiography that restores agency to the subaltern classes. Such a project, however, is fraught with difficulties, since the

---

[8] James Clifford and George Marcus, eds, *Writing Culture: The Poetics and Politics of Ethnography* (Berkeley: University of California Press, 1986), p. 2.

[9] Hulme, 'Introduction', p. 1.

[10] For an excellent introduction to postcolonial theory, see Ania Loomba's *Colonialism/Postcolonialism* (London: Routledge, 1998).

[11] Gyan Prakash, 'Subaltern Studies as Postcolonial Criticism', *American Historical Review*, 99:5 (December 1994), p. 1475.

historian challenges the contours of academic history while 'reading' records not regarded as constitutive of that history. Neither élite nor nationalist historiography, subaltern history attempts the history of the subaltern classes even as it deals with the theoretical issues attendant on determining just what materials constitute the historical record. In his Foreword to the volume *Selected Subaltern Studies*, Edward Said discusses the inaccessibility of the sources of subaltern history:

> We find frequent reference to such things as gaps, absences, lapses, ellipses, all of them symbolic of the truths that historical writing is after all writing and not reality, and that as subalterns their history as well as their historical documents are necessarily in the hands of others. ... In other words, subaltern history in literal fact is a narrative missing from the official story.[12]

Attempting to write the missing narrative, the subaltern historian inevitably struggles with theoretical questions regarding historiography. Doing so naturally demands revisions of form and content. Such revisionary impulses also describe postcolonial literature. While no simple definitions of postcolonial literature are possible, critics would agree that it has made a tremendous impact – both within and outside the academy – in the last two decades. Described as a 'writing back' by the Australian critics Bill Ashcroft, Gareth Griffiths, and Helen Tiffin, postcolonial literature does much more than 'write back', although this remains an important distinguishing feature of contemporary postcolonial literature. At their best, the contributions made by postcolonial writers have challenged traditional literary forms as well. These writers have forced a rethinking of many of the structures defining inherited literary genres. Rushdie and Ghosh, for instance, seamlessly weave together history and fiction to highlight the traits of both. Both writers, using very different techniques, question such notions as nationhood and nationalism as they tell stories that reveal the fabulous fictions of post-Enlightenment history and literature.

The rethinking of form is, of course, not in itself a postcolonial project. However, in conjunction with the many other features that describe postcolonial writing, formal innovation can become an important tool for subverting received knowledge. A work of many formal affiliations, *In an Antique Land* challenges the boundaries of the many genres on which it relies. In so doing, Ghosh's book forces us to rethink traditional disciplinary forms from a postcolonial perspective. The result – an amalgamated text – offers a distinct form of travel writing that might best be called postcolonial.

## In an antique land

Discovered as a footnote in a document, Bomma – the Indian slave to the Tunisian Jew, Abraham Ben Yiju – is a mysterious and compelling figure. Bomma initially

---

[12]   Edward Said, 'Foreword', in *Selected Subaltern Studies*, ed. Gayatri Chakravorty Spivak and Ranajit Guha (New York: Oxford University Press, 1988), p. vii.

appears in the written record in a letter penned in 1148 by the trader Khalaf ibn Ishaq to his friend, Abraham Ben Yiju. The letter, bearing the catalogue number MS H. 6 of the National and University Library in Jerusalem, was published in the Hebrew journal *Zion* in 1942. As a young student at Oxford, Ghosh first encountered Bomma in 1978 in a book of translations titled *Letters of Medieval Jewish Traders*, by Professor S. D. Goitein, although Bomma in this second published reference is several years younger. This initial encounter provided Ghosh with the impetus to track Bomma's trail, a trail with virtually no signposts, but a journey that Ghosh meticulously shares in *In an Antique Land*. From being merely a 'name and a greeting',[13] Bomma, through Ghosh's efforts, gains a geographical home, a personality, and a professional life.

Reminiscent of the work of the late postcolonial poet, Agha Shahid Ali (1949–2001), Ghosh's interest in Bomma parallels Ali's wonder at an extant sculpture of a servant girl from 2500 BC. Just as Ali marvels, 'No one keeps records/of soldiers and slaves' in his poem 'At the Museum',[14] Ghosh is cognisant of the rarity of his find. Introducing Bomma, Ghosh says:

> But the reference comes to us from a moment in time when the only people for whom we can even begin to imagine properly human, individual, existences are the literate and the consequential ... the people who had the power to inscribe themselves physically upon time. But the slave of Khalaf's letter was not of that company; in his instance it was a mere accident that those barely discernible traces that ordinary people leave upon the world happen to have been preserved. It is nothing less than a miracle that anything is known about him at all. (pp. 16–17)

Even as it is miraculous that any trace of Bomma exists in the written record, it is almost as miraculous that any sort of story could be written around him. It is little wonder, though, that Bomma is elusive. A few fragments, scattered in a few documents, are all that exist officially. To retrieve him from his status as a footnote and make him one of the primary subjects of the historical narrative is an affirmation of his life and an acknowledgement of the many histories erased by official narratives. By taking on an enormous, even an impossible task – to craft a story for a twelfth-century slave – Ghosh shares the process of his/story making. Although his task is daunting, creating Bomma's story vindicates the human traces left upon history.

Ghosh's process of tracking down Bomma's traces is a laborious, difficult one. It has as much to do with a scholarly world of manuscript chasing and reading as it does with Ghosh's own site(s) of knowledge production as an anthropologist in the 1980s. Throughout, the construction of Bomma's story is informed by the anthropologist discovering and inventing that story. Almost as though it were an

---

[13]  Amitav Ghosh, *In an Antique Land* (Delhi: Ravi Dayal, 1992), p. 16. All subsequent references to this work appear parenthetically within the text.

[14]  Agha Shahid Ali, *The Country Without a Post Office* (New York: Norton, 1997), p. 65.

interleaved book, we have this weave between Bomma and Ghosh, two Indians, one a slave from the twelfth century and the other a privileged anthropologist, even as the former grants the latter a justification for being in Egypt conducting his fieldwork. This interweaving is premised on the long reach of the historical arm, so that Ghosh's world is clearly shown as shaped by Bomma's eight hundred years earlier.

Much of Ghosh's narrative is built upon the careful piecing together – over a ten-year period – of details in manuscripts. In this process, the slave Bomma gains a name, an occupation, travels, and even emotions. The preservation of the documents themselves makes a compelling story. Most of the documents that interest Ghosh come from the Geniza of the Synagogue of Ben Ezra outside Cairo, in Fustat. Ben Yiju belonged to the congregation of this synagogue, which he joined when he moved to Cairo from what was known in mediaeval times as Ifriqiya and is now Tunisia. For more than eight hundred years, writings were deposited in the Geniza, stemming from a widespread custom at the time and one still practised among Jewish groups today. The practice of depositing their writings was 'intended to prevent the accidental desecration of any written form of God's name. Since most writings in that epoch included at least one sacred invocation in the course of the text, the custom effectively ensured that written documents of every kind were deposited within the synagogue' (p. 56). The Geniza, or the chambers where these documents were housed, remained miraculously untouched until 1890, when the old building that Ben Yiju saw in the early 1100s was torn down.

The story of the dispersal of the documents from the Geniza is a fascinating one. In the eighteenth century, the documents began to be collected (or stolen) by Europeans who were responding to the waves of Egyptomania that swept Europe at the time. Ghosh suggests that the 'discovery' of Egypt was 'by the end of the eighteenth century ... the scholarly counterpart of those great landmasses that were then being claimed and explored by European settlers' (p. 82). By 1864, when the construction of the Suez Canal was well underway, Egypt was under British control and crucial to becoming the stepping-stone to India. At around this time, the documents of the Geniza caught the attention of the scholarly world, and news of their wealth spread throughout Europe. The single largest collection is housed at Cambridge: it was within these papers that Ghosh first encountered a reference to the Slave of MS H. 6. The irony of the journey of these documents, which came from all over the world to the Geniza in Fustat, is that not a single one remains in Egypt, the place that nurtured them for eight hundred years.

From an incidental encounter in a manuscript, Ghosh tracks the lives of Ben Yiju and Bomma. The trail is not only incomplete, but fraught with linguistic and other difficulties as well. Ghosh shares with us in detail the slow, laborious journey tracing the few clues he is given. Since the fact of Bomma's existence in the historical record is itself a surprise, Ghosh offers the story peppered with doubt and questioning, always asking whether a conclusion he draws is or is not convincing. Much of Bomma's life and that of his Jewish master, Abraham Ben Yiju, is sheer speculation. Consider Ghosh's careful anatomizing of Ben Yiju's marriage. Having brought Ben Yiju from Cairo to the Malabar Coast of India via Aden, Ghosh pauses on a document revealing that Ben Yiju freed a slave named Ashu. Building on this seemingly inconsequential detail, Ghosh is able to suggest that Ashu bore Ben Yiju's children, that they probably married, and that Ashu probably came from the matrilineal Nair community along the Malabar coast. Even as this story gains roundness, Ghosh reminds us of its speculative nature. Other options to the story exist, and Ghosh offers them to us before selecting his preferred one. He admits his interpretation of Ben Yiju's personal life could be wrong. Perhaps there was no marriage to Ashu, although she seems to have borne Ben Yiju's children. Yet Ghosh urges us towards believing that Ben Yiju chose to marry Ashu, a woman outside his community. He ends the section devoted to exploring the relationship between Ben Yiju and Ashu thus: 'If I hesitate to call it love it is only because the documents offer no certain proof' (p. 230). Yet, since he has evocatively created a love story, Ghosh seduces the reader with it as he suggests its tenuousness, even its falsity. In the process, the production of both history and fiction is laid bare. Remarkably, while revealing the tentative nature of his conclusions, Ghosh manages to give moments such as the one above the mantle of facticity.

We usually expect our historical documents and the stories they tell to have a polished completion. Since we assume this coherence, we are willing to accept the historian's creation of completion even where there is none. Of course, the reader is not usually made privy to the incompleteness of the historical record. Ghosh gives us none of that comfort. The story he creates is plausible but by no means more so than the many others suggested in *In an Antique Land*. The book is thus both subaltern history and also a reminder that history and fiction are inseparable. That history is story – the Italian word *storia* makes no distinction between the two – is by now a commonplace. Yet, the revelation of details that make up that fabrication affords the reader a different participatory process. The book demonstrates how the subaltern historian contends with the incompleteness of historical records. No passive consumer of a well-crafted story, the reader of Ghosh's *In an Antique Land* must pause to reflect on the conjectural nature of stories and find his/her pleasure in the interaction between the tale and its tenuous telling.

The pre-colonial world Ghosh creates in *In an Antique Land* challenges many of the assumptions we make about it, about the advent of colonialism and indeed about the postcolonial world. Bomma's mediaeval society is richly seen by Ghosh as a vital, cosmopolitan one that puts to shame our current notions of cosmopolitanism. Intermarriage between communities and peoples is just a small instance of that cosmopolitanism. Speaking of the unusual linkages between the Tunisian Ben Yiju, his Nair wife, and his Indian slave, Bomma, Ghosh says that the confluence that brought them together ended with the coming of Vasco da Gama in 1498:

> Within a few years of that day the knell had been struck for the world that had brought Bomma, Ben Yiju and Ashu together, and another age had begun in which the crossing of their paths would seem so unlikely that its very possibility would all but disappear from human memory. (p. 286)

Ghosh relates the difference between the mediaeval world and his own eight hundred years later: the 'intertwined histories, Indian and Egyptian, Muslim and Jewish, Hindu and Muslim, had been partitioned long ago' (p. 286). By recovering the memory of this intertwining, Ghosh travels across space and time. Even as he journeys forward in space, covering ground, he travels backward in time, just as nineteenth-century explorers and anthropologists did. However, unlike the tales produced by these nineteenth-century travellers where such trajectories would reveal a 'primitive' world, Ghosh, in his process of journeying, discovers a world more cosmopolitan, nuanced, and complex than the progressivist narratives of post-Enlightenment history and literature would have us believe. If no obvious traces of the complex relations between peoples and cultures in mediaeval times exists in the late twentieth century, it is not because those relations did not thrive for years. Instead, the advent of European colonialism severed pre-existing relations and structures to create a fissure that has almost erased the histories Ghosh recovers.

The long-lasting impact of the arrival of the Portuguese in India cannot be overstated. Upon their arrival in 1498, they gained control of the Indian Ocean trade, which had not till then been subjected to control through the force of arms. For centuries before that date, peoples had traded on the Indian Ocean respecting the laws of peace that governed the waters, careful not to allow the militaristic nature of land-battles onto the laws of the water. The Portuguese changed that. The mediaeval world of trade between Egypt and India had been running smoothly and graciously when it was interrupted by the Portuguese and brought under a system of military dominance. That single shift led to a new set of rules that governed trade, and these new rules – dominance and autonomy – altered the history of the world. The radical alteration of the older structure led, as Ghosh puts it, to the 'unquenchable, demonic thirst that has raged ever since, for almost 500 years, over the Indian Ocean, the Arabian Sea, and the Persian Gulf' (p. 288).

This is how Ghosh describes the changes in power over the sea and trade that result from the arrival and intervention of the Portuguese:

> Within the Western historiographical record the unarmed nature of the Indian Ocean trade is often represented as a lack, or failure, one that invited the intervention of Europe, with its increasing proficiency in war. ... Yet it is worth allowing for the possibility that the peaceful tradition of the oceanic trade may have been, in a quiet and inarticulate way, the product of a rare cultural choice – one that may have owed a great deal to the pacifist customs and beliefs of the Gujarati Jains and Vanias who played such an important part in it. (p. 287)

Rather than viewing colonialism as a response to a lack, Ghosh rewrites the advent of the Portuguese as a violent, meditated encounter, one that highlights the distinctions between different modes of cultural organization. The allegiances between the Egyptians, Tunisians, Indians and others in mediaeval times are revealed to have been based on relations other than power and possession, relations the European powers had no terms to understand. Nor is the pre-colonial, mediaeval world the society of the dark ages created by the fictions and histories written by Europeans. The dominant narratives we have all inherited, as a result of the wide reach of Western systems of knowledge production and education, underscore the European need to pull the colonized regions of the world out of their 'darkness'. That this 'darkness' is as much a fabrication as the 'light' brought to it becomes abundantly clear throughout the book. The grand idea that fed the civilizing mission of the Europeans (as constructed through the eighteenth and nineteenth centuries and inherited by us in the twentieth) is unmasked in *In an Antique Land* as naked greed:

> Consider, for example, our understanding of just the name Egypt. Masr is the name by which the country has been known, in its own language, for at least a millennium, and most of the cultures and civilizations with which it has old connections have accepted its own self-definition. ... Only Europe has always insisted on knowing the country not on its own terms, but as a dark mirror for itself. (p. 32)

So even the name Egypt contains an alternative history. Ghosh makes us consider the phrases 'Egyptian darkness' and 'Egyptian bondage'. Both locate Egypt within the Biblical narrative. European languages derive Egypt from the 'Greek Aegyptos, a term that is related to the word "Copt," the name generally used for Egypt's indigenous Christians' (p. 32). Words like 'gypsy' and 'gitano' are derived from Egyptian (p. 33). As Ghosh sums it up, 'Europe's apparently innocent "Egypt" ... is almost as much a weapon as a word' (p. 33). Ghosh's detour into the etymology of Egypt reveals the history embedded in an apparently innocent name. *Masr* offers an alternative history of Egypt.

By offering a glimpse into the cosmopolitan, humane circuit of relations prevalent in mediaeval India up to the moment when European dominance via colonialism enters its history, Ghosh poses a postcolonial challenge via the pre-colonial. In Ghosh's telling of this history, an alternative picture emerges, one that is tantalizing and heartbreaking because it offers a picture of the world and of relations between peoples which might have unfolded had the rupture introduced by colonialism not occurred. Indeed, at a particular historical moment, it was possible that the Indian Ocean trade routes not be brought under the Portuguese with their need to include all trade within a single dominating structure. Contained within this moment is the possibility of an alternative history. That human societies have functioned – even in competitive arenas such as trade – with pacifist dignity and generosity is a reminder at once poignantly painful and exhilaratingly optimistic. Although European colonialism and imperialism have been written as having a historical inevitability to them, Ghosh's pre-colonial world questions that inevitability. The world he creates reveals the possibility of futures and histories other than the one we have come to regard as inevitable.

James Clifford, discussing *In an Antique Land*, says: 'The story delivers a sharp critique of a classic quest – exoticist, anthropological, orientalist – for pure traditions and discrete cultural differences.'[15] Indeed, Ghosh's text reveals the impossibility of finding any pure traditions or discrete differences. When he first goes to Egypt for his fieldwork, he expects to find in that ancient land, a settled and rooted people. He could not have been more wrong. Not only was everyone (male) in the village travelling, but they had been doing so for centuries:

> This ethnographer [was] no longer a (worldly) traveler visiting (local) natives, departing from a metropolitan center to study in a rural periphery. Instead, his 'ancient and settled' fieldsite opens onto complex histories of dwelling and traveling, cosmopolitan experiences.[16]

Eight hundred years before the anthropologist's arrival at his fieldsite, people had been travelling, merchants and traders involved with the trade between the Mediterranean and the Indian Ocean. Not privileged men, these small traders nevertheless moved regularly between continents and challenge the anthropologist's expectations of the rootedness of his site's inhabitants. Fieldwork, in Ghosh's account, says Clifford, is 'less a matter of localized dwelling and more a series of travel encounters. Everyone's on the move, and has been for centuries: dwelling-in-travel.' And he goes on to argue for 'a view of human location as constituted by displacement as much as by stasis', so that 'practices of displacement might emerge as constitutive of cultural meanings rather than as their simple transfer or extension'.[17] For Clifford in *Routes*, and Ghosh in *In an Antique Land* as well as his other works, travel is a compelling metaphor for knowing.

*In an Antique Land* complicates more usual understandings of home and away, positions that have been crucial to earlier anthropological modes. In Ghosh's *The Shadow Lines*, first published in 1988, his narrator meditates on the difference between coming and going in the context of his grandmother's journey to the town of her birth, Dhaka, but a town that post-1947 and Indian independence has become a foreign place to her. Is the narrator's grandmother going home or coming home? The narrator says: 'Every language assumes a centrality, a fixed and settled point to go away from and come back to, and what my grandmother was looking for was a word for a journey which was not a coming or a going at all; a journey that was a search for precisely that fixed point which permits the proper use of verbs of movement.'[18] Beyond the specific historical realities which have complicated the distinction between going and coming in *The Shadow Lines*, these verbs of movement remain troublesome in other contexts as well; in *In an Antique Land* coming and going, home and abroad, blend into each other. If Ghosh in 1980 is away from home in Egypt, by 1988 he is at home there and his Egyptian friends are abroad in Iraq. In the eight years that have passed since Ghosh's fieldwork of

15    James Clifford, *Routes: Travel and Translation in the Late Twentieth Century* (Cambridge, Mass.: Harvard University Press, 1997), p. 5.

16    Clifford, *Routes*, p. 2.

17    Clifford, *Routes*, pp. 2–3.

18    Amitav Ghosh, *The Shadow Lines* (London: Penguin, 1990), p. 150.

1980, Isma'il and Nabeel, his two closest friends and companions, have left their homes in Lataifa and gone abroad to work in Iraq. As the war between Iraq and Iran intensified in the late 1980s, many men had left Egypt to go 'outside' (p. 321). Ghosh describes the changes money earned outside has produced in Lataifa in the years since 1981 'as though the village had been drawn on to the fringes of a revolution – except that this one had happened in another country, far away' (p. 321). When Ghosh goes back to Egypt in 1988, and then three weeks after the Gulf War has started in 1990, he goes to a place or comes to a place that is both home and abroad.

In 1988, Ghosh visits Isma'il's and Nabeel's families, in the small town Lataifa, and remarks on the dramatic changes all around him. Nabeel's house, once made up of mud-walled rooms, is now a 'large new bungalow' (p. 318). Built by the money Nabeel sent home from Iraq, the house contains all the trappings of modernity – a television set, washing machine, and a tape recorder on which the family plays the tapes Nabeel sends from Iraq with news of himself. Ghosh listens to one of these tapes with the family but is unable to answer whether or not Nabeel is happy in Iraq. Offered only as the briefest glimpse, Nabeel and Isma'il's life in Iraq is sketched, nevertheless, with its evident strains. Isma'il describes the resentment Iraqi men feel towards Egyptian workers, which is never far from exploding. On one occasion, when it does, Isma'il decides to return home; Nabeel decides to stay a bit longer so the modernization of his house in Lataifa can be completed. In this interim, the Gulf War breaks out and there is no longer news of Nabeel. When Ghosh returns to Lataifa in 1990, three weeks after the Gulf War started, nobody has heard from Nabeel. 'Nabeel had vanished into the anonymity of History', says Ghosh (p. 353). His capitalized History – the master narrative – spared little time and attention on those thousands of workers who walked out of Iraq searching for some safety. Many died on their journeys towards refuge; their homes in Egypt (and elsewhere) were arrested in mid-development. Ghosh offers no better symbol for the effects of the Gulf War on foreign workers than Nabeel's new house, unfinished, as the money dried up.

Long past his fieldwork, Ghosh's return to Egypt reveals that though his interest in the stories that most propel his book forward – his own and Bomma's – might have ended, at least within the demands of the narrative shared in *In an Antique Land*, the stories of those he encountered during the time of his fieldwork in the 1980s continue. The most poignant of these is focused on Nabeel, a story that cannot end except in the questioning way Ghosh does, letting Nabeel vanish into history. The anonymity of history claims Nabeel, just as it had claimed Bomma. However, having taken on two historical periods for decipherment – the one Ghosh attempts to discern through his manuscript chasing, and the current one when his fieldwork takes place – Ghosh travels beyond the boundaries that shape the genres and disciplines that inform his text. He offers us alternative histories, plucking Bomma out of the anonymity of History and suggesting the possibility of Nabeel's similar removal from obscurity.

If an earlier body of knowledge production erased the subjectivity of the 'native', Ghosh's work reveals the native returning the gaze, time and again, even as the 'native' is revealed as a cosmopolitan traveller. As Ghosh, the anthropologist, poses questions, the villagers question him back, and produce, at times, great discomfort and anxiety. One of the most memorable examples is the discussion of circumcision and the anthropologist's inability to answer the question about his own circumcision. When later his friend Nabeel says, 'They were only asking questions ... just like you do; they didn't mean any harm' (p. 204), the moment forces a profound focus on the subjectivity of this anthropologist. Using the occasion as a detour into his own life, Ghosh returns to a moment he describes as an 'Indian's terror of symbols' (p. 210). The occasion is his reflection on a childhood memory that is significant in *The Shadow Lines* as well, the riots in Calcutta and Dacca in 1964. At the early age of six, Ghosh is thrown into the tension between Hindus and Muslims, a tension that breaks out so frequently in the Indian subcontinent. Because it does, and is often sparked by the weight of a symbol, 'a cow found dead in a temple or a pig in a mosque ... men dismembered for the state of their foreskins' (p. 210), Ghosh is unable to answer the question posed to him. Only by comprehending that the revelation of circumcision can mean the difference between life and death can one understand Ghosh's reluctance to answer an apparently innocent question. Nevertheless, the moment draws attention to the discomfort produced by the ethnographic mode, presumably as much for the participant/observer as for the observed.

Even more memorable is Ghosh's exchange with the Imam. The latter baits Ghosh with sarcastic comments on the peculiar customs of Indians – the worshipping of cows and the burning of the dead – customs that many others Ghosh has met have commented on earlier. Before Ghosh knows what is happening, he is engaged in a verbal battle with the Imam, the two men arguing over the military strengths of Egypt and India, 'two superseded civilizations' (p. 236). Ghosh says: 'We were both travelling, he and I: we were travelling in the West' (p. 236), as he realizes how easily he has slipped into a familiar vocabulary of progress and development. As Ghosh leaves this encounter, he sadly acknowledges that both he and the Imam participated in erasing the inheritance of a centuries-old legacy of friendship between Egypt and India. 'We had acknowledged that it was no longer possible to speak, as Ben Yiju or his Slave ... might have done: of things that were right, or good, or willed by God [for those words] belonged to a dismantled rung on the ascending ladder of Development' (pp. 236–7). Whether or not Ben Yiju and Bomma's world allowed for the sort of dialogue Ghosh imagines, our world certainly conspires to make such dialogues difficult, even impossible. The centrality of the West in determining the contours of cultural exchange, such as in the moment above, underscores the difficulty of challenging our inherited structures. *In an Antique Land* deliberately draws attention to some of these structures.

In an influential essay, Dipesh Chakrabarty has argued that 'insofar as the academic discourse of history ... is concerned, "Europe" remains the sovereign, theoretical subject of all histories, including the ones we call "Indian", "Chinese",

"Kenyan", and so on'.[19] His call to 'provincialize Europe' is fraught with difficulty, a project doomed to failure. Yet Chakrabarty calls for a 'history that deliberately makes visible … its own repressive strategies and practices' so that 'the modern is inevitably contested'.[20] Works such as *In an Antique Land* go some distance towards taking on such a task. The book offers us alternative histories and does so, in part, by challenging not only the boundaries of travel writing, but also those of fiction, anthropology, and academic history writing. Indeed, Ghosh's travels across space and time offer a counterpoint to his travels across the borders and boundaries of disciplines. He thereby poses a postcolonial challenge to the already slippery categories of travel writing, anthropology and history.

---

[19]   Dipesh Chakrabarty, 'Postcoloniality and the Artifice of History: Who Speaks for "Indian" Pasts?', *Representations*, 37 (Winter 1992), p. 1.
[20]   Chakrabarty, 'Postcoloniality', p. 23.

Chapter 12

# Where Are We Going? Cross-border Approaches to Travel Writing

## Tim Youngs

### Travelling disciplines

In academic terms travel writing has travelled. As an object of study it has crossed disciplines. Given its broader context, this is no surprise. Insights from sociology and cultural studies into the experience and consequences of travel are relevant to colleagues across a range of subjects, including Literature. The textual detail of travel writing itself, however, has now become the focus of scholars in many fields besides literary criticism. The editors and most of the contributors to a recent volume of essays, subtitled 'Reading Travel Writing', are geographers;[1] as are the authors of two monographs on women travellers in Africa.[2] The editors of another collection of essays subtitled 'Towards a Cultural History of Travel' are an art historian and a historian.[3] The editor of the definitive edition of Ralegh's *Discoverie of Guiana* is an anthropologist.[4] Contributors to the journal *Studies in Travel Writing* have been drawn from anthropology, history and sociology, besides American, Arctic, British, communications, comparative, cultural, English, French, and Italian Studies. In large part this disciplinary crossing is a result of the crisis in the humanities of the 1970s and of shared interests in gender and in (post)colonialism.

My essay will address some of these questions about disciplinary identity in relation to travel and will ask what travel *writing* and its criticism leave out.

My thanks to Carl Thompson and Peter Hulme for helpful comments on this essay. The views expressed in it are my responsibility.

[1] James Duncan and Derek Gregory, eds, *Writes of Passage: Reading Travel Writing* (London: Routledge, 1999).
[2] Alison Blunt, *Travel, Gender, and Imperialism: Mary Kingsley and West Africa* (New York: Guilford Press, 1994); Cheryl McEwan, *Gender, Geography and Empire: Victorian Women Travellers in West Africa* (Aldershot: Ashgate, 2000).
[3] Jas Elsner and Joan Pau Rubiés, *Voyages & Visions: Towards a Cultural History of Travel* (London: Reaktion Books, 1999).
[4] Sir Walter Ralegh, *The Discoverie of the Large, Rich and Bewtiful Empyre of Guiana*, transcribed, edited and introduced by Neil L. Whitehead (Manchester: Manchester University Press, 1997). Moreover, in his acknowledgements, Whitehead remarks that 'the interdisciplinary nature of this project means that my debt is not to anthropologists alone' (p. vii).

**Travel and anthropology**

Since the humanities and social sciences began to re-examine themselves in the 1970s, impelled by their responses to US intervention in Vietnam, by the Civil Rights movement and by the new wave of feminism, issues of power and of representation (in both main senses of the word) have been a common concern.[5] The study of travel writing has reflected these developments in the attention paid to the relationship between the visitor and visited. Of particular importance has been the turn in anthropology towards a critique of ethnography and the adoption by those in literary studies of elements of that critique. Yet the place where these subjects converge is the written text and one needs to ask, as John Hutnyk has done, what is missed out when we look at travel *writing*.[6] Especially influential in providing a bridge between literary and cultural studies and anthropology has been the work of James Clifford.[7] Clifford has been criticized on a number of grounds, however. Most relevant to the present discussion is the charge that he remains silent on the economic context and political practice of his own travel and writing.[8] These accusations do not stand against Clifford alone, of course. Hutnyk's comment that 'travel stories ... are the

---

[5]     See Chapter 1, 'A Crisis of Representation in the Human Sciences', George E. Marcus and Michael M. J. Fischer, eds, *Anthropology as Cultural Critique: An Experimental Moment in the Human Sciences* (Chicago: University of Chicago Press, 1986), pp. 7–16. The chapter displays some of the features of the move towards the discursive that I address later in this essay. Marcus and Fischer's reference to the 'unfavorable shift in the relative position of American power and influence in the world' (p. 9) was a baffling one to have made even in 1986 and finds a most surprising echo ten years later in Caren Kaplan's, in many ways radical, always invigorating and often excellent, *Questions of Travel* when she remarks that 'we have seen the "superpowers" lose some of their hegemonic social, economic, and political control over the rest of the world'. Well, one of the superpowers anyway. Caren Kaplan, *Questions of Travel: Postmodern Discourses of Displacement* (Durham: Duke University Press, 1996), p. 15.

[6]     Remarks made by John Hutnyk at 'Representing Culture: Travel and Anthropology', a colloquium held at The Nottingham Trent University, 8 May 2002.

[7]     James Clifford and George E. Marcus, eds, *Writing Culture: The Poetics and Politics of Ethnography* (Berkeley: University of California Press, 1986); James Clifford, *The Predicament of Culture: Twentieth-Century Ethnography, Literature, and Art* (Cambridge, Mass.: Harvard University Press, 1988); James Clifford, *Routes: Travel and Translation in the Late Twentieth Century* (Cambridge, Mass.: Harvard University Press, 1997). It is important to note that Clifford's writing is not as representative of anthropology as those, like myself, who are outside the discipline often take it to be. I present an over-simplified picture here, and in so doing illustrate my point that cross-disciplinary bridges can have weaknesses. Anthropology is not what it seems to those who come at it from English or cultural studies. My larger point in this essay is that a desire for a meeting of disciplines, though in many cases enriching, can diminish us by leading to a kind of disciplinary nowhere in which specialist skills cannot be employed.

[8]     For a sense of the criticism see John Hutnyk, 'Argonauts of Western Pessimism: Clifford's Malinowski', in Steve Clark, ed., *Travel Writing and Empire: Postcolonial Theory in Transit* (London: Zed Books, 1999), pp. 45–62, esp. p. 47.

stuff of contemporary travel economics' points to the fact that academics who travel and who write about travel are no less implicated in structures that maintain power inequalities than those they criticize.[9] It is difficult to disagree with this diagnosis, though Hutnyk's remedy is not one that all would want to take:

> Without a critical perspective grounded in a practical politics dedicated to changing ... troubles, and transforming the conditions of inequality, exploitation and oppression from which they arise, anthropology (multi-site or bounded), travel (alternative or mainstream) and 'the history of ethnography' (orthodox or Cliffordian) remains only so much sight-seeing.[10]

Setting aside for the moment the call to action, Hutnyk is surely right to suggest the limitations of a critical practice which, despite its calls for self-reflexivity, ignores its own material conditions. The so-called crisis in anthropology has not stopped government intelligence agencies seeking their recruits from among its number.[11] Perhaps the simple picture of a subject that has freed itself from its colonial legacy through greater introspection needs to be redrawn. On the other hand, anthropologists can assist the powerless, monitor human rights violations, and have their work support those who seek redress through the courts.[12] Pronouncements about anthropology's loss of authority ought to be received with some scepticism: both conservative and radical examples attest to the contrary.

The role of anthropology in gaining and transmitting local knowledge is stressed in its defence. The editors of a volume of essays on eighteenth- and nineteenth-century Pacific encounters compare anthropology favourably with subaltern studies and postcolonial discourse theory, which, 'while insisting on representing their clients in the global terms of the subject/other binarism, maintain an agenda peculiar to specific economic and political regions, chiefly postcolonial India, the Middle East, and the former slave economies of the Caribbean and the Americas'.[13] According to these same editors:

---

[9]  Hutnyk, 'Argonauts', p. 60.

[10]  Hutnyk, 'Argonauts', p. 62.

[11]  For example through the advertisement placed by Britain's Defence Evaluation & Research Agency (DERA) in the *Times Higher Education Supplement* of 29 January 2001 for visiting senior fellows. The advert states that appointees will work mainly through the Centre for Defence Analysis, which carries out studies and analyses of defence and security issues for the Ministry of Defence and other Government Departments. Applicants must hold a senior post in universities or research institutions. (The other eligible subjects, besides anthropology, were modern world history and politics, strategic and war studies, social science, operational research and management science, economics, and statistics.) My point here is not to condemn those who wish to defend their nation's security (though how that is conceived, what it involves, and how it is done is another matter) but to suggest that anthropology is not as powerless as some would claim.

[12]  Jeremy MacClancy, 'Keeping watch on the seats of power', *Times Higher Education Supplement*, 21 June 2002, p. 20.

[13]  Alex Calder, Jonathan Lamb, and Bridget Orr, eds, *Voyages and Beaches: Pacific Encounters, 1769–1840* (Honolulu: University of Hawai'i Press, 1999), p. 5.

> In awareness of what it costs to posit an accurately observing and judging subject, anthropology has been ahead of the game that postcolonial discourse theory and cultural nationalism only hesitantly play in the South Pacific. As well as being properly cautious about the gaze they turn to the periphery, anthropologists make no generalizations about hegemony, or about the coherence of European designs upon Oceania.[14]

The focus on local detail is admirable: a welcome corrective to ill-informed generalizations. To add to the disciplinary confusion, however, none of the three editors is an anthropologist: all are specialists in literature! Furthermore, the two essays that are singled out for their examination of the '*textual* record of European discovery' are by anthropologist Nicholas Thomas and anthropologist/archaeologist Ian Barber.[15] Indeed, we are told that:

> Like Shakespearean textual scholars, these anthropologists examine variants, emend the corrupt memory of actors, and explore other versions of the 'same' story. Out of these possible readings, they reconstruct the ragged *ur*-text of contact, a patchwork of investigation and inference that is assessed finally on how adequately it represents the interactive complexities of encounter.[16]

Apart from the fact that such a reconstruction is made using the tools and assumptions of modern critical and cultural theory and so *creates* its urtext after the event, this cross-disciplinary travel, with anthropologists and literary critics visiting one another's territory, further provokes the question of what each discipline brings to travel studies that is distinct and useful.

## The place of travel study

Nicholas Thomas has posed a similar question in noting the wave (especially since the mid-1980s) of new studies of race, imperialism, Orientalism and related topics, and comments that:

> Much of this work has necessarily been interdisciplinary; it has almost created a postdisciplinary humanities field, in which histories, cultural studies, cultural politics, narratives and ethnographies all intersect and are all open to being challenged. If there is something basically enabling and positive in the undoing of disciplinary boundaries, authoritative privileges and canonical sources and modes of presentation, it may nevertheless be too easy to celebrate this new fluidity, this new scope for exhilarating trespasses. It would be a pity if the spectacle of intellectual plurality fostered a relativist permissiveness, that acknowledged the fertility of diverse agendas and refused to discriminate among them.[17]

---

[14] Calder, Lamb, and Orr, eds, *Voyages and Beaches*, p. 6.

[15] Calder, Lamb, and Orr, eds, *Voyages and Beaches*, p. 15, my emphasis.

[16] Calder, Lamb, and Orr, eds, *Voyages and Beaches*, pp. 15–16.

[17] Nicholas Thomas, *Colonialism's Culture: Anthropology, Travel and Government* (Cambridge: Polity Press, 1994), p. 19.

Thomas advocates arguing about the 'effectiveness of different disciplinary technologies; about the politics of analytical strategies; about priorities among different ways of contextualizing texts and events; about the appropriateness of particular theoretical languages'.[18] He explains that in *Colonialism's Culture* he calls for and practises a 'historicization of colonialism' but not one that promotes an idea of progress, and he argues against certain deconstructive and psychoanalytical approaches.[19] He stresses the importance of a 'nuanced understanding of the plurality of colonizing endeavours and their continuing effects' and the 'overarching value of political relevance'.[20] By the latter he means intellectual projects, exemplified by Raymond Williams and Edward Said, which address the contexts of scholars and their work, and of their audiences; not a jumping to political correctness or the pseudo-radicalism of academics who 'after all, are engaged in privileged work at some remove from the most consequential theatres of political debate and action'.[21] Thomas means the privileged position of academics in the West (or North) in general terms, rather than suggesting that some have rather different political beliefs in private than are indicated by their publications. If we take Hutynk's point, however, and examine the circumstances of production of work on travel writing, we are faced with the uncomfortable truth that, like postcolonial studies, with which it shares a sometimes strained relationship, travel writing studies is now in fashion. It is true that the subject has not (yet) become institutionalized in the way that postcolonial studies has. A count of advertised posts in English (in Britain at least) that call for a specialism in postcolonialism compared with those that ask for expertise in travel writing is proof of that (though I concede that another way of looking at things would be to say that in their many recent postcolonial appointments English departments are simply making good a lack of provision in what is still a new – and revisionist – field). Indeed, travel writing is even nowadays looked down upon by traditionalists as not-quite-literature. Conversely, there seems to exist within cultural theory an inverted snobbery towards literary texts *per se* (as well as a resistance to historical topics); and in postcolonial theory a feeling that unless the texts studied are those that 'write back' they are not worth looking at. Thus, despite the increased opportunities afforded by travel writing criticism for funding, research, publication and promotion, and by travel to international conferences, to other universities, and to libraries, those who work on travel writing may find themselves occupying an ill-defined space between disciplines. I mean 'find themselves' in both senses: what might appear to be an academic displacement into a zone without demarcation can also provide a platform for self- (or rather group-) identification.

Looking at the material circumstances and benefits of work on travel writing need not mean that we should chastise ourselves or become self-indulgently

---

18 Thomas, *Colonialism's Culture*, p. 19.
19 Thomas, *Colonialism's Culture*, p. 19.
20 Thomas, *Colonialism's Culture*, p. 20.
21 Thomas, *Colonialism's Culture*, p. 20.

introspective. The increasing commercialization of universities – the emphasis on education as a product to be packaged, bought and sold like any other commodity – has all salaried academics complicit to some degree in the structures of capitalism that many would condemn in other manifestations. Rather, it is more the case that greater awareness of the conditions in which we write and read about travel writing (including in books at prices that only university libraries in wealthy countries can afford) should lead to further thought about how we frame our object of study and to the realization, urged on us by John Hutnyk, that travel writing misses out a great deal that matters. Recognition of material conditions can help situate travel, its writing, and its criticism.

## Travel and language

The question of what the specialist disciplinary tools are that could be brought to the study of travel writing is not a straightforward one. Developments in the criticism of travel writing have been influenced by transitions in European intellectual culture and, in particular, by the impact of French structuralist and poststructuralist ideas on the European and US academies. While one might have assumed, for example, that a thorough attention to textual detail would be the domain of literary scholars, this is not so. Reminders of the importance of archive research and of the comparison of different manuscript and printed versions have come from historians,[22] while some literary studies have sometimes theorized on the basis of primary materials quoted second-hand (acknowledged as such) from others' monographs. The turn to discourse analysis has helped direct the gaze of critics to representation and ideology. Two of the three studies that more than any other have moved the academic study of travel writing along are authored by linguists.[23] All three are concerned with power. Yet another approach is taken by Michael Cronin, whose important book concentrates on translation and proceeds from the premise that: 'Indifference to the question of language in many of the

---

[22]  See R. C. Bridges, 'Nineteenth-Century East African Travel Records', *Paideuma*, XXXIII (1987), pp. 179–96, and the same author's essay, 'Explorers' texts and the problem of reactions by non-literate peoples: some nineteenth-century East African examples', *Studies in Travel Writing*, 2 (1999), pp. 65–84; also David Henige, 'Putting the horse back before the cart: recent encouraging signs', *History in Africa*, 13 (1986), pp. 177–93; 'In quest of error's sly imprimatur: the concept of "authorial intent" in modern textual criticism', *History in Africa*, 14 (1987), pp. 87–112; and 'Ventriloquists and wandering truths', *Studies in Travel Writing*, 2 (1998), pp. 164–80.

[23]  Sara Mills, *Discourses of Difference: An Analysis of Women's Travel Writing and Colonialism* (London: Routledge, 1991); Mary Louise Pratt, *Imperial Eyes: Travel Writing and Transculturation* (London: Routledge, 1992). Mills discusses her Foucauldian framework on pp. 6–19. The other of the three titles, and the earliest of them, is Peter Hulme, *Colonial Encounters: Europe and the Native Caribbean 1492–1797* (London: Methuen, 1986).

key texts on writing and travel that have been published over the last two decades has led to a serious misrepresentation of both the experience of travel and the construction of narrative accounts of these experiences.'[24] Cronin has in mind the centrality of language to the doing and telling of travel and the act of translation that all travellers make. A particular target of his attack (as it was for Hutnyk) is James Clifford, who, in his book *Routes*, 'managed to completely ignore the entire body of scholarly work on translation in a work allegedly discussing the question of translation and travel'.[25] Making good this neglect, Cronin draws on Roman Jakobson's identification of three kinds of translation:

> *Intralingual translation* or translation within a language is the interpretation of verbal signs by means of other signs belonging to the same language. *Interlingual translation* or translation between languages is the interpretation of verbal signs by means of verbal signs from another language. Lastly, *intersemiotic translation* or translation into or from something other than language is the interpretation of verbal signs by means of signs belonging to non-verbal sign systems.[26]

In practice the traveller might range across all three during an act of travel.

Cronin's book extends the interdisciplinarity of travel writing criticism and takes it in another direction, comparing the traveller with the translator, who 'ceaselessly moving between languages and cultures is reflected at another level in translation studies, a discipline that travels continuously between disciplines' (p. 4). One might also note that in his acknowledgements Cronin says he has learnt much from the undergraduates who have studied on his Travel Literature course – students who are taking Applied Languages, International Marketing and Languages and Applied Computational Linguistics (p. ix). But even though he is careful not to reduce the complexity of translation to a simple metaphor and he refuses to 'trivialise translation ... by merely using it as a synonym for any kind of transformation' (p. 17), it is noticeable that he adopts the problematic symbol of the nomad to describe the position of the translator. Cronin posits a 'nomadic theory of translation', in which:

> The translating agent like the traveller straddles the borderline between the cultures. A nomadic theory of translation proposes the translator-nomad as an emblematic figure of (post)modernity by demonstrating what translation can tell us about nomadism and what nomadism can tell us about translation and how both impinge on contemporary concerns with identity. (p. 2)

It is unfortunate that Cronin should deploy this image of the nomad since its romantic appropriation by Bruce Chatwin and other travel writers, and its questionable use in cultural theory, removes from the label the economic realities of the existence of

---

[24] Michael Cronin, *Across the Lines: Travel, Language, Translation* (Cork: Cork University Press, 2000), p. 2.
[25] Cronin, *Across the Lines*, p. 4.
[26] Cronin, *Across the Lines*, p. 2.

those to whom it properly belongs.[27] Elsewhere in *Across the Lines* Cronin shows an eye for the economic by complaining about the restrictions on foreign language learning placed on and by universities and by reminding us of the conditions faced by refugees.

Two other arguments in *Across the Lines* are worth mentioning here. One is Cronin's criticism of sociologists Chris Rojek and John Urry's edited collection of essays, *Touring Cultures* – a book that highlights yet another aspect of travel: this time the idea that culture travels and that tourism contributes to the construction of national cultures – for its favouring 'an overly visual reading of the travel phenomenon in cultural formation' at the expense of language.[28] Through our communication about places, language is fundamental to our experience and to our perception of them. The other aspect is technological innovation. In particular, Cronin considers how the development of the internet and the opening up of cyberspace has affected the modes and language of travel.

What Rojek and Urry do write is that: 'All cultures get remade as a result of the flows of peoples, objects and images across national borders, whether these involve colonialism, work-based migration, individual travel or mass tourism.'[29] That they should have to remind us of this is itself a sign of what much commentary on travel has ignored, as well as of the fixity falsely foisted on cultures by some (post)colonial discourse criticism that has a short historical memory. Evidence of ancient and more recent cultural remaking can be heard every time we open our mouths to speak or can be read in each sentence we write. (Taking just this last sentence, 'evidence' is from the Latin, 'ancient' from French and Latin, 'speak' from Old English, 'can' from Old English and German, 'write' from Old English and Old Norse, and so on.) Such depth of contact can be heard in many languages. Linguists, archaeologists and classical historians can testify to a cultural travelling on a scale that might throw into question some of the assumptions about modern globalization. A historical perspective should help us to qualify some of the claims that we make about modern travel and contemporary culture.

Nonetheless, it is surely true, as several scholars have noted, that the technological changes of the last one hundred and fifty years have had a profound effect not only on the way that people travel (from industrialized countries at least) but also on the way that they perceive and narrate their journeys. In her book *Moving Lives*, Sidonie Smith considers how 'technologies of motion transform narratives of

---

[27]   See Tim Youngs, 'Where has all the baggage gone? Relabelling the nomad in contemporary travel writing and criticism', in David Jarrett, Tomasz Kowaleski and Geoff Ridden, eds, *Packing and Unpacking Culture: Changing Models of British Studies* (Torun: Uniwersytet Mikolaaja Kopernika Press, 2001), pp. 105–14.

[28]   Cronin, *Across the Lines*, p. 21.

[29]   Chris Rojek and John Urry, 'Transformations of Travel and Theory', in Chris Rojek and John Urry, eds, *Touring Cultures: Transformations of Travel and Theory* (London: Routledge, 1997), p. 11.

travel'.[30] Changes in the way people travel alter their identities and relationships. In particular Smith's interest is in gender: on 'how women travel and how those [new modern] modes of mobility affect the stories women narrate about gender and bodies in motion in the twentieth century'.[31]

Since travel writing in its broadest sense must, like all literature, reflect the society in which it is produced and consumed, multifarious elements of culture are contained within it. They are there to be uncovered and teased out. Of course, the travels of many groups in society are written about by others, often prejudicially. Apart from migrants and refugees an example in Britain might be the 'New Age' travellers, an obsession of the popular – and populist – media in the 1980s and 1990s. Such groups do not generally tell their stories in literary form for public consumption. Their stories are rarely heard by those who readily tell stories about them, and when they are they are usually told orally and transcribed by others.[32] Others might record their journeys in writing but in private and for themselves.[33]

## Travel and metaphor

A further reason for the growing popularity of travel in academia is undoubtedly its appeal as metaphor, a device which comes close to combining language with visual image.[34] Margins and borders have been centralized (both as part of the postcolonial project described above but also due to their symbolic value); exile is embraced; displacement has found a home; nomadism is everywhere; migrancy is concentrated into many a forum. At its best the utilization of these terms accompanies serious attention to those who are invoked by them; at worst the terms are separated from the people and employed without meaningful reference to the often brutal realities behind them. Or, as a middle way, the labels are stuck on for fashion.

In a much-quoted essay that serves as a kind of position paper, Janet Wolff has commented on the use of these metaphors. Indeed, her article is as prescient as it is a commentary on an existing state of affairs: it was published in 1993 and the usage that she describes has become more pervasive since then:

---

[30] Sidonie Smith, *Moving Lives: Twentieth-Century Women's Travel Writing* (Minneapolis: University of Minnesota Press, 2001), p. xii. (Smith also has a coda on the internet.)

[31] Smith, *Moving Lives*, p. xiii.

[32] See Kevin Hetherington, *New Age Travellers: Vanloads of Uproarious Humanity* (London: Cassell, 2000).

[33] Inderpal Grewal has been working on the diaries of Sikh immigrant women to the US, for example.

[34] Of course, the editors of the present volume admit their own promotion of such metaphors: as mentioned in the Introduction to this volume, the conference which gave rise to this volume was titled 'Borders and Crossings'.

> Vocabularies of travel seem to have been proliferating in cultural criticism recently: nomadic criticism, traveling theory, critic-as-tourist (and vice versa), maps, billboards, hotels and motels. ... I want to suggest that these metaphors are *gendered*, in a way which is for the most part not acknowledged. ... My argument is that just as the practices and ideologies of *actual* travel operate to exclude or pathologize women, so the use of that vocabulary as metaphor necessarily produces androcentric tendencies in theory.[35]

It is an important argument but its challenge seems not to have been taken up. Wolff argues that the metaphors are so encumbered by their gender baggage that they cannot be shifted and should be dropped. Wolff acknowledges that, besides gender, '[d]isparities of wealth and cultural capital, and class difference generally, have ensured real disparities in access to and modes of travel' (p. 224), and that the ways in which people travel are diverse. She admits that her focus is on 'a single notion of travel, which for the most part rests on a Western, middle-class idea of the chosen and leisured journey' (p. 225). This admission is welcome since, in travel writing criticism, as in other areas of study, there has sometimes been a tension between gender- and class-based approaches. Wolff's openness about the limits of her focus suggests that these approaches are not incompatible but implies, sensibly, that the issues are too large for them to be easily combined (except, perhaps, one infers in a closely defined case study).

Noting the tendency of travel theorists to quote the works of travel writers, Wolff observes that: 'Clearly this is a restless moment in cultural history' (p. 225). The idea might be driven further. Wolff does not comment on the fact that the volume containing the essay to which she refers is titled *Traveling Theories/Traveling Theorists*.[36] One might speculate here on the appeal to contemporary theories and theorists of being elsewhere; of being *Other*, as well as being on the move.[37] In their preface to *Traveling Theories*, the editors assert that:

> If theories no longer totalize, they do travel. Indeed, in their diverse rootings and uprootings, theories are constantly translated, appropriated, contested, grafted. Theory travels; so do theorists. (p. v)

But ideas have always travelled and so have those who hold and exchange them. 'Theory' is no different in this respect. What strikes one here is the totalizing assumption that it represents a departure (as it were), and the desire that it should, when it does not.[38]

---

[35] Janet Wolff, 'On the road again: metaphors of travel in cultural criticism', *Cultural Studies*, 7:2 (May 1993), p. 224.

[36] James Clifford and Vivek Dhareshwar, eds, *Traveling Theories/Traveling Theorists*, *Inscriptions*, 5 (1989).

[37] Steve Clark's edited book is subtitled *Postcolonial Theory in Transit*; a more recent collection of essays promotes motion to its main title: Helen Gilbert and Anna Johnston, eds, *In Transit: Travel, Text, Empire* (New York: Peter Lang, 2002).

[38] 'Travel is very much a modern concept', writes Kaplan in *Questions of Travel* (p. 3). Again, this is (in my view) a minor lapse in an important book, with whose general argument I largely agree.

Wolff concentrates on the vocabularies of travel in postcolonial criticism, postmodern theory and poststructuralism, and traces the possibility of a feminist critique of travel metaphors. Admitting the appeal of metaphors of movement over stasis and fixity, she warns against an abandonment of the rooted and the solid: 'From the point of view of engaged politics, and here specifically in relation to feminism, a certain postmodern stance is incompatible with the fundamental commitment to a critique which is premised on the existence of systematically structured, actual, inequalities (of gender)' (p. 228). Wolff explores the possibility that there is an intrinsic relationship between masculinity and travel, by which she means not that there is an essential connection between them, but that travel may be central to a constructed masculine identity.[39] Wolff does not deny that when nineteenth-century women travellers encountered 'native' subjects, considerations of authority overrode those of gender. Rather, reminding us that 'many feminists have made the point about poststructuralist theory that just as women are discovering their subjectivity and identity, theory tells us that we have to deconstruct and de-centre the subject', she suggests that: 'The already-gendered language of mobility marginalizes women who want to participate in cultural criticism' (p. 234). Wolff's objection seems to be that postmodern theory undermines the solid subject position and the specific narrative that feminism needs. The rush to terms such as 'nomad', 'maps' and 'travel' has, she feels, given a false impression of movement because 'we don't all have the same access to the road' (p. 235). If metaphors of displacement and destabilization are to be used, she believes we should not be deceived by them into thinking that they are not themselves situated somewhere. The dominant centre, she remarks, is what must be criticized; and it should be acknowledged that the criticism comes from a place: the margins. She indicates a preference for the metaphors of 'borderlands', 'exile', and 'margins' in that they 'are premised on the fact of dislocation from a given, and excluding, place' (p. 235).

Wolff implores us to challenge the 'exclusions of a metaphoric discourse of travel', and remarks that in a patriarchal culture not everyone is 'on the road' together: 'We therefore have to think carefully about employing a vocabulary which, liberatory in many ways, also encourages the irresponsibility of flight and misleadingly implies a notion of universal and equal mobility' (p. 235). It is an important argument and one that has not really been acted upon despite the frequency with which her article is cited. If anything, the urge to embrace these metaphors has grown stronger. Pointing out that metaphors are not static, Wolff proposes that rather than reject all travel metaphors we should reappropriate them: 'a good postmodern practice which both exposes the implicit meanings in play, and produces the possibility of subverting those meanings by thinking against the grain' (pp. 235–6). But this strategy still leaves the power of (re)appropriation in the hands of those who have the luxury of travelling voluntarily.

---

[39] cf. Karen R. Lawrence, *Penelope Voyages: Women and Travel in the British Literary Tradition* (Ithaca: Cornell University Press, 1994).

Whether reappropriation of them is possible or not, the metaphors of travel migrate and put down new roots. It is worth remembering their original contexts, which are often considerably harsher than our celebration of mobility and fluidity suggests.

## Travelling capital

To criticize these practices is not to overlook one's own involvement in them: to do so would be as self-deluding as to attack capitalism without simultaneously admitting one's own immersion in the system. Again, I take my lead from John Hutnyk, whose compelling and self-critical study *The Rumour of Calcutta* demonstrates the importance of a material view of travel culture. Hutnyk's 'ethnography of budget travel' is a 'study of the ways in which particular Western visitors understand Calcutta; how writing, photography and film condition this process; and how touristic representations fit into the practices and ideologies of aid work and cultural imperialism'.[40] Hutnyk acknowledges 'my own complicities in writing on this topic' and hopes to further, 'in however small a way, an anti-imperialist project that is *not just mere writing*, and is not naive about representation and presentation' (p. ix, my emphasis). He wants to explore, too, his own 'involvement in an entire industry of description and explanation implicated within an international inscribing apparatus which constituted the many "meanings" of Calcutta' (p. 4). He admits that his project, 'broadly that of representation, of travel and of perception or interpretation', risks slipping into 'a study of international capitalism' (p. 2). It is a risk worth taking, however, and one that yields valuable results. For one thing, Hutnyk's approach allows him to look at a considerably larger picture than is presented only by travel writing. Indeed, he supplies a kind of Barthesian reading of cultural artefacts with the result that he scales down travel *writing* to just one, rarefied, expression of travel. Hutnyk's aim is certainly not to reduce everything to discourse or representation. He is more interested in the material as well as symbolic function of things like souvenirs; in what they tell us about their place of origin and their new home.

Hutnyk, too, has statements to make about travel and theory; about travelling theory. Refreshingly eclectic, he has 'souvenired' from '[a]mong the book production industry that is theory today' some 'fashionable items': 'I want to set out my work under the sign of both Marx and an analysis of processes of commodification and the world market, and Heidegger in so far as he was concerned with technology and the "production" of how we live in the world' (p. 14). Hutnyk will not consider discourse and representation without paying particular attention to the material technologies with which 'conceptual matters are inextricably linked' (p. 15). One need not be a

---

[40]   John Hutnyk, *The Rumour of Calcutta: Tourism, Charity and Representation* (London: Zed Books, 1996), p. viii.

Marxist to acknowledge that '[t]echnologies of representation are major channelling factors which determine, to some extent, what kind of representations of Calcutta can be produced' (p. 20) – and, of course, not only Calcutta – but it probably helps to be one to agree that:

> The rumour of Calcutta coexists with a mobile capital which chases all around the globe, making commodities of all it sees. The technological channels through which this rumour passes – the machineries of traveller perception, writing, camera, etc. – are the tools by which capitalism transmutes all culture, emotion, identity into a form open to exchange. (p. 21)

This mobile capital reminds us that it is not just individuals that travel: culture travels with them and – a fact that often gets missed out – people and their culture travel economically. Yet travel writing criticism often lets this drift out of view.

Whether metaphors of travelling capital risk slipping away from the material into the discursive is another and a larger question to do with the problems – and potential – of framing *things* in language. Metaphors are necessary to understanding and description, but their application to travel and to travel writing can distract from the specific material contexts in which travel happens and from the relationship between the language employed to describe it and the actualities of that travel.[41]

Further evidence of the slipperiness of travel is provided by a recent anthology of travel writing edited by Robyn Davidson. In her introduction, Davidson, herself the author of two accomplished and important books of travel,[42] writes rather grandly that:

> The metaphor of the journey is embedded in the very way in which we conceive of life – a movement from birth to death, from this world to the next, from ignorance to wisdom. In Aboriginal philosophy, its metaphorical possibilities extended to include the earth itself – Australia *is* a travel narrative.[43]

Davidson's aim is laudable: to make travel writing more inclusive. But to extend travel metaphorically to any and every life event, and to the nation itself, is to dematerialize travel and to make of it a huge and empty metaphor. Davidson's

---

[41]   For more on travel and metaphor, in the context of French philosophical literature of the late Renaissance and the Enlightenment, see Georges Van Den Abbeele, *Travel as Metaphor: From Montaigne to Rousseau* (Minneapolis: University of Minnesota Press, 1992). Van Den Abbeele notes that: '"Metaphor" comes from *metaphorein*, to transfer or transport' (p. xxii).

[42]   Robyn Davidson, *Tracks* [1980] (London: Vintage, 1992); *Desert Places* [1996] (London: Penguin, 1997). See also her collection of articles, *Travelling Light* [1989] (Pymble: Collins Angus & Robertson, 1993). Of her novel *Ancestors* (London: Vintage, 1989), it might softly be observed that the border between travel writing and fiction is sometimes best left preserved. For a discussion of Davidson and nomadism see Youngs, 'Where has all the baggage gone?'

[43]   Robyn Davidson, ed., *The Picador Book of Journeys* (Basingstoke: Macmillan, 2000), p. 4.

justified complaint against a tight restriction on the definition of travel writing leads to exactly the free-floating identity that I have questioned earlier in this essay. She defines travel writing as 'a non-fiction work in which the author goes from point a to point b and tells us something about it' (p. 3). She includes in this 'literature of movement', involuntary travellers, 'tugged around the world by circumstances over which they have no control – slaves, soldiers, and the victims of war' (p. 3). Those unfortunates make few appearances in travel writing, despite the minor tradition of domestic travel that uncovers the socially excluded. Their representation is more common in photography where it raises the difficult question of the commodification and aestheticization of suffering, a tension that exists most famously nowadays in the portraits of the dispossessed by the socialist photographer Sebastião Salgado.[44] Whatever one's position in that debate, we see in Salgado's subjects something staring us in the face: that the background to academic celebrations of fluidity, movement, intermixing, and the collapse of borders is the racially and politically-motivated reinforcement of borders – in Europe, Australia, and the US – against those who would enter. That is a closure and it has popular support, especially now that terror and refugees are officially conflated. While we write about global movements and the collapse of disciplinary boundaries, the very nations in which we write are policing those boundaries with state discipline and (in the case of English scares about refugees travelling illegally from France through the Channel Tunnel) berating foreign governments for their indiscipline in holding people back. This is something that travel writing and much of its criticism leaves out. Travel writing need not be blamed for this: we should not expect it to read like political economy. But viewing it in a broader context allows us to see points of detail against larger backdrops and might make us review both the points from which we approach it and how we travel between our intellectual and disciplinary positions.

---

[44] Collected in, among other works, Sebastião Salgado, *Other Americas* (New York: Pantheon Books, 1986); *Terra: Struggle of the Landless* (London: Phaidon, 1997); *Migrations: Humanity in Transition* (New York: Aperture, 2000).

# Select Bibliography

'A tour through Brittany made in the year 1829', in *The Literary Remains of the Rev. Thomas Price, Carnhuanawr*, 2 vols (Llandovery: William Rees/London: Longman & Co., 1854), vol. 1

Adams, Percy, *Travel Literature and the Evolution of the Novel* (Lexington: University Press of Kentucky, 1983)

Almeida, Paulo Mendes de, ed., *Semana de 22*, catalogue, trans. Edwina Jackson (São Paulo: Museo de Arte de São Paulo, 1972)

Andrade, Joaquim Pedro de, 'New Line Cinema Corporation', broadsheet (circa 1978)

Andrade, José Oswald de Sousa, *Pau Brasil: Cancioneiro de Oswald de Andrade* (Paris: Au Sans Pareil, 1924)

——, 'Contra os emboabas', *O Minas Gerais*, 13 May 1928, p. 5

——, *Serafim Ponte Grande* (Rio de Janeiro: Ariel, 1933)

——, 'Manifesto antropófago', *Revista de Antropofagia*, 1 May 1928, pp. 1–3; rpt. *Obras completas*, 11 vols (Rio de Janeiro: Editôra Civilização Brasileira, 1971), vol. VI, pp. 13–19. Trans. Leslie Bary as 'Cannibalist Manifesto'. *Latin American Literary Review* [Pittsburgh, PA], XXXVIII (July–Dec. 1991), pp. 35–47

Andrade, Mário Raúl de Morais, *Macunaíma, o Herói sem nenhum caráter* (São Paulo: Livraria Editôra Martins, 1965)

——, *Poesias completas* (São Paulo: Editôra Itatiaia, 1987)

Arnold, Matthew, *The Study of Celtic Literature* (London: Smith & Elder, 1912)

Ashworth, John Hervey, *The Saxon in Ireland: or, the Rambles of an Englishman in Search of a Settlement in the West of Ireland* (London: Murray, 1851)

Aurégan, Pierre, *Des récits et des hommes – Terre Humaine: un autre regard sur les sciences de l'homme* (Paris: Nathan/Plon, 2001)

Barbotin, Père Maurice, 'Arawaks et Caraïbes à Marie-Galante', *Bulletin de la Société d'histoire de la Guadeloupe*, 11–12 (1976), pp. 77–118

Barreiro, José, 'Indians in Cuba', *Cultural Survival Quarterly*, 13:3 (1989), pp. 56–60

Batten, Charles L., Jr, *Pleasurable Instruction: Form and Convention in Eighteenth-Century Travel Literature* (Los Angeles: University of California Press, 1978)

Baudrillard, Jean, *America*, trans. Chris Turner (London: Verso, 1988)

Behdad, Ali, *Belated Travelers: Orientalism in the Age of Colonial Dissolution* (Durham, NC: Duke University Press, 1994)

Bell, H. Hesketh, *Glimpses of a Governor's Life: From Diaries, Letters and Memoranda* (London: Sampson Low, Marston & Co., 1946)

Bell, R., *Wayside Pictures Through France, Belgium, and Holland* (London: Richard Bentley, 1850)

Berger, James, *After the End: Representations of Post-Apocalypse* (Minneapolis: University of Minnesota Press, 1999)

Berkhofer, Robert F., Jr, *The White Man's Indian: Images of the American Indian from Columbus to the Present* (New York: Vintage, 1978)

Berman, Antoine, *Pour une critique des traductions: John Donne* (Paris: Gallimard, 1995)

Black, Jeremy, *Maps and Politics* (Chicago: University of Chicago Press, 1997)

Blanco, Gladys, 'Indians of Cuba', *Granma Weekly Review*, International Edition, no. 25 (18 June 1989), p. 4

Blunt, Alison, *Travel, Gender, and Imperialism: Mary Kingsley and West Africa* (New York: Guilford Press, 1994)

Bond, Richmond P., *Queen Anne's American Kings* (Oxford: Clarendon Press, 1952)

Bopp, Raúl, *Cobra Norato e outros poemas* (Rio de Janeiro: Block Editôres, 1951)

Borer, Alain, *et al.*, eds, *Pour une littérature voyageuse* (Paris: Editions Complexe, 1992)

Borm, Jan, 'In-Betweeners?', *Studies in Travel Writing*, 4 (2000), pp. 78–105

Boswell, James, *The Journal of a Tour to the Hebrides with Samuel Johnson* (Edinburgh: Canongate, 1996)

Boym, Svetlana, *The Future of Nostalgia* (New York: Basic Books, 2001)

Bridges, R. C., 'Nineteenth-Century East African Travel Records', *Paideuma*, XXXIII (1987), pp. 179–96

——, 'Explorers' texts and the problem of reactions by non-literate peoples: some nineteenth-century East African examples', *Studies in Travel Writing*, 2 (1999), pp. 65–84

Brinton, Daniel G., 'The Archaeology of Cuba', *American Archaeologist*, 2:10 (October 1898), pp. 253–6

Bryan, William S., ed., *Our Islands and Their People as seen with Camera and Pencil*, 2 vols (St Louis: N. D. Thompson, 1899)

Bryson, Anna, *From Courtesy to Civility: Changing Modes of Conduct in Early Modern England* (Oxford: Clarendon, 1998)

Burke, Wayne, 'Double G(l)azing: Regarding a Colonial Imagination in Patrick Fermor's *The Traveller's Tree*', *Caribbean Quarterly*, 46:2 (2000), pp. 67–84

Byron, Robert, *The Road to Oxiana* (London: Picador, 1994)

Calder, Alex, Lamb, Jonathan, and Bridget Orr, eds, *Voyages and Beaches: Pacific Encounters, 1769–1840* (Honolulu: University of Hawai'i Press, 1999)

Caminha, Pero Vaz de, 'Letter to King Manoel', 1 May 1500, trans. William Brooks Greenlee, *The Voyages of Pedro Álvarez Cabral to Brazil and India*, 2nd ser., 81 (London: Hakluyt Society, 1937), pp. 3–33

Campbell, Mary B., *The Witness and the Other World: Exotic European Travel Writing 400–1600* (Ithaca: Cornell University Press, 1988)

Campos, Haroldo de, 'Serafim: Um grande não-livro'. Oswald de Andrade, *Obras completas*, vol. II (Rio de Janeiro: Editôra Civilização Brasileira, 1971)

Canziani, Estella, *Through the Apennines and the Land of the Abruzzi* (Cambridge: W. Heffer and Sons, 1928)

——, *Altraversogli Appenninie le terre degli Abruzzi*, trans. Allesandra Iommi (Fermo: Andrea Livi, 1996)

——, *Round About Three Palace Green* (London: Methuen, 1939)

'Carib Identity in the New Millenium', *Koudmen: Issues in Development*, 9:2 (2000)

Castronovo, David, *The English Gentleman: Images and Ideals in Literature and Society* (New York: Ungar, 1987)

Cendrars, Blaise, *Trop c'est trop. Œuvres complètes*, vol. VIII (Paris: Denoël, 1960–65)

Chakrabarty, Dipesh, 'Postcoloniality and the Artifice of History: Who Speaks for Indian Pasts?', *Representations*, 37 (Winter 1992), pp. 1–26

Chatwin, Bruce, *The Songlines* (New York: Viking Penguin, 1987)

——, Introduction to Robert Byron, *The Road to Oxiana* (London: Picador, 1994), pp. xi–xx.

——, *Anatomy of Restlessness: Uncollected Writings*, ed. Jan Borm and Matthew Graves (London: Picador, 1997)

Clark, Steve, ed., *Travel Writing and Empire: Postcolonial Theory in Transit* (London: Zed Books, 1999)

Clifford, James, *The Predicament of Culture: Twentieth-Century Ethnography, Literature, and Art* (Cambridge, Mass.: Harvard University Press, 1988)

——, 'Notes on Travel and Theory', *Inscriptions* 5 (1989), pp. 177–88.

——, *Routes: Travel and Translation in the Late Twentieth Century* (Cambridge: Harvard University Press, 1997)

——, and George E. Marcus, eds, *Writing Culture: The Poetics and Politics of Ethnography* (Berkeley: University of California Press, 1986)

——, and Vivek Dhareshwar, eds, *Traveling Theories/Traveling Theorists*, *Inscriptions* 5 (1989)

Cocker, Mark, *Loneliness and Time: British Travel Writing in the Twentieth Century* (London: Secker & Warburg, 1992)

Colley, Linda, *Britons, Forging the Nation* (London: Pimlico, 1992)

Colombo, Cristoforo, *Epistola Christofori Colom: cui etas nostra multum debet: de insulis Indie supra Gangem nuper inventis* (Rome: Stephan Plannck, 1493)

Conrad, Joseph, *Heart of Darkness* with the *Congo Diary* (London: Penguin, 1995)

*Contributions from the Heye Museum*, vol. 1 (New York: Heye Museum, 1913–15)

Cortesão, Jaime, *A carta de Pero Vaz de Caminha* (Lisbon: Livros de Portugal, 1943)

Costello, Louisa Stuart, *A Summer Amongst the Bocages and the Vines*, 2 vols (London: Richard Bentley, 1840)

Cronin, Michael, *Across the Lines: Travel, Language, Translation* (Cork: Cork University Press, 2000)

Culin, Stewart, 'The Indians of Cuba', *Bulletin of the Free Museum of Science and Arts, University of Pennsylvania, Philadelphia*, III:4 (1902), pp. 185–226

Dampier, William, *A New Voyage Round the World: The Journal of an English Buccaneer* (London: hummingbird press, 1998)

Davidson, Robyn, *Tracks* (London: Vintage, 1992)

——, *Travelling Light* (Pymble: Collins Angus & Robertson, 1993)

——, *Desert Places* (London: Penguin, 1997)

——, ed., *The Picador Book of Journeys* (Basingstoke: Macmillan, 2000)

Davies, E. W. L., *Wolf-Hunting and Wild Sport in Lower Brittany* (London: Chapman and Hall, 1875)

Duncan, James, and Derek Gregory, eds, *Writes of Passage: Reading Travel Writing* (London: Routledge, 1999)

Dunlop, Madeline Ann Wallace, and Rosalind Harriet Maria Wallace Dunlop, *How we Spent the Autumn; or, Wanderings in Brittany* (London: Richard Bentley, 1860)

Dunn, Oliver, and James E. Kelley, Jr, eds, *The Diario of Christopher Columbus' First Voyage to America: 1492–1493* (Norman: University of Oklahoma Press, 1989)

Eckhout, Albert, *Pássaros do Brasil. Reprodução dos quadros existentes no castelo de Hofloessnitz na Saxônia* (Rio de Janeiro: Agir, 1970)

Edwards, Matilda Betham, *A Year in Western France* (London: Longman, Green and Co., 1877)

Elsner, Jaś, and Joan Pau Rubiés, *Voyages & Visions: Towards a Cultural History of Travel* (London: Reaktion Books, 1999)

Fermor, Patrick Leigh, *The Traveller's Tree: A Journey through the Caribbean Islands* (Harmondsworth: Penguin, 1984)

Fewkes, J. Walter, 'Prehistoric Puerto Rico', *Proceedings of the American Association for the Advancement of Science*, LI (1902), pp. 487–512

——, 'Prehistoric Culture of Cuba', *American Anthropologist*, n.s. VI:4 (1904), pp. 535–8

Fewkes, Jesse W., 'Preliminary Report on an Archaeological Trip to the West Indies', *Smithsonian Miscellaneous Collections*, Quarterly Issue, 45 (Washington, 1903), pp. 112–33

Fischermann, Thomas, 'Flucht in den Cyberspace', 19 April 2001, <www.zeit.de/2001/17/staatenlose>

Forbes, John, *Memorandums made in Ireland in the Autumn of 1852*, 2 vols (London: Smith, 1853)

Forsdick, Charles, '*Viator in Fabula*: Jean-Didier Urbain and the Cultures of Travel in Contemporary France', *Studies in Travel Writing*, 4 (2000), pp. 141–64

Foster, Shirley, *Across New Worlds: Nineteenth-century Women Travellers and their Writings* (London: Harvester, 1990)

Foucault, Michel, *Surveiller et punir. Naissance de la prison* (Paris: Gallimard, 1995)

Frederick, Hilary, *The Caribs and their Colonizers* (London: EAFORD, 1983)

Freuderico [pseudonym for Oswald de Andrade], 'De Antropofogia', *Diário de São Paulo*, 17 March 1929

Frow, John, 'Tourism and the Semiotics of Nostalgia', *October* (Fall 1990), pp. 127–54

Frye, Northrop, *Anatomy of Criticism* (New Jersey: Princeton University Press, 1957)

Fussell, Paul, *Abroad: British Literary Traveling Between the Wars* (New York: Oxford University Press, 1980)

Gates, R. Ruggles, 'Studies in Race Crossing: VI. The Indians of Eastern Cuba', *Genetica*, XXVII (1954), pp. 65–96

Genette, Gérard, *Figures II* (Paris: Seuil, 1969)

——, *Nouveau discours du récit* (Paris: Seuil, 1983)

Genette, Gérard, *et al.*, eds, *Théorie des genres* (Paris: Seuil, 1986)

Ghosh, Amitav, *The Shadow Lines* (London: Penguin, 1990)

——, *In an Antique Land* (Delhi: Ravi Dayal, 1992)

Gilbert, Helen, and Anna Johnston, eds, *In Transit: Travel, Text, Empire* (New York: Peter Lang, 2002)

Grant, Anne, *Letters from the Mountains: Being the real Correspondence of a Lady between the Years 1773 and 1803*, 3 vols (London: Longman, 1806)

——, *Memoirs of an American Lady with Sketches of Manners and Scenery in America, as they existed previous to the Revolution*, 2 vols (London: Longman, 1808)

——, *Essays on the Superstitions of the Highlanders of Scotland*, 2 vols (London: Longman, 1811)

——, *Memoir and Correspondence of Mrs. Grant of Laggan*, ed. J. P. Grant, 3 vols (London: Longman, 1844)

Grant, Mary Anne, *Sketches of Life and Manners, with delineation of scenery in England, Scotland and Ireland* (London: Cox, 1810)

Greenblatt, Stephen, *Marvelous Possessions: The Wonder of the New World* (Oxford: Clarendon Press, 1988)

Grewal, Inderpal, *Home and Harem: Nation, Gender, Empire, and the Cultures of Travel* (London: Leicester Press, 1996)

Gutiérrez, Pedro Juan, 'Have Cuban aborigines really disappeared?', *Granma Weekly Review*, International Edition, no. 20 (24 May 1987), p. 12

Hadfield, Andrew, *Literature, Travel and Colonial Writing* (Oxford: Clarendon, 1998)

Hakluyt, Richard, *The Principal Navigations, Voyages, Traffiques and Discoveries of the English Nation*, 8 vols (London: Dent, 1907)

Harley, J. B., 'Maps, Knowledge and Power', in S. Daniels and D. Cosgrove, eds, *The Iconography of Landscape* (Cambridge: Cambridge University Press, 1988), pp. 277–312

Harrington, Mark R., *Cuba before Columbus*, 2 vols (New York: Museum of the American Indian Heye Foundation, 1921)

Haslip-Viera, Gabriel, ed., *Taíno Revival: Critical Perspectives on Puerto Rican Identity and Cultural Politics* (New York: Centro de Estudios Puertorriqueños, 1999)

Head, Francis Bond, *A Fortnight in Ireland* (London: John Murray, 1852)

Helgerson, Richard, *Forms of Nationhood* (Chicago: Chicago University Press, 1992)

Henige, David, 'Putting the horse back before the cart: recent encouraging signs', *History in Africa*, 13 (1986), pp. 177–93

——, 'In quest of error's sly imprimatur: the concept of "authorial intent" in modern textual criticism', *History in Africa*, 14 (1987), pp. 87–112

——, 'Ventriloquists and wandering truths', *Studies in Travel Writing*, 2 (1998), pp. 164–80

Hetherington, Kevin, *New Age Travellers: Vanloads of Uproarious Humanity* (London: Cassell, 2000)

Hinsley, Curtis M., Jr, *Savages and Scientists: The Smithsonian Institution and the Development of American Anthropology 1846–1910* (Washington, DC: Smithsonian Institution Press, 1981)

Holland, Patrick, and Graham Huggan, *Tourists with Typewriters: Critical Reflections on Contemporary Travel Writing* (Ann Arbor: University of Michigan Press, 1998)

Hulme, Peter, *Colonial Encounters: Europe and the Native Caribbean 1492–1797* (London: Methuen, 1986)

——, *Rescuing Cuba: Adventure and Masculinity in the 1890s* (College Park, MD: Latin American Studies Center, 1996)

——, 'In the Wake of Columbus: Frederick Ober's Ambulant Gloss', *Literature and History*, 6:2 (1997), pp. 18–36

——, *Remnants of Conquest: The Island Caribs and their Visitors, 1877–1998* (Oxford: Oxford University Press, 2000)

——, and William Sherman, eds, *'The Tempest' and Its Travels* (London: Reaktion Books, 2000)

——, and Tim Youngs, eds, *The Cambridge Companion to Travel Writing* (Cambridge: Cambridge University Press, 2002)

Hutnyk, John, *The Rumour of Calcutta: Tourism, Charity and Representation* (London: Zed Books, 1996)

——, 'Argonauts of Western Pessimism: Clifford's Malinowski', in Steve Clark, ed., *Travel Writing and Empire: Postcolonial Theory in Transit* (London: Zed Books, 1999), pp. 45–62

Islam, Syed Manzurul, *The Ethics of Travel: From Marco Polo to Kafka* (Manchester: Manchester University Press, 1996)

Jameson, Fredric, *Postmodernism, or, the Cultural Logic of Late Capitalism* (Durham: Duke University Press, 1991)

Jerrold, William Blanchard, *On the Boulevards; with Trips in Normandy and Brittany*, 2 vols (London: Wm. H. Allen & Co, 1867)

Johnson, Amryl, *Sequins for a Ragged Hem* (London: Virago, 1988)

Johnston, Johanna, *The Life, Manners and Travels of Fanny Trollope* (London: Constable, 1979)

Kaplan, Caren, *Questions of Travel: Postmodern Discourses of Displacement* (Durham: Duke University Press, 1996)

Kearns, Richard, 'The Return of the Taínos: Our Own "Lost Tribe"', *Issues in Caribbean Amerindian Studies*, II (October 1999–October 2000) (http://www.centrelink.org/KearnsA.html)

Lacarrière, Jacques, *L'Été grec* (Paris: Terre Humaine/Plon, 1975)

Lawrence, Karen R., *Penelope Voyages: Women and Travel in the British Literary Tradition* (Ithaca: Cornell University Press, 1994)

Le Bris, Michel, 'Fragments du royaume', in Alain Borer *et al.*, *Pour une littérature voyageuse* (Paris: Editions Complexe, 1992), pp. 119–40

Le Disez, Jean-Yves, 'Un victorien au pardon: le Révérend Phillip W. de Quetteville', in *Hauts lieux du sacré en Bretagne* (Brest: CRBC-UBO, 1997), pp. 191–206

——, 'L'Autre des Victoriens. Récits de voyageurs britanniques en Bretagne (1830–1900)', Ph.D. thesis, Université de Bretagne Occidentale (Brest), 1997

——, *Étrange Bretagne* (Rennes: P.U.R, 2002)

Leed, Eric, *The Mind of the Traveler: From Gilgamesh to Global Tourism* (New York: Basic Books, 1991)

Lejeune, Philippe, *Le pacte autobiographique* (Paris: Seuil, 1975)

Léry, Jean de, *Histoire d'vn voyage fait en la terre dv Brésil* (La Rochelle: Antoine Chuppin, 1578)

——, *Historia navigationis in Brasiliam quae et America dicitur* (Geneva: Heirs of Eustache Vignon, 1594)

——, *Histoire d'vn voyage fait en la terre dv Brésil* ([Geneva]: Heirs of Eustache Vignon, 1599–1600)

——, *História de uma viagem faita à terra do Brasil*, ed. Monteiro Lobato (Rio de Janeiro: Companhia Editôra Nacional, 1926)

——, *History of a Voyage to the Land of Brazil, Otherwise Called America*, trans. Janet Whatley (Berkeley: University of California Press, 1990)

Lewis, W., *The Complete Wild Body, 1907–27*, ed. Bernard Lafourcade (Santa Barbara: Black Sparrow Press, 1982)

Lippard, Lucy, *Dadas on Art* (Englewood Cliffs: Prentice Hall, 1971)

Lodge, David, *The Practice of Writing* (London: Penguin, 1997)

Lowth, George T., *The Wanderer in Western France* (London: Hurst and Blackett, 1863)

Lussagnet, Suzanne, *Le Brésil et les Brésiliens*, vol. II (Paris: Presses Universitaires de France, 1953)

Macfarlane, Alan, *Witchcraft in Tudor and Stuart England* (London: Routledge, 1970)

Macpherson, James, *Fragments of Ancient Poetry, collected in the Highlands of Scotland, and translated from the Galic or Erse Language* (Edinburgh: Hamilton, 1760)

Malaurie, Jean, *Les Derniers Rois de Thulé* (Paris: Plon/Terre Humaine, 5th edition, 1989; English translation *The Last Kings of Thule*, New York: E. P. Dutton, 1982)

——, *Hummocks*, 2 vols (Paris: Terre Humaine/Plon, 1999)

Malheiro Dias, Carlos, ed., *História da colonização portuguesa do Brasil. Edição Monumental comemorativa do Primeiro Centenário da Independência do Brasil*, vols I–II (Porto: Litografia Nacional, 1921–23)

Marandon, Sylvaine, *L'image de la France dans l'Angleterre victorienne* (Paris: Armand Colin, 1967)

Marcos, Subcomandante Insurgente, *Our Word Is Our Weapon* (New York: Seven Stories Press, 2001)

Marcus, George E., and Michael M. J. Fischer, eds, *Anthropology as Cultural Critique: An Experimental Moment in the Human Sciences* (Chicago: University of Chicago Press, 1986)

Marshall, Roderick, *Italy in English Literature, 1755–1815: Origins of the Romantic Interest in Italy* (New York: Columbia University Press, 1934)

Martineau, Harriet, *Letters from Ireland*, ed. Glenn Hooper (Dublin: Irish Academic Press, 2001)

McEwan, Cheryl, *Gender, Geography and Empire: Victorian Women Travellers in West Africa* (Aldershot: Ashgate, 2000)

McLeod, Bruce, *The Geography of Empire in English Literature* (Cambridge: Cambridge University Press, 1999)

McMillan, Dorothy, 'Some Early Travellers', in Douglas Gifford and Dorothy McMillan, eds, *A History of Scottish Women's Writing* (Edinburgh: Edinburgh University Press, 1997)

Miller, Thomas, *The Agricultural and Social State of Ireland in 1858* (Dublin: Thom, 1858)

Mills, Sara, *Discourses of Difference: An Analysis of Women's Travel Writing and Colonialism* (New York: Routledge, 1991)

Morel, Michel, *Praxis de la lecture*, unpublished Ph.D. dissertation, 2 vols (Paris: Université de la Sorbonne Nouvelle – Paris III, 1989)

Morgan, Marlo, *Mutant Message Down Under* (New York: HarperCollins, 1994)

Naipaul, V. S., 'Death of the Novel' [interview by Ahmed Rashid], *The Observer* (Review), 25 February 1996, p. 16

Nerval, Gérard de, *Œuvres*, vol. 1 (Paris: Garnier, 1958)

Newby, Eric, *A Short Walk in the Hindu Kush* (London: Penguin, 1958)

——, *A Traveller's Life* (London: Pan, 1982)

Nixon, Rob, 'Preparations for Travel: The Naipaul Brothers' Conradian Atavism', *Research in African Literatures*, 22 (1991), pp. 177–90

Norton, Caroline Elisabeth Sarah [Lady Stirling Maxwell], *The Lady of La Garaye* (London: Macmillan, 1862)

Nuñéz Jiménez, Antonio, *Geografía de Cuba: Adaptada al Nuevo Programa Revolucionario de Bachillerato* (Havana: Editorial Lex, 1959)

Odjaun [pseudonym for Oswald de Andrade], 'Revistofagia, comendo estrêlas', *Diário de São Paulo*, 1 May 1929

Ortiz, Fernando, *Historia de arqueología indocubana* (Havana: Imprenta 'Siglo XX', 1922)

——, *Contrapunteo cubano del tabaco y el azúcar* (Havana: Editorial de Ciencias Sociales, 1991)

——, *Cuban Counterpoint: Tobacco and Sugar*, trans. Harriet de Onís (Durham: Duke University Press, 1995)

Palliser, Mrs Bury, *Brittany and its Byways: Some Account of its Inhabitants and its Antiquities* (London: John Murray, 1869)

Patterson, Thomas C., *Toward a Social History of Archaeology in the United States* (Fort Worth: Harcourt Brace College Publishers, 1995)

Peppercorn, Lisa M., *The World of Villa-Lobos in Pictures and Documents* (Aldershot: Scolar Press, 1996)

Perry, Nick, *Hyperreality and Global Culture* (London: Routledge, 1998)

Pichardo Moya, Felipe, *Los indios de Cuba en su tiempos históricos* (Havana: Academia de la Historia de Cuba, 1945)

Porter, Dennis, *Haunted Journeys: Desire and Transgression in European Travel Writing* (New Jersey: Princeton University Press, 1991)

Prakash, Gyan, 'Subaltern Studies as Postcolonial Criticism', *American Historical Review*, 99:5 (December 1994), pp. 1475–90

Pratt, Mary Louise, 'Fieldwork in Common Places', in James Clifford and George Marcus, eds, *Writing Culture: The Poetics and Politics of Ethnography* (Berkeley: University of California Press, 1986), pp. 27–50

——, *Imperial Eyes: Travel Writing and Transculturation* (London: Routledge, 1992)

Purchas, Samuel, *Hakluytus Posthumus or Purchas His Pilgrimes* (Glasgow: MacLehose, 1905)

Raban, Jonathan, *Coasting* (London: Collins & Harvill, 1986)

——, *For Love & Money: Writing – Reading – Travelling 1968–1987* (London: Picador, 1988)

Rabaté, Etienne, 'Littérateurs de voyage', *Revue de littérature générale 2* (Paris: P.O.L., 1996), n. p.

Ralegh, Sir Walter, *The Discoverie of the Large, Rich and Bewtiful Empyre of Guiana*, transcribed, edited and introduced by Neil L. Whitehead (Manchester: Manchester University Press, 1997)

Raspail, Jean, *Bleu Caraïbe et Citrons Verts: Mes Derniers Voyages aux Antilles* (Paris: Éditions Robert Laffont, 1980)

Rivero Calle, Manuel de la, 'Los indios cubanos de Yateras', *Santiago*, 10 (1973), pp. 151–74

Rogin, Michael Paul, *Fathers and Children: Andrew Jackson and the Subjugation of the American Indian* (New Brunswick: Transaction Publishers, 1991)

Rojek, Chris, and John Urry, 'Transformations of Travel and Theory', in Chris Rojek and John Urry, eds, *Touring Cultures: Transformations of Travel and Theory* (London: Routledge, 1997), pp. 1–19

Rosaldo, Renato, *Culture and Truth: The Remaking of Social Analysis* (London: Routledge, 1993)

Roudaut, Jean, 'La littérature et le voyage', *le magazine du Centre 94* (Paris: Centre Georges Pompidou, July/August 1996), pp. 7–8

Rouse, Irving, *Archaeology of the Maniabón Hills, Cuba* (New Haven: Yale University Publications in Anthropology, no. 26, 1942)

Rushdie, Salman, 'Outside the Whale', in *Imaginary Homelands: Essays and Criticism 1981–1991* (London: Granta, 1991), pp. 87–101

Ryle, Martin, *Journeys in Ireland: Literary Travellers, Rural Landscapes, Cultural Relations* (Aldershot: Ashgate, 1999)

Said, Edward W., *Orientalism* (New York: Vintage-Random, 1979)

Schaeffer, Jean-Marie, *Qu'est-ce qu'un genre littéraire?* (Paris: Seuil, 1989)

——, *Pourquoi la fiction?* (Paris: Seuil, 1999)

Smith, Sidonie, *Moving Lives: Twentieth-Century Women's Travel Writing* (Minneapolis: University of Minnesota Press, 2001)

Smollett, Tobias, *Travels through France and Italy* (Oxford: Oxford University Press, 1981)

Solnit, Rebecca, *A Book of Migrations: Some Passages in Ireland* (London: Verso, 1997)

Spix, Johann Baptist von, *Reise in Brasilien: 1817–1820* (Munich: M. Lindauer, 1830)

Spurr, David, *The Rhetoric of Empire: Colonial Discourse in Journalism, Travel Writing, and Imperial Administration* (Durham: Duke University Press, 1993)

Staden, Hans, *Warhaftig Historia un Beschreibung eyner Landtschafft der Wilden Nacketen Grimmigen Menschfresser Leuthen in der Newenwelt America gelegen ...* (Marburg: Andreas Kolbe, 1557)

Stafford, Fiona, *The Last of the Race* (Oxford: Clarendon Press, 1994)

Stevenson, Robert Louis, *Travels with a Donkey in the Cévennes* (London: Arrow Books, 1879)

Stewart, Susan, *On Longing: Narratives of the Miniature, the Gigantic, the Souvenir, the Collection* (Baltimore: Johns Hopkins University Press, 1984)

——, *Crimes of Writing: Problems in the Containment of Representation* (Oxford: Oxford University Press, 1991)

Sugnet, Charles, 'Vile Bodies, Vile Places: Travelling with *Granta*', *Transition*, 51 (1991), pp. 70–85

Swift, Jonathan, *Gulliver's Travels* (Oxford: Oxford University Press, 1994)

Taylor, David, 'Bruce Chatwin: Connoisseur of Exile, Exile as Connoisseur', in Steve Clark, ed., *Travel Writing and Empire: Postcolonial Theory in Transit* (London: Zed Books, 1999), pp. 195–211

Theroux, Paul, *The Great Railway Bazaar: By Train Through Asia* (London: Penguin, 1979)

Thesiger, Wilfred, *Desert, Marsh and Mountains* (London: Collins, 1979)

Thevet, André, *Les singularités de la France Antarctique autrement nommée Amerique: & de plusieures terres et îles decouvertes de nostre temps* (Anvers: Christophle Plantin, 1557)

Thomas, Nicholas, *Colonialism's Culture: Anthropology, Travel and Government* (Cambridge: Polity Press, 1994)

Thompson, F. M. L., *The Rise of Respectable Society: A Social History of Victorian Britain, 1830–1900* (London: Fontana, 1988)

Tocqueville, Alexis de, *Democracy in America* [1831–32] (Garden City, NY: Anchor Books, 1969)

Trollope, Thomas Adolphus, *A Summer in Brittany*, ed. Frances Trollope, 2 vols (London: Henry Colburn, 1840)

Tylor, Edward B., *Anthropology: An Introduction to the Study of Man and Civilization* (London: Macmillan and Co., 1892)

Urbain, Jean-Didier, *Secrets de voyage: Menteurs, imposteurs et autres voyageurs invisibles* (Paris: Payot, 1998)

Van der Post, Laurens, *The Lost World of the Kalahari* (New York: Morrow, 1958)

Venuti, Lawrence, 'Introduction', in Lawrence Venuti, ed., *Rethinking Translation. Discourse, Subjectivity, Ideology* (London: Routledge, 1992)

von Martels, Zweder, ed., *Travel Fact and Fiction: Studies on Fiction, Literary Tradition, Scholarly Discovery and Observation in Travel Writing* (Leiden: Brill, 1994)

Waldseemüller, Martin, *Cosmographiae introductio cum quibusdam geometriae ac astronomiae principiis ad eam rem necessariis ...* (Saint-Dié: Gautier Lud, 1507)

Waugh, Evelyn, *When the Going Was Good* (London: Duckworth, 1946)

Wehler, Hans-Ulrich, *Nationalismus: Geschichte, Formen, Folgen* (München: Beck, 2001)

White, Hayden, *Tropics of Discourse. Essays in Cultural Criticism* (Baltimore: Johns Hopkins University Press, 1978)

Wiener, Martin J., *English Culture and the Decline of the Industrial Spirit, 1850–1980* (London: Penguin, 1985)

Wilkie, Tom, *Perilous Knowledge: The Human Genome Project and Its Implications* (Berkeley: University of California Press, 1993)

Williamson, Tom, *Polite Landscapes: Gardens and Society in Eighteenth-Century England* (Baltimore: Johns Hopkins University Press, 1995)

Wolff, Janet, 'On the road again: metaphors of travel in cultural criticism', *Cultural Studies*, 7:2 (May 1993), pp. 224–39

Wood, Frances, *Did Marco Polo Go to China?* (London: Secker & Warburg, 1995)

Wordsworth, Dorothy, *Journal of My Second Tour in Scotland, 1822*, ed. Jiro Nagasawa (Tokyo: Kenkyusha, 1989)

Wordsworth, William, 'Elegiac Stanzas', *Poetical Works* (London: Moxon, 1847)

Youngs, Tim, *Travellers in Africa: British Travelogues, 1850–1900* (Manchester: Manchester University Press, 1994)

——, 'Where has all the baggage gone? Relabelling the nomad in contemporary travel writing and criticism', in David Jarrett, Tomasz Kowaleski and Geoff Ridden, eds, *Packing and Unpacking Culture: Changing Models of British Studies* (Torun: Uniwersytet Mikolaaja Kopernika Press, 2001), pp. 105–14

# Index

Illustrations are indicated by use of bold.